Praise for *The Next Evolution of Marketing*

"Advertising is changing rapidly and the old formulas don't work anymore. Bob Gilbreath's new book is loaded with ideas and concepts that will help you deal with the new realities in the marketing arena. It is well written too."

—**Al Ries,** coauthor of *War in the Boardroom*

"As the world becomes more immune to 'advertising as usual,' the urgency for finding new and better ways to connect with consumers is rapidly increasing. Recognizing the need and responding with a solution, Bob Gilbreath introduces Marketing with Meaning, a fantastic way to earn consumer attention and make the world a better place in the process."

—**Kevin Doohan,** Director, Digital Marketing,
Red Bull North America

"This immensely important book presents a new marketing model in sync with today's new consumers hungry for meaning in their lives. It's a behind-the-scenes look at how the greatest brands are leveraging their power and an essential read for anyone looking to add value to their business, career, and life."

—**Jim Heekin,** Chairman and CEO, Grey Group

"I thoroughly recommend this book. Bob Gilbreath demonstrates how marketing can go beyond interruption to add value for both consumers and brand owners. He illustrates his case with a rich and diverse set of case studies complemented by guidelines designed to help others create Marketing with Meaning."

—**Nigel Hollis,** Chief Global Analyst, Millward Brown,
and author of *The Global Brand*

"Today's technologies have shifted power to consumers. *The Next Evolution of Marketing* shows how companies can leverage that power to benefit both their customers and themselves."

—**Peter Golder,** Professor of Marketing, Tuck School of
Business at Dartmouth, and coauthor of *Will and Vision:
How Latecomers Grow to Dominate Markets*

"Bob Gilbreath has written an exciting and articulate guide to the future of marketing in the new media environment. Kudos!"

—**Bruce Owen,** Morris M. Doyle Professor
in Public Policy, Stanford University

"The world has changed, consumer expectations have changed, and as a result, traditional, interruptive marketing is significantly less effective. In his book, Bob Gilbreath not only defines and makes the case for the evolution to Marketing with Meaning, he provides a strategic framework, excellent real-life examples, and a clear road map to deliver, all in an insightful and engaging way."

—**Brian McNamara,** President Europe,
Novartis OTC Business Unit

"Tell and sell was never authentic. Smart companies have watched their products soar by adopting a more meaningful approach, but no one has named the new model, codified it, or provided any guidelines for implementing it. Until now, right here in this book, where Bob Gilbreath does all three."

—**Pete Blackshaw,** EVP, Digital Strategic Services,
Nielsen Online, and author of *Satisfied
Customers Tell Three Friends, Angry
Customers Tell Three Thousand*

"Gilbreath is onto something important with *The Next Evolution of Marketing*. I can't recall a book that contains more actionable, real-world examples."

—**Tim Kopp,** CMO, ExactTarget

"This is a comprehensive and practical approach to marketing connectivity. With media no longer 'dumb,' marketers must truly connect their brands with their key customers. The plethora of new media vehicles fragments the marketplace, but also creates a tremendous opportunity. Bob skillfully uses real-time examples of how we can capitalize with richer and deeper connections."

—**Mark Chmiel,**
Chief Marketing & Innovation Officer,
The Denny's Corporation

"Ten years after *Permission Marketing*, Bob Gilbreath takes the idea to a new level. Must reading for anyone who buys a lot of advertising."
—**Seth Godin,** author of *Tribes*

"Bob is one of the marketing industry's young bright lights. *The Next Evolution of Marketing* is a true beacon for all brand builders—many books claim that, Bob's book delivers. It is part inspirational stories, part handbook for change . . . change we must embrace if we are to grow brands into the future."
—**Jim Stengel,** former Global Marketing Officer, Procter & Gamble

"Some timeless truths restored for modern marketing—and many new ones added. An inspiring reminder of the value of brand behavior and how to make it happen."
—**Sir Martin Sorrell,** CEO, WPP

"In the always on, text-messaged, TiVo-infested, social media–driven world of today, traditional advertising has been rendered virtually meaningless. Bob Gilbreath brilliantly shows why we're no longer living in our fathers' marketing era. Better yet, he details how marketing works best when it adds value to people's lives, and he provides a playbook for success."
—**David Meerman Scott,** bestselling author of *The New Rules of Marketing & PR* and *World Wide Rave*

"One of the many illuminating insights in Bob Gilbreath's important new book is that many marketers are finding success in social media because they're rediscovering their generosity. Persuasion has given way to sharing, and marketing will never be the same."
—**John Gerzema,** Chief Insights Officer, Young & Rubicam, and coauthor of *The Brand Bubble*

"At The Coca-Cola Company we believe that nurturing brand love and advocacy is critical to building brands in this age of social media. This book provides a framework and compelling examples for creating the next generation of culture-leading brands."
—**Mark Greatrex,** Senior Vice President, Marketing Communications and Insights, The Coca-Cola Company

THE NEXT
EVOLUTION OF
MARKETING

CONNECT WITH
YOUR CUSTOMERS
BY MARKETING
WITH MEANING

BOB GILBREATH

New York   Chicago   San Francisco
Lisbon   London   Madrid   Mexico City   Milan
New Delhi   San Juan   Seoul   Singapore
Sydney   Toronto

The **McGraw-Hill** Companies

Copyright © 2010 by Bridge Worldwide. All rights reserved. Printed in the United States of America. Except as permitted under the United States Copyright Act of 1976, no part of this publication may be reproduced or distributed in any form or by any means, or stored in a database or retrieval system, without the prior written permission of the publisher.

1 2 3 4 5 6 7 8 9 0   DOC/DOC   0 1 6 5 4 3 2 1 0 9

ISBN 978-0-07-162536-4
MHID 0-07-162536-4

McGraw-Hill books are available at special quantity discounts to use as premiums and sales promotions, or for use in corporate training programs. To contact a representative please e-mail us at bulksales@mcgraw-hill.com.

This book is printed on acid-free paper.

Library of Congress Cataloging-in-Publication Data

Gilbreath, Bob.
   The next evolution of marketing : connect with your customers by marketing with meaning / by Bob Gilbreath.
      p. cm.
   ISBN 0-07-162536-4 (alk. paper)
   1. Marketing.   2. Advertising.   3. Customer relations.   I. Title.
   HF5415.G467 2010
   658.8—dc22

                                                                          2009011087

FOR EVERY BRIDGE WORLDWIDE EMPLOYEE AND

CLIENT WHO INSPIRED THIS IDEA AND CREATES

MEANINGFUL MARKETING EACH DAY

CONTENTS

ACKNOWLEDGMENTS

Whenever my friends and colleagues hear that I have been working on a book, they nearly always say that they are amazed that I have found the time and energy over more than two years to make it happen. Looking back, it has been the biggest project I have ever taken on in my life—a kind of mental marathon that has taken years of training and enormous effort in writing, all the while holding down a day job at a fast-growing, fast-changing business. But, as nearly any marathoner will agree, it is my friends and family and the people I have met along the way who have given me the strength and support to accomplish this feat.

First, I must deeply thank my "book team," which I have worked closely with for months to successfully create the work you are holding in your hands. I began working with my agent, Lisa Dimona, nearly two years ago, and from the first discussion, I found her to be a wonderful guide on my first journey through the publication process. She pushed me to perfect my thinking and managed my expectations and emotions wonderfully. Our most recent team member, Donya Dickerson at McGraw-Hill, was a great addition to the process and the project. She had energy for this work from our first discussion, and she has been a great partner in both the editorial and business aspects of the publishing process. Thanks also go to McGraw-Hill team members Mary Glenn, Heather Cooper, Jane Palmieri, and Staci Shands. And Mark Fortier has been an outstanding guide on the PR front.

My very special thanks go to Laureen Rowland, my editor and all-around all-star partner, who took on the project with great passion, thorough organization, and even some personal counseling along the way. Laureen took the work to heart and complemented my style and perspective perfectly. She was the biggest fan of the work, yet she brought needed realism on how the publishing world works. Despite ice storms on both of our ends, hundreds of miles of distance between us, and never meeting in person until after the book was complete, I really could not have delivered this book without Laureen. For this she will always hold a special place in my heart.

Another person who made this dream real is my best friend since freshman hall at Duke University, who now happens to be my boss at Bridge Worldwide: Jay Woffington. As much as I thought this concept had legs and high potential, I lacked the confidence to take it to the next level until Jay encouraged me to make it big. I still remember him kicking me and challenging me to write a book—something he knew I had always wanted to do at some point in my life. Jay has always been someone who believes in making a difference in the present, rather than putting it off into the murky future. Not only did Jay challenge me to make this happen, but he supported me during the times when work on the book distracted me from my day job.

Along with Jay, I have much thanks for the rest of our executive team at Bridge Worldwide. Peter Schwartz, Michael Graham, and Steve Wolf all bought into the idea at an early stage and helped me refine my thinking throughout. They, too, took on more work when I was slaving away at researching or writing. Other key company leaders in this effort include Michael Wilson, a fellow thought leader and supporter; Jonathan Richman, who volunteered to help promote the concept in countless ways; and my left- and right-hand client service leaders, Jodi Schmidtgoesling and Jason Ruebel, who not only managed but improved our service levels while I was otherwise occupied.

There are many, many others at Bridge Worldwide who helped me bring this book and this concept to market. It has truly been a company project that hundreds of past and present Bridge employees have touched over the past two-plus years. Alex Rolfes has led a team of people throughout the company who have put in extra passion to make this concept a success, including, in no particular order, Shannon Lanner, Erik Shrewsberry, Carole Amend, Taylor Cline, Marc Connor, Tiffany Bruning, Tracey Dye, Ryan Kolbe, Brad

Mahler, Sarah Medley, John Stichweh, Jason Van Cleave, Chris Zievrink, Debbie Effler, Don Huesman, James Marable, Jared Bauer, Ian "Trey" Dahlman, David Shepherd, Margaret Russo, Becky Gruebmeyer, Dennis Chacon, Gretchen Conner, Ray Seguin, Jessi Link, Nick Schultz, Brad Lark, and Rebekah Kluesener. I must also thank two "unofficial" Bridge employees, Carolyn Hennessy and Teresa Litzler, who helped turn this idea into the driving force behind our company.

In addition to the immediate Bridge Worldwide family, I owe great thanks to our parent company, WPP, and the many agency brothers, sisters, and cousins who have been extremely giving of their time and talent. Since the day we first joined WPP, I have been amazed at how responsive and helpful 100,000 employees around the world can be. I think this is a credit to our leader, Sir Martin Sorrell, who sets this expectation of his people—and sets an example by replying to any e-mail within minutes!

Within WPP, I have special thanks for Tamara Ingram, the leader of WPP's Team P&G. Tam supported our project by opening doors and purse strings. I also greatly appreciate the advice that I received from others within WPP who have written successful books, including Jon Steel (*Truth, Lies and Advertising and The Perfect Pitch*), Allen Adamson (*BrandSimple* and *BrandDigital*), Shane Atchison (*Actionable Web Analytics*), David Nicols (*Brands and Gaming*), Jim Taylor (*Space Race*), John Gerzema (*The Brand Bubble*), and Nigel Hollis (*The Global Brand*). Lee Aldridge took me under his wing and provided invaluable marketing guidance for our launch. Richard Westendorf and his team and Landor jumped in to help on cover art. I also appreciate the time from Ryan Turner, Gilad Kat, and Maria Mandel, who shared inside examples of their experience with meaningful marketing.

There are a handful of other friends and partners who were especially giving in this project. Kevin Doohan, formerly at ConAgra and now at Red Bull, was especially encouraging and supportive. I found important fellow believers at Procter & Gamble with Jim Stengel and Matt Carceri. Pete Blackshaw challenged me to create change while we were both at P&G, and he has been a role model as I have gone to the client service side. Sanjay Puligadda at Miami University has been a terrific partner as we have worked on academic research to support the marketing with meaning concept. And I will always treasure the encouragement I received from Jory Des Jardin, founder and president of BlogHer, who saw my presentation of this concept in Athens, Greece, in 2007. It was the first time I had shared the idea at a public conference, and when she said it was one of the best presentations she had seen in some time, I felt that we really had a chance to make it big.

My deepest thanks go to my family for their support over the years. My dad, Robert Gilbreath Sr., was an inspiration for my writing and put the passion for print into my life at an early age. Growing up as a child, I watched him bang out the books *Forward Thinking*, *Save Yourself*, and *Escape from Management Hell* on an early Epson word processor. I marveled at his effort in the home office, and I cheered as he achieved success as an author. While I drew writing lessons from my father, my mother, Linda Gilbreath, was always the proud and encouraging parent who made me feel good about my creative work. She still recalls and praises my third-grade short story about a boy who survived a tornado—and has probably kept it somewhere. I hope I have made them both proud with this work.

I have so much appreciation for and so many hours that I owe to my wife, Stephanie, and my girls, Grace and Ella. On weekends, evenings, and holidays, they often saw only the back of my head in my office as I cranked away. They were incredibly supportive through it all, and I hope that I have done their sacrifice justice through this work. I promise to wait a few years before the next book!

Finally, I thank you, dear reader, for recognizing the need for change and spending your valuable time reading this book. I hope that you find return on your investment in the form of better business results and a more meaningful career and life. If you need more assistance along the way, do not hesitate to contact me through www.marketingwithmeaning.com.

INTRODUCTION

THE SEARCH FOR
MEANING

What we really need is a mind-set shift, a mind-set shift that will make us relevant to today's consumers, a mind-set shift from "telling and selling" to building relationships.

—Jim Stengel, Global Marketing Officer,
Procter & Gamble, February 2007

I have a confession to make: I lead a double life.

Yes, my wife knows about it. So do my friends. Even my children, who are eight and six, know that by day, Daddy makes marketing. And at night, on his own time, Daddy does everything he can to avoid it.

As a marketing professional—specifically, as chief marketing strategist at Bridge Worldwide, an interactive and relationship-marketing advertising agency in Cincinnati that's part of WPP, one of the world's largest agency holding companies—I spend much of my time creating campaigns to convince people to buy my clients' products and services. Throughout my 15-year career in business, I have made my fair share of annoying commercials and even approved a few pop-up ads. But as a consumer, I ignore or actively avoid interruptive advertising as much as possible. I was an early adopter of TiVo, and I now employ three DVRs in my home. I subscribed to the federal Do-Not-Call list on the first day it was offered. I even pull over to the side of the road when I'm driving to tear down those "Earn Money at Home" signs from telephone poles.

I'm certainly not the only one. Today's consumer is retaliating against traditional marketing with TiVo, iPod, and the remote control. People are reading blogs instead of newspapers and playing *Madden NFL 08* on Xbox instead of watching *Monday Night Football*. Rather than waiting up for the regional weather forecast on the 11 o'clock news, they're uploading real-time local Doppler scans on AccuWeather.com.

At a time when creating and sharing content is cheap—if not free—and access to information has no boundaries, people have learned, at best, to avoid marketing, and at worst, to hate it. And it's not just because they're being spammed virtually everywhere, from urinals to pizza boxes.

It's because most traditional advertising is meaningless.

When I, along with 295 million other people who do not have erectile dysfunction, am forced to sit through a series of Viagra ads during a Sunday football game, I'm bound to get a little annoyed—especially when I then have to try to explain ED to my daughters (true story). When my wife is contemplating the situation in Darfur while listening to news radio, she's not exactly primed to reevaluate her choice of margarine. Nor am I in the right frame of mind to consider new job listings on CareerBuilder when I am checking the scores on ESPN.com.

So what's a marketer to do when consumers are not just immune to our messages, but are ignoring us completely?

Create marketing that's *meaningful*.

What Is Meaningful Marketing?

When your marketing is meaningful, people choose to engage with you in an exchange that *they* perceive as valuable. But engagement is only the beginning. Whatever your product or service may be, when your marketing is meaningful, *the marketing itself adds value to people's lives, whether or not they immediately buy what you're selling*. Make no mistake: meaningful marketing is not pro bono marketing, nor is it cause marketing (although cause marketing can certainly be meaningful). To be sure, moving product and making money are still the goal and usually the result; if they aren't, it's not marketing.

But the numbers prove that the more meaningful people find your marketing, the more they'll be willing to pay for your stuff, and the more loyal they'll become to your brand. They'll make more of an investment in your brand emotionally, and they'll be more motivated to choose it and spread the word about it. If you don't believe me, take a look at the results of companies such as Coca-Cola, American Express, Dove, Nike, Kraft, General Mills, Intel, Monster.com, and Dell, to name a few.

Just as I am not the first person to wield my TiVo as a weapon, I'm also not the first person to recognize the need for a new marketing model. In February 2007, Jim Stengel, global marketing officer for none other than Procter & Gamble, the world's largest advertiser and the veritable creator of mass marketing, stood before representatives from the more than 1,200 member organizations of the American Association of Advertising Agencies and practically pleaded for a new marketing model that would "meet the needs of a new consumer." Calling for a break from the historical "telling and selling" approach, he said that he spoke as a "representative of all companies" and that he was seeking "a model based on relationships and making meaning."

Separately, the *New York Times*, the *Wall Street Journal*, and *BusinessWeek* have all chronicled the rise of digital and other "nontraditional" marketing, featuring examples of companies that are shifting their focus so that they can better engage with potential customers and add value to their lives. Every day, insider publications and blogs such as *Advertising Age*, *Brandweek*, *MarketingVOX*, and *AdRants* provide more evidence that the mass, interruptive approach to advertising is failing, and that new, more meaningful approaches are succeeding by connecting brands more directly with their target audiences.

My own epiphany came in 2003, after six years of spending my time perfecting the art of the 30-second ad. At the time, I was brand manager for Mr. Clean at P&G, and we were about to launch a new

> *The future of marketing isn't in new and exciting technology; it is in what we say, not where it is said.*
> —TODD COPILEVITZ, DIRECTOR OF DIGITAL
> STRATEGY, JWT/RMG CONNECT

product called the Mr. Clean Magic Eraser. Less than a year earlier, our R&D team had found a unique product during a scouting trip to Japan. It was a cube of foam that, when wet, would "erase" dirt, grime, and marks from a variety of surfaces around the home. The product had had only modest sales in Japan, but we were looking for something, *anything*, to help resurrect a brand that was the number three player behind Lysol and Pine-Sol in the shrinking liquid cleaner category. After acquiring the rights to this foam substance, someone on the team came up with the name "Magic Eraser," and we rushed it to market in record time in order to try to boost our sagging sales.

Unfortunately, our speed to market was greater than our ability to produce a proper television spot. Anyone who has worked on a commercial lately knows that it can take four to six months to get something on the air. Meanwhile, I knew that we needed some kind of marketing activity to drive enough sales to keep the product on the shelves. After all, thanks to sophisticated scanner data and prediction modeling, key retailers like Target and Wal-Mart were increasingly looking at the rate of sales in the first week after launch as a testament to a new product's eventual success. So we had to make *something* happen, and fast.

Oh, and did I mention that we had a very small budget?

I wish I could say that our efforts were deliberately brilliant, strategic, and well executed, but the truth is, it was out of sheer desperation that we chose to invest our first few months of marketing spending in an online sampling program, using the handful of product that had come from our production line setup. Our hope was that consumers who requested samples online would try the product and tell others about it. We first tapped into a program called Home Made Simple (www.homemadesimple.com), an online relationship-marketing program that P&G's collective home care brands had launched four years earlier. Home Made Simple had 6 million members in its database who had opted in to receive monthly e-mail newsletter content on topics such as home organization, decorating, cooking, and family living. Along with nonbranded content, the program provided offers for brands such as Mr. Clean, Dawn, Cascade, Febreze, and Swiffer to a receptive audience.

In August 2003, we launched the free Magic Eraser offer on Home Made Simple.

While my team and I continued to tweak the edits of our television ad, our online "request a sample" offer was exceeding our predictions. Within two months, we had exhausted our budgeted supply of 1 million samples. However, while giving away samples was easy, we had no idea if the samples would motivate people to pick up the product in stores. With fingers crossed, we called out to our customer teams and asked for sales results—and they told us it was working. Sales were blowing away both our expectations and those of our retailer customers. Retailers were asking for more product so that they could promote it further with special offers and end-caps. Meanwhile, consumers and media alike came out of the woodwork with personal tales of how the Mr. Clean Magic Eraser had removed just about anything they tried to clean with it.

In two months we had to double, then triple our production capacity. Even with the factory running 24/7, we still came very, very close to running out of product to ship to our retail customers. And our television ad? It finally made it to the airwaves nearly three months after launch—and while we saw some effect, the Magic Eraser momentum was already gaining speed, thanks solely to the online sampling campaign.

By the end of 2003, after it had been on shelves for only five months and with very little traditional advertising, a national survey showed that the Magic Eraser had made several "Product of the Year" lists, and its growth continued, thanks to word of mouth. In part because of the success of this campaign, I was fortunate enough to make the *Advertising Age* list of the top 50 marketers of the year. Mr. Clean went from being an also-ran in liquid cleaners to a leader in innovation and a favorite of our retail buyers.

It was at this point that I realized that we had a new marketing model on our hands—one that broke just about every rule I had learned from the playbooks of the world's top marketers. Using an age-old advertising tactic, request sampling, combined with a modern approach, online relationship marketing, had allowed a large number of very interested buyers to request the product, have a great experience with it, rush to the store, and tell their friends. At the time, this campaign was born of necessity and common sense, but looking back, it could be called a brilliant strategic shift for the dawn of the new millennium of marketing. Whether it was dumb luck or mad genius, the lesson is the same: marketing works best when it adds value to customers' lives. And if a mere free sample could work wonders, I imagined what even more valuable, higher-level marketing could do.

I'm certainly not the first one to experience this new marketing epiphany. In fact, thousands of other marketers are having similar results. And there is a consensus forming around the idea that marketing must do more than interrupt, tell, and (try to) sell products and services in broad, sweeping, tsunami-like strokes. Clearly, we are evolving toward a new kind of marketing, something that people choose to engage with, something that offers meaning in exchange for their attention. Yet no individual or organization has stepped up to deliver a model or an idea set that could truly change marketing as we know it, until now.

There Are No New Ideas in Advertising (or, What's Old Is New)

I think it was actually a poet named Audre Lord who first said, "There are no new ideas," but, as would seem fitting, most marketers consider it an old advertising saw. Regardless, it happens to be true, and so it stands to reason that the idea behind this so-called new model is really quite old.

When I left Procter & Gamble in 2004 to join an advertising agency (Bridge Worldwide) for the first time, I spent my nights reading the classics in order to prepare for this new aspect of my career. My favorite guide was *Ogilvy on Advertising* by the legendary adman

> *Marketing, when it works, transcends any discussion of the benefits of the product or the service.*
> —SETH GODIN, MARKETING GURU AND BESTSELLING AUTHOR

David Ogilvy. Although it was written in 1983 about a career that was made during the *"Mad Men"* days of the 1950s and 1960s, it appears that Ogilvy was practicing meaningful marketing back when my father was still in diapers.

In 1951, at the age of 39, David Ogilvy created a print ad for Guinness Stout, his first assignment as the head of his own agency, and thus an incredibly important piece of work. In a full-page print ad, Ogilvy showed nine types of oysters—Cape Cods, Bluepoints, Delaware Bays, and so on. A finely detailed photo of each was accompanied by a paragraph describing its history and nuances of flavor. At the top, in clean, straightforward text was the headline: "Guinness Guide to Oysters." In the bottom right-hand corner, a small photo of a Guinness bottle and glass appeared beside a single, simple line of copy claiming, "All oysters taste their best when washed down with drafts of Guinness." The fine print even offered to mail a free copy of the poster to anyone who requested it.

While it seems modest—and part of the point is that it *is* modest—this print ad doesn't shout, "Buy Guinness!" More reference guide than product message, the ad clearly aims to "suggest Guinness" by offering even the casual reader some useful information—not on the virtues of beer, but on the varieties of mollusks. Early on, Ogilvy learned that advertising must be respectful ("The consumer isn't a moron; she is your wife"), that it must actually sell product ("If it doesn't sell, it isn't creative"), and that we marketers should aim high with our work ("Don't bunt. Aim out of the ball park. Aim for the company of immortals").

More than 50 years after its creation, Ogilvy's Guinness ad offers a simple, elegant example of meaningful marketing and points, historically, to many others. My mother-in-law has a framed print of a Goetz Beer ad from the 1950s that highlights the landmarks and mileage between towns along U.S. Route 36 (from Hannibal, Missouri, to Denver, Colorado). The first refrigerators and electric ovens came with complimentary recipe books to help buyers learn how to cook with their new appliances. And in the 1920s, in the first loyalty campaign on record, every Betty Crocker purchase featured a stamp that could be collected and redeemed at the supermarket for free silverware.

One of the best historical examples of marketing with meaning that's still relevant today is the Michelin Guide, which dates back to the turn of the twentieth century and the start of the automobile revolution. Michelin made tires—a commodity even back then—and knew that it needed to find a way to stand out among several identical competitors in what was then a dynamic market. So in 1900, André Michelin came up with the idea of producing and distributing the first-ever travel guide for car owners in France, complete with information about auto maintenance, lodging, restrooms, and restaurants.[1] The free, one-of-a-kind guide not only created brand awareness for the Michelin product and loyalty among its customers, but also emboldened new motorists, giving them the know-how to take to the roads more confidently and more often—all the while wearing down their tires!

The popularity of the Michelin guide grew steadily over time, and in 1920, André Michelin started charging for the guide in order to fight the perception that a free guide had no value. In the years that followed, the three-star restaurant ranking system was introduced, and the guide was produced in different languages for different countries. Today, in addition to the many European editions that exist, there are Michelin guides to San Francisco, New York City, Las Vegas, and Tokyo. The endorsement of Michelin stars is more significant than ever, often making or breaking a chef's career. The Michelin endorsement signifies quality, consistency, and excellence in cuisine and accommodations—attributes that would rarely be associated with a tire manufacturer.

Today, Michelin continues to capitalize on this brilliant piece of meaningful marketing handed down by its founders more than 100 years ago. Beyond the original "sales goal" of helping to get drivers to buy more tires, the guides build brand awareness and customer affinity by offering real value and a real service, independent of purchase, to loyal and would-be Michelin customers. And their success doesn't involve paying a celebrity or interrupting a football game.

> I believe that if he were alive today, David Ogilvy would agree that we are in the midst of a sea change in marketing, one that will exceed television's impact by at least tenfold—very likely, for the better.

The Journey of a Thousand Marketers Can Start with One Speech

Generations of marketers have risen to the heights of hall-of-fame greatness by relying on simple measures such as reach, frequency, purchase intent, redemption rate, and recall—and, as we all know from Marketing 101, changing habits is difficult and usually takes a long time. Jim Stengel's words at that February 2007 conference were aimed at no fewer than 300 P&G brand teams in 100 countries, not to mention the thousands of advertising agency and media partners that support them. His very purposeful, public call for a new model was aimed to light the fuse of change.

In that same eponymous text, David Ogilvy wrote, "When I set up shop on Madison Avenue in 1949, I assumed that advertising would undergo several major changes before I retired. So far, there has been only one change that can be called major: Television has emerged as the most potent medium for selling products." I believe that if he were alive today, David Ogilvy would agree that we are in the midst of a sea change in marketing, one that will exceed television's impact by at least tenfold—very likely, for the better.

Some people in the marketing world point out that TV commercials still work for a lot of brands, and I remember another industry guru who said that we just had to "hold on" until the coming generation of plugged-in Millennials join our companies and figure out "the new, new thing" for us. But our brands and our jobs may not still be here if we continue to hold onto old models or wait for the world to deliver the answer to our doors. The time for change is now.

The move to digital is not in itself the biggest sea change that David Ogilvy would identify today. Digital means many things and is constantly evolving and revolving. Digital technology is a means, a catalyst, a Promethean fire that is driving a bigger change to our entire marketing model. It is providing consumers with the freedom to avoid our messages altogether, all the while enabling an unprecedented level of service to customers and bonding with brands. Digital gives us the ability to *measure* how many people are actually avoiding our messages—and how many are professing their love for our work.

Those of us who "grew up" in digital marketing found early on that the only way to get people to visit our Web sites, open our e-mails, or install our widgets was to actually create something that added value to their lives. We learned that digital can be a powerful means to the true end goal of a marketing revolution.

Another promising (and growing) change in the marketing world is a call for businesses and brands to refocus on a core purpose. Purpose-based brands exist to meet higher-level needs and therefore organize their entire business around those needs. Jim Stengel championed this cause in his final years at Procter & Gamble, helping the Pampers brand move from a benefit focus on "dry bottoms" to a fundamental purpose of "helping moms develop healthy, happy babies." This is no mere language change: According to the Millward-Brown annual BrandZ study of the world's most valuable brands, Pampers today has a value of $19 billion—up from $3.5 billion three years ago.

Another industry legend, Roy Spence, the chairman and CEO of GSD&M Idea City, claims that the only brands that will be left standing after the current economic challenges will be those that are "in the life improvement business." Case in point: Spence's agency helped Southwest Airlines deliver on its purpose, "to democratize air travel."

Unfortunately, too many brands still believe that the best way to bring their purpose to life is with a 30-second ad campaign that announces this "new approach" to branding. But talk alone does not convince today's cynical and careful consumers. As Emerson said, "Without action, thought can never ripen into truth."

Actions speak louder than advertising, and meaningful marketing is the natural next step for brands that are seeking to deliver on a higher level. Purpose describes the new *thinking* that brands need; and "marketing with meaning" codifies the kind of *action* they must take if they are to deliver.

•　•　•

The goal of this book is to outline the reality of this marketing revolution, introduce a model for developing meaningful marketing, and help you—whether you are a multi-billion-dollar marketer, a middle manager, or an entrepreneur—to forge a new path to success in a marketplace that is literally demanding it. Beginning with a brief obituary for the traditional interruptive marketing model, Part I further explores the concept of meaningful marketing, illustrating, through numerous real-world case studies, what it can do for your customers and your bottom line. This part also introduces the model we at Bridge Worldwide have developed—the Hierarchy of Meaningful Marketing—which serves as both a road map to help you meet your customers' "higher-level" needs and a gauge with which to measure just how meaningful your marketing is and can be.

Part II provides a step-by-step guide for marketing with meaning—our process for setting objectives, conducting research, generating and evaluating ideas, and measuring both the customer value meaning and business success of your marketing investment. Then we'll take a look at changes in technology and globalization, and how they will shape, and be shaped by, this new approach to marketing. Finally, I will share the bonus benefit of a marketing with meaning approach: not only will it improve your business results, but it can have a positive impact on your organizational culture and help you feel more engaged in and motivated by the work you do every day.

My life's purpose is to do whatever I can to leave the world a better place than I found it—or, as Steve Jobs says, to "make a dent in the universe." Like many readers, I was attracted to a career in marketing because it allowed me to use my skills to understand people's needs and improve their lives on a large-scale basis. I have been fortunate to achieve success in my consumer marketing career, launching products and marketing that have positively touched the lives of millions of people around the world. My most sincere hope is that this book adds value to your business, your career, and your life—and that you, too, will be inspired to make a dent in the universe through the marketing that you do every day.

But this book is really just a signpost. Ultimately, you have to do the hard work—and it will be you who will deserve all the credit for your success. Good luck; read on, and remember that more help from me and a community of fellow trailblazers is available online at www.marketingwithmeaning.com. I hope you will join us there.

PART I

WHAT IS
MARKETING
WITH
MEANING?

WHY TRADITIONAL MARKETING IS MEANINGLESS

AND WHY EVOLUTION IS ESSENTIAL

It's Everywhere, and It's Intrusive

Whether they're on pumps at the gas station, on turnstiles at the football stadium, or on the flanks of sheep grazing along highways in the Netherlands, it will come as a surprise to no one to learn that today's consumer is accosted by an average of 3,000 advertisements per day, at a cost to advertisers of more than $244 billion.[1] In spite of our best efforts to achieve media saturation as a means of boosting sales—or, perhaps more accurately, *because* of those efforts—consumers have learned to ignore the majority of our marketing efforts at best, and at worst to hate them.

Think I'm exaggerating? The numbers don't lie. A survey jointly conducted by *AdWeek* and advertising agency J. Walter Thompson in 2007 revealed that 84 percent of people believe, "Too many things are over-hyped now." Another 72 percent admitted that they are "tired of people trying to . . . sell me stuff." That's not hard to imagine, given the efforts that some companies are making to infiltrate even our most sacred spaces with advertising. A company appropriately called Mangia Media sells ad space on pizza boxes, connecting with consumers, "*In their hands. In their homes*" (italics *not* mine).[2] Another company is selling ad space on floating displays alongside lakes and ocean beaches. Ah, the beauty of the great outdoors, brought to you by the Principal Financial Group.[3]

Some industries are going so far as to use what they consider "innovative" advertising to keep their businesses afloat. Take the airlines. Airlines that are in trouble are using their captive audiences to generate advertising revenue from brands such as Hewlett-Packard, Microsoft, and ING.[4] At a time when the airlines are removing the free drinks and complimentary peanut packs from your tray table, they're slapping ads onto it. And if the white space on the baggage compartment doors, napkins, and airsickness bags is already taken, you can now buy space *outside* the window. A new start-up called Ad-Air has bought or leased $10 million in real estate next to landing strips and will sell you space in one of its 30 airport slots for $100,000 per month.[5] A real estate company in Dubai was the first taker, placing a two-football-field-sized ad that broke the Guinness World Record for banner size.[6] Even the Transportation Security Administration is getting in on the game by advertising on its plastic security bins.

> *Advertisers distract users; users ignore advertisers. Advertisers distract better; users ignore better.*
> —SETH GOLDSTEIN, SOCIALMEDIA NETWORKS

Another business that is in trouble, network television, not only is taking advantage of its captive audience to advertise products and services during (widening) commercial breaks, but is increasingly utilizing the unused physical space during programming with none other than pop-up ads. "Snipes" is the actual name for these graphics, which creep onto the screen and into your peripheral vision as you attempt to enjoy whatever show you are watching.[7] Lewis Black perhaps best represented the general viewing public's frustration with snipes in a three-minute rant during the Emmys in October 2007:

> Your job is to tell stories; it's not to tell us in the middle of the story what show is coming on next or which one is premiering two weeks from now! What do you want me to do, stop and get a pencil and write it down?[8]

Perhaps because of the all-time low ratings it received, Fox took things a step further when it aired the 2007 World Series between the Rockies and the Red Sox. In its broadcast of Game Two, at the bottom of the seventh inning, at a time usually reserved for the American ritual of stretching and singing "Take Me Out to the Ballgame," Fox announcer Joe Buck instead directed viewers to the giant high-definition screen on the DirecTV blimp for a special preview of the new season of *24*.[9]

The full blitz interruptive approach of traditional advertising is also catching on globally. *BusinessWeek* recently reported on the rise of 35-year-old entrepreneur Jason Jiang, a new advertising mogul in China who built a $6 billion company in five years by installing 190,000 advertising video screens in 90 cities. Like many people before him, Jiang discovered that there was money to be made by putting ad messages in front of a large, captive audience. Business is very good for Jiang, who is now worth $1.8 billion and counting, as global brands are vying for ad space on his network and bidding up the price in hopes of winning in the world's hottest economy. "'I am very hungry and ambitious,' says Jiang, who wants to put screens everywhere. 'I see a golden age for advertising.'"[10] I suppose the 1 billion Chinese consumers should prepare for their 3 trillion ad impressions per day. Is this really the kind of cultural contribution we should be exporting?

It's Irrelevant, and It's Offensive

The problem isn't just that we are spamming people in countless ways; hundreds of billions of dollars are wasted every year on marketing that either misses its target audience completely or, worse, delivers a useless message to someone who might otherwise be compelled to purchase. When a woman with cats is interrupted by a commercial for dog food, or when a man is forced to stare at a tampon billboard while sitting in traffic, that's both a wasted buck and a wasted impression.

And it's not just that our ads hit the wrong people; even the "right," or targeted, consumers often find our ads irrelevant for reasons that have absolutely nothing to do with the quality of the creative output. One big reason for this is that *interruption itself is irrelevant.* When there's an abrupt break in the continuity of a particular activity, we're trained to look past the interruption and resume whatever it was we were doing, thinking, or watching before. A study conducted by Moshe Bar, director of the Visual Neurocognition Laboratory at Harvard Medical School, shows that when we force viewers to watch ads, we actually end up hurting our sales. According to Bar:

> Cognitive psychology experiments have shown that when people have to ignore a stimulus on the way to achieving another goal, not only do they get annoyed, they end up really disliking the distraction. And this disliking is very specific to that stimulus. So, if I am interested in the latest Red Sox score, but am forced to watch a commercial for a new merlot first, chances are that I will develop an aversion to that very brand of merlot, which will create for the advertiser the opposite effect of what was intended.[11]

Another reason that traditional ads have become irrelevant is that most of us are fairly set in our ways as far as our purchasing patterns are concerned. We are pretty much satisfied with the cars we're driving, the deodorant we're using, and the life insurance company we send checks to every month. Others may disagree with me, but I have found in my experience that no amount of one-sided selling and telling will break through a satisfied consumer's hardened mind until and unless he himself has experienced, firsthand, a real reason to change banks, toilet tissue, or dog food. And even then, it often takes more than one disappointing situation to motivate a person to spend the time and energy (yes, even changing brands of dog food generally requires a little bit of contemplation) to make the switch.

Beyond irrelevance, it seems that many of the so-called advertising innovations that were created to cut through the clutter in the marketplace have backfired, succeeding only in offending the very people that the companies had hoped to win over with their Clio award–winning efforts. Sellers of winter clothes advertising on city snowplows and pharmaceutical companies emblazoning their taglines on the tissue paper covering doctors' examination tables may seem harmless enough, but McDonald's underwriting the cost of printing report cards for schools in exchange for the right to feature Happy Meal coupons on the covers? Not so much. More than 2,000 angry calls and protests from parents in Seminole County, Florida, brought the McDonald's program to an abrupt halt, despite the $1,600 that the endeavor had added to an admittedly tight school budget.

> No amount of one-sided selling and telling will break through a satisfied consumer's hardened mind until and unless he himself has experienced, firsthand, a real reason to change.

In New York City, people protested an ad for the A&E network's new show *Paranormal State* that used a hypersonic speaker to literally beam messages into the skulls of passersby on the corner of Prince and Mulberry Streets in Manhattan's fashionable SoHo neighborhood.[12] San Francisco residents complained about the cookie-scented strips featured in "Got Milk?" bus stop ads, alleging that the aroma could cause allergy or asthma attacks in the "scent sensitive." The California Milk Processor Board pulled the ads after only one day.[13] In January 2007, a guerrilla marketing campaign for Cartoon Network's show *Aqua Teen Hunger Force* caused the city of Boston to declare a terror alert after police officers mistakenly identified small electronic devices (actually LITE-BRITE toys) found throughout the city as improvised explosive devices. Bostonians who were stuck in traffic for hours failed to appreciate the cleverness of the campaign. According to the Associated Press, parent company Turner Broadcasting paid a $2 million fine to the Massachusetts attorney general to settle potential civil or criminal charges. The CEO of Cartoon Network resigned shortly after the stunt. That's what I call an ad backfiring.

The fact is, traditional broadcast advertising often succeeds in offending people, even when we marketers don't really mean to. Every race, sex, religion, and sexual orientation has felt the sting of bad jokes and stereotyping through advertising, and now it seems as if every cause has its own special-interest group, ready to leap to the defense when advertising treads on its sacred ground. When I worked on the Tide brand at P&G, we created a print ad for our new tablet product that proclaimed: "The Best Tablets Since Moses Returned from Mount Sinai." It was a classic reference that we assumed would make anyone smile. But we were wrong; 10 people called to complain about the inappropriate religious reference, and we felt compelled to pull the ad. When GM showed a dreaming robot leaping to its death during a 2006 Super Bowl spot, the American Foundation for Suicide Prevention immediately gained a platform for its message and its fund-raising.[14] In an effort to change the marketplace perception that it was a laxative for senior citizens, Metamucil launched a campaign highlighting the benefits of daily fiber therapy—complete with the medical studies to back it up. The ads featured healthy-looking thirty-something women and the headline "Beautify Your Inside," but the brand was immediately accused of encouraging and profiting from weight loss disorders.

Even the last group that advertisers could safely make fun of is fighting back. A group called Fathers and Husbands regularly protests ads that poke fun at white males.

Amazingly, protests now spring up when marketers do something as simple as run an annoying ad too often. In the fall of 2008, Toyota publicized its no-interest loans with an ad that poorly reworked the song "Saved by Zero" from the 1980s band The Fixx. After the ad ran dozens of times during college football games, a protest group sprang up on Facebook that ultimately included 9,000 members. Small numbers, sure, but the group gained media coverage from *Time* magazine, the *Wall Street Journal*, and the popular auto blog Jalopnik. Now it seems that you cannot even hit your gross rating point goal without risking bad publicity!

The result of all of this? Oversensitized, politically correct marketers, closely watched by their conservative legal and PR departments, are producing bland ads that neither capture interest nor move cases of product.

But even that's not the real problem.

The real problem isn't that people hate marketing, or that most of traditional marketing today is ubiquitous, ineffective, irritating, and/or dull. It's also not that we are wasting 50 percent or more of our budgets on nontargeted mass advertising that seems to convince no one and aggravate everyone. You could argue that advertising has always done this; historic figures have spilled a lot of ink deriding our profession—from Mark Twain ("Many a small thing has been made large by the right kind of advertising") to pudding-pop-peddler Bill Cosby ("The very first law in advertising is to avoid the concrete promise and cultivate the delightfully vague"). Yet despite the contempt, "traditional" advertising has "traditionally" worked, as some small percentage of people who see or hear ads ended up buying enough product to pay for more ads.

But nothing lasts forever. The real problem is that consumers have changed—both in terms of how they expect to be approached with marketing, and the tools they are using to avoid it. They now have the power to control what they allow into their eyes and ears—and most of those 3,000 messages we deliver each day are not making the cut.

Permission + Technology = A Whole New World

According to Forrester Research, 48 percent of consumers today now believe that they have the right to decide whether or not to receive advertising. And this shift of power from consumer as passive receiver of marketing messages to consumer as active controller of those messages can be attributed largely to the pervasiveness of permission marketing.

Permission marketing, a term coined in the late 1990s by marketing guru and bestselling author Seth Godin, is an approach to marketing that maintains that businesses should treat prospective customers with respect by seeking their consent, via e-mail or phone, before approaching them with marketing, then giving them incentives to anticipate receiving it. The "give and take" of the dialogue that emerges is customized, cost-effective, and relevant for both marketers and consumers. In addition to driving the growth of e-mail marketing, which is now a $5 billion global industry, permission marketing has literally altered how people demand that marketers behave; they now expect to have to entertain marketing *only if* they are asked, and agree to grant, permission to do so. This, in turn, has fueled the attitude that consumers have the power to opt out of advertising altogether, and are well within their rights in doing so.

> *We still spend so much time trying to figure out how to intrude into people's lives, that we don't think about what to do so we're invited in.*
>
> —DAVID POLINCHOCK, BRAND EXPERIENCE LAB

Now factor in technology, which allows people to opt out at the touch of a button, and marketers are faced with a whole new breed of consumer—a consumer who has the power, the gadgets, and, often, the will to actively avoid advertising messages altogether.

And we're not talking about a handful of anticonsumerist zealots whom we can handily ignore. IDC Research, the global market intelligence firm, shows that two-thirds of DVR (digital video recorder) owners skip commercials *all or most of the time*. This figure soars to 80 percent among viewers 30 years old and younger. Nielsen Media Research reports that "as much as one-fifth of the audience for television's most popular shows are skipping commercials." That's not 20 percent of DVR owners; that's 20 percent of *all* television viewers.[15] What's worse, this 20 percent is largely made up of high-income, college-educated consumers who tend to buy lots of products and services. More than 50 percent of households with incomes over $100,000 have a DVR. So regardless of how hard you're working to reach that demographic, the chances that its members will ever see your well-polished, multi-million-dollar television ad are fading rapidly.

Digital technology is also empowering potential target consumers to block marketers' efforts *online*. Yes, the latest, greatest hope for buying eyeball time is already faltering just as we are discovering that people spend hours in front of their computer screens. According to Forrester Research, 81 percent of broadband users deploy spam filters and pop-up blockers. Nearly 40 percent of Internet users regularly delete "cookies" from their computer,[16] a technology that Web advertisers depend upon to deliver relevant banners to site visitors. A collaborative tool called BugMeNot arms visitors with a false username and password combination so that they can gain access to sites that require mandatory user registration (culled for advertising and e-mail pushes, naturally).

The latest assault on Internet advertising comes in the form of a free plug-in tool called Adblock Plus. Configured to pair with the popular non-Microsoft browser Firefox, after a one- to two-minute installation process, Adblock Plus literally erases all the banner ads on any Web site you visit from that point forward. Introduced in 2007 (and named a "best product" by *PC World* magazine), it has already attracted more than 4 million users worldwide, and it is adding 300,000 to 400,000 new users *per month*, perhaps in part because of an endorsement by the *New York Times*, which said that the consumer experience improves dramatically when there aren't a legion of banners begging for our attention:

> What happens when the advertisements are wiped clean from a Web site? There is a contented feeling similar to what happens when you watch a recorded half-hour network TV show on DVD in 22 minutes.[17]

And what of those attempts by marketers and advertisers to thwart Adblock Plus? The service provides rapid software updates, leading some Webmasters to become so frustrated that they are denying all Firefox browser users access to their sites, which amounts to about 20 percent of all consumers in the United States and 30 percent in Europe.[18] A self-defeating tactic, perhaps, but what's a marketer to do?

Now that technology has liberated consumers from the tyranny of the networks and the advertisers that support them, they are exacting revenge by exercising their freedom. And, as in any newly democratized society, there is no going back to the old way of doing things.

The People versus Meaningless Marketing

Many marketers would love to imagine a future similar to the one envisioned in the movie *Minority Report*. (Steven Spielberg actually enrolled a think tank of MIT futurists to help him come up with a vision of what advertising might look like in the year 2054.[19]) The result was a world in which an outdoor ad for Aquafina splashes you with holographic water, a subway ad remarks, "Hey, Bob, you look like you could use a Guinness" (hear that? It's the sound of David Ogilvy rolling over in his grave), and an American Express ad observes, "It looks like you need an escape, and Blue can take you there." But this future will never exist, because people won't let it. As it is, people today are fighting back against meaningless, interruptive marketing with their own strategic "campaign" through the power of democracy.

Consider what happened to telemarketing, which was, until 2003, when the United States passed the Do-Not-Call List Implementation Act, an $80.3 billion business. If you happen to be reading this book at home after 7 p.m., stop for a moment and listen. Do you hear your phone ringing? Probably not, because you are probably one of the 76 percent of Americans who took the time to register more than 150 million phone numbers on the Do-Not-Call List, which afforded people freedom and peace of mind by opting out of unwanted tele-marketing solicitations.[20] What was most impressive was the widespread success of this program: there was no major awareness campaign or media splash, just tens of millions of irritated consumers, all of whom yearned for fewer angry confrontations with salespeople and fewer interruptions during the dinner hour.

American citizens are now starting to use federal government bailouts as another reason to call for less marketing; both members of Congress and grassroots groups of taxpayers called on Citigroup to pull back from its $400 million contract for naming rights to the New York Mets stadium. Since Citi accepted $45 billion in bailout money from the U.S. government and the citizens it represents, giant marketing expenditures like this are now part of the public debate. General Motors, a regular NFL sponsor and Super Bowl advertiser, chose not to advertise in or attend the big game in 2009, in part because of public pressure resulting from its own multi-billion-dollar taxpayer bailout.

We marketers should be more afraid of the signal that the success of the Do-Not-Call list sent to our elected officials: that restricting advertising is an easy way to whip up support among constituents, as there are few or no staunch defenders of it. Just as with bills that raise mandatory prison sentences, limit CEO pay, or reduce the legal blood-alcohol level while driving, government officials love the chance to show that they are doing something important about an issue that people broadly care about—and about a practice that few will step up to defend. Is it any wonder that bills against advertising outdoors, through the mail, and online are making their way through local, state, and federal bodies?

> *I've been in this business for 29 years and have never seen a more competitive marketplace. The industry has changed more in the past two years than in the previous twenty-five.*
> —WALLY SNYDER, PRESIDENT EMERITUS,
> AMERICAN ADVERTISING FEDERATION

Not only are people using digital technology to enjoy the content they want (without the ads they don't want) in the privacy of their own homes, but they are also using it as a tool to disparage our brands and boycott our products in the public forum. Why? Consider it payback for the onslaught of all of the meaningless marketing they've been subjected to for years. Remember the panic to snap up the "sucks.com" URLs that could be attached to a company, brand, or product name and used against it? A quick Google search turns up 164,000 links to sites with "sucks.com" ("Disney-sucks.com," "All stateInsuranceSucks.com," and "PayPalSucks.com" are a few examples.) Short of a complete and dramatic shift in marketers' approach to traditional advertising, there is no stopping motivated, disgruntled consumers from building brand protest sites, which also tend to appear high in online search results. (Home Depot, for example, tried to sue the environmental group that runs HomeDepotSucks.com and failed to win. So a consumer using Google to find the official Home Depot Web site is also exposed to a site that touts the message "Home Depot Sucks for sourcing and selling old growth lumber.")

Various interest groups, too numerous to mention, are banding together and attacking marketing of all kinds. Adbusters, for example, is a not-for-profit, anticonsumerist "global network of artists, activists, writers, pranksters, students, educators, and entrepreneurs who want to advance the new social activist movement of the information age."[21] Its more than 100,000 members are devoted to international social marketing campaigns such as "Buy Nothing Day" and "TV Turnoff Week." Another recent campaign for "Mental Environmentalism" is aimed at taking back the public space occupied by unwanted (especially outdoor) advertising. And the group sells a $25 device called TV-B-Gone that blasts multiple infrared signals to turn off virtually any nearby ad-supported television. Other groups include the Campaign for a Commercial-Free Childhood, which is fighting against bus radio advertising, and Commercial Alert, a group formed by Ralph Nader that is pushing for legislation that would force movie theaters to publish the actual times when movies begin—meaning, when the ads (or trailers) are finally over.[22]

Why Content Is King

Digital technology is doing more than helping people actively block our advertising; it is also arming them with the tools to enjoy content that is not ad-supported. This, in turn, is significantly influencing how much time people spend watching TV, reading magazines and newspapers, and listening to radio in general. A research report by New York–based Veronis Suhler Stevenson (VSS) showed that from 2001 to 2006, U.S. consumers spent 6.3 percent less time with ad-supported media. According to VSS, this is the result of "changing consumer behaviors and digital media efficiencies," and that digital media is helping people better manage their increasingly valuable time:

> The drop in consumer media usage was driven by the continued migration of consumers to digital alternatives for news, information, and entertainment, which require less time investment than

their traditional media counterparts. For example, consumers typically watch broadcast or cable television at least 30 minutes per session while they spend as little as five to seven minutes viewing consumer-generated video clips online.[23]

This analysis jibes entirely with an oft-heard quote from TiVo owners: "I don't watch more TV. I watch *better* TV." Since digital content is readily available, consumers can search, view, and listen when and how they wish—without having to sit through a word from their sponsors.

Those sponsorship ads aren't persuading them to buy anyhow. Product reviews and peer reviews—be they from family, friends, or total strangers—are equally accessible on the Web, available in an instant, and obviously more credible than the carefully worded, benefit-driven copy points that agency writers make their living crafting. These reviews are simple to create through blogs, discussion boards, and online customer comments and ranking; they are simple to discover, as search engine algorithms give higher weight to consumer-generated content; and they are simple to verify and compare, through reviews of individual reviewers and features such as "Top Reviewers."

Why Just "Going Digital" Isn't Enough

> *I guess the most important thing that I would be asking myself is: How can I make advertising something that people are not only willing to put up with but actually have positive willingness to take?*
>
> —BRUCE OWEN, MEDIA ECONOMIST, STANFORD[24]

Historically, marketers have always looked at revolutions in media and marketing as a way of anticipating where consumers' eyeballs and attention would go next. When a critical mass of people started listening to radio, marketers followed, establishing a universal set of advertising tools, such as sponsorships and commercial breaks. When people upgraded to television, again we followed, tweaking the model to allow for the sight, sound, and motion of the modern commercial. So as consumers' attention has shifted to digital media such as online video and social networking sites, our instinct is to, yet again, move in the same direction and follow the same steps. But simply "going digital" is not working.

Traditional marketers' first instinct when it came to going digital was to try banner advertisements. Billions of dollars have been moved from print, television, and radio to these ads, which are the online equivalent of outdoor billboards. Marketers hoped that their customers would see these ads of many shapes and sizes and "click here" to unlock countless Web site visits, but, unfortunately for us, people have better things to do with their lives, and the percentage of people who click on these ads is less than 1 percent and falling.

> *The Internet is not replacing advertising but shattering it, and all the king's horses, all the king's men, and all the creative talent of Madison Avenue cannot put it together again.*
> —ERIC CLEMONS, PROFESSOR OF OPERATIONS AND INFORMATION MANAGEMENT, WHARTON SCHOOL OF BUSINESS

Hot social networking sites such as MySpace and Facebook were supposed to solve the banner ad problem by mining user profiles and serving up relevant ads. The valuations of these sites once shot up into the billions, with Google and Microsoft signing massive deals for the right to serve ads on them. But just as the ads have appeared, members seem to be abandoning this "next big thing." On January 31, 2008, Google admitted that, like its $1.65 billion purchase of YouTube, the $900 million it committed to serve ads on MySpace was not paying off. According to Google cofounder Sergey Brin, "I don't think we have . . . the best way to advertise and monetize the social networks yet." Even Facebook's own chief operating officer, Sheryl Sandberg, admitted that traditional banner ads will not work for its users or advertisers.[25]

In fact, it could be argued that advertising is killing the social networks. In 2007, advertising on these media grew 155 percent, to $1.2 billion, and it was projected to grow another 75 percent, to $2.1 billion, in 2008. But in roughly that same time frame—October 2007 to January 2008—consumer interest in these sites is down 14 percent, and MySpace membership has fallen from its all-time peak. As membership decreases, advertising prospects further worsen. Instead of 75 percent growth in 2008, as was originally projected, the actual number was 33 percent, and eMarketer now expects average single-digit growth each year through 2013.[26]

The numbers prove that, no matter what new tools and technologies we marketers use to get in front of their eyes, consumers are increasingly immune—and increasingly hostile—to our messages. Veteran brands whose names you know well won't ever admit this publicly, but they are, for the first time in decades, unable to reach their targets (and this was before the recent economic downturn).

Marketing as we have known it for decades is no longer sustainable in its current form. Society has learned that it cannot continue its current pace of resource consumption and environmental impact. Interruptive advertising is increasingly viewed as yet another source of unwanted pollution. While we could once rely on a steady stream of sales with a continuous flow of ad dollars, advertising as it is practiced today is viewed as a noisy negative externality pushed onto people we are meant to serve. And our sales results, brand value, and career prospects are suffering.

Chief marketing officers today last an average of 24.8 months in the job before they leave to "spend more time with their families" and a hopeful new superstar is plucked for the position. Ad agencies are turning over clients in less than four years, while in David Ogilvy's day, the client relationship was for life. Everyone is anxious, and everyone agrees that something has to change. But hardly anyone knows what to do—or how to do it.

I have met and worked with some of the world's largest marketers, including Johnson & Johnson, General Mills, Anheuser-Busch, Visa, and Ford—and I've walked in their shoes as a brand manager at Procter & Gamble. The people who work in these and other large, great companies are smart, well trained, and capable of deftly handling millions of marketing dollars for multi-billion-dollar brands. One of their common personal strengths is their reliance on data, success models, and research. They are savvy enough to limit their risks and maximize their results by consulting historical playbooks and backward-looking ROI models. But what happens when the old models don't work anymore?

In the absence of a new model, the tendency is to continue to follow the historical formula, even when it fails to deliver the same results. As stewards of multi-billion-dollar companies, these marketers see the stakes as being simply too high for them to follow every other marketing guru's call to "Cross the Chasm" or "Break the Rules." Real organizational change requires more than a keynote address and a handful of case studies; it demands a new toolkit and a new process that is just as structured, proven, and measurable as the old one. The purpose of this book, and the focus of every page that follows, is to present one such model. I believe that marketers at companies large and small, from local to global in sales, and focusing on end consumers or on business customers can use this model to successfully shift from a failing world of interruptive advertising into a new world of marketing with meaning. And, as you'll see in the pages and examples that follow, the quality of marketing—and the resulting numbers—proves this belief.

So what are you waiting for? Turn the page to uncover just what marketing with meaning can do for your customers, your business, your bottom line, and your world.

WHAT MARKETING WITH MEANING CAN DO FOR YOU

What if we started over? What if we threw out the textbooks and the flowcharts and rose above the snazzy jingle, the celebrity bribe, the empty sizzle, and the ad accost? What if we stopped trying (and failing) to be all things to all people and instead tried to create something of meaning? What if we stopped interrupting people to tell them how great our products are and actually *did* something to prove our greatness?

I believe that in a world in which consumers can actively choose to avoid marketing, the only way to win is to create marketing that they actively choose to engage with. Akin to the industry-altering significance of direct marketing in the 1950s and permission marketing in the 1990s, marketing with meaning is the next logical step in an evolutionary process. If direct marketing was about approaching strangers individually, and permission marketing was about turning strangers into friends and friends into customers, marketing with meaning is about improving customers' lives *through the marketing itself*.

Direct Marketing	Permission Marketing	Marketing with Meaning
Approach the consumer directly, using targeted information.	Seek consumer approval and input prior to the approach.	Create marketing that invites consumer participation.
"Advertising arrives at my home, whether I like it or not."	"I can choose whether or not to receive relevant advertising."	"The marketing itself improves my life, so I will both notice you *and* give you my business."
"Tell and sell" monologue	"Give and take" dialogue	"Value-added" benefit
Interruption	Authorization	Service
Focus on medium	Focus on message	Focus on meaning

Direct marketing was widely adopted in the 1950s, thanks to bulk postage rates, cheaper mailing materials, and the use of some of the first computers available to businesses. The concept offered several unique benefits as compared to broadcast media like print and radio: companies could reach out more specifically to the individual households that most interested them, they could include much more information by mail, and they could begin to measure the responsiveness to individual offers, a breakthrough in judging return on marketing investment. For consumers, direct marketing by mail or phone brought some added value—it provided more relevant messages and offers, along with some freedom to ignore the sales pitches altogether. But the industry also abused people's phone lines and mailboxes at an early stage. No wonder the term *junk mail* was first used in 1954.

Permission marketing, as mentioned in Chapter 1, is the brainchild of marketing maverick Seth Godin, and it succeeded in tilting both the advertising playing field and the relationship between marketers and consumers in the people's favor. Permission marketing is what created (and continues to drive) the expectation that we shouldn't, can't, and won't simply interrupt people with marketing via e-mail or phone unless we first ask them and are given their permission to do so. Permission marketing represents a distinct improvement over the traditional "tell and sell" approach to marketing, but in many ways it has made our jobs harder, as it has fueled consumers' desire and motivation to opt out of marketing altogether.

> Marketing with meaning is the antidote to opting out; it adds value to people's lives independent of purchase.... It's marketing that is often more meaningful than the product it aims to sell.

Marketing with meaning is the antidote to opting out; it adds value to people's lives independent of purchase—which, as it turns out, is far more likely to win their business. It's marketing that is often more meaningful than the product it aims to sell. It's Samsung, providing not 1 but 50 eight-foot electrical charging stations for cell phones and laptops at LAX and JFK (with Dallas–Fort Worth, LaGuardia, and Orlando next in the queue). It's Charmin, underwriting restrooms in Times Square, providing, shall we say, a much-needed service in exchange for the opportunity to connect the toilet with the tissue in people's minds. It's a company that makes matches—a commodity, to be sure—that partners with a grill company and sponsors a "stop, drop, and roll" fire-safety program in elementary schools, creating marketing that is far more meaningful than the simple flame the match produces.

What can marketing with meaning do for you and your business? Our research at Bridge Worldwide and dozens of successful projects for our customers show that the more meaningful people find your marketing, the more they'll be willing to pay for your stuff, the more of an investment they'll make in it emotionally, and the more motivated they'll become to spread the word. This means that you'll be improving your customers' lives, your bottom line, and the world at large.

Admittedly, the word *meaning* carries some baggage; some people believe that it narrowly suggests cause marketing or that it calls for the abandonment of conspicuous consumption, neither of which is true in our use of the word. Here, *meaning* translates to "personal value." What people find meaningful is very personal, and this chapter will demonstrate, in particular, how marketing your brand can be meaningful in different ways, to various degrees.

Of course, this suggests that meaning can vary from person to person, which is frankly part of the point—your brand probably has a unique target market that's different from mine. A teenage boy finds a sexy, funny viral video amusing, while the rest of the world turns up its nose. A person with diabetes becomes deeply engaged with articles about how to manage her disease, while the rest of the world has no clue to—nor any interest in—what an A1C is. Although meaning can vary by brand and target, I have found in our work with clients that true marketing with meaning has two consistent traits:

1. *It's marketing that people choose to engage with.*
   It involves creating something that people find is worthy of their time and attention, rather than continuing to look for ways to cleverly (or not so cleverly) interrupt them.

2. *It's marketing that itself improves people's lives.* Many a marketer goes to bed at night, proud to support products and services that add value. Indeed, they may remove tough stains, put a smile on faces, or enable priceless purchases, but we too often utilize the old interruption approach to present these products and services to our customers. Instead, we must create advertising that actually adds value—without necessarily forcing a sale.

An initial fear for some is that the idea of "meaning" is too high level and far away from the dollars and cents that people are most concerned about during this difficult economy. Brands feel pressured to go back to traditional TV commercials with product-benefit and value messaging to connect with price-sensitive buyers. But practicing meaningful marketing is at its heart about understanding consumer needs and delivering value through the marketing itself.

As you will read in the chapters ahead, free samples and offers are strong examples of meaningful marketing, but in today's economy people are still responding to cause-related campaigns and sustainability messages. The new bottom line for consumers is that they expect more from their brands on many levels—and this model will help your company bring marketing itself into the value equation.

The best way to illustrate the value of meaningful marketing is to look deeply within pioneering brands that are charting a unique but consistent course. Dove, Nike, Burger King, and the Partnership for a Drug-Free America are but four examples of major brands that are executing this new approach in truly significant ways. They have abandoned interruption, created marketing that people choose to engage with, connected with them in a variety of innovative new forums, and successfully launched meaningful campaigns that have positively affected both their numbers and the quality of life of the people they're targeting.

Reinventing Beauty Gives a Lift to Dove's Bottom Line

In 2002, in the face of slow growth, diminishing market share, and eye-opening research that revealed that more than 50 percent of women say that their body "disgusts them," Dove stopped talking about soap for its own sake, quit perpetuating a beauty myth that was potentially damaging to girls and women, and started a movement to help improve self-esteem.

In lieu of the size-one fashion models who have come to be expected—and ignored—in advertising, Dove's original "Real Beauty" campaign featured real women of all ages, sizes, and ethnicities in print ads, online banners, and Times Square billboards. Its marketing featured people such as a 90-year-old woman, with copy that asked the question: "Wrinkled or wonderful?" In what would later become the "Campaign for Real Beauty," Dove crashed the stereotypes of beauty product advertising forever, creating a national debate among women about what beauty is and what it means. The initial success of the campaign fueled the brand to go further into the digital realm, creating a Web site and mobile-enabled billboards where consumers could continue the discussion with others and download tools to help moms and mentors talk with girls about accepting and celebrating themselves. Then Dove took the campaign viral.

In 2006, its Canadian agency, Ogilvy Toronto, created a time-sped video to dramatize the process that beauty-product advertisers go through to turn a simple woman into a Photoshopped fashion model, ending with: "No wonder our perception of beauty is distorted. Every

"Evolution" . . . has achieved over 500 million views—and counting. This cost Dove . . . a mere $50,000.

girl deserves to feel beautiful just the way she is." On October 6, 2006, the agency released the video, called "Evolution," on YouTube with no other support or fanfare. Traffic began to build, and a week later, *Good Morning America* featured it. Free views and free press coverage continued unabated for months. According to Maria Mandel, executive director for digital innovation at Ogilvy, the video has achieved over 500 million views—and counting.

This cost Dove little more than the price of the video's production, a mere $50,000, in comparison to the $1.3 million to air a single 30-second ad once during the *American Idol* season finale. Not to mention the fact that a consumer who chooses to engage in meaningful marketing is obviously more open to the message than someone who is likely to use the bathroom, get a snack, or TiVo through a commercial break.

In summer 2007, even the old guard of advertising recognized the campaign with its highest honor, a Cannes Grand Prix. But the Dove Real Beauty advertising campaign did more than win eyeballs and creative awards. It drove the company's business, resulting in double-digit sales growth for this 54-year-old brand in 2005 and 2006. And it made an impact on society by igniting a debate about our culture's definition of beauty, shining a spotlight on how the media's portrayal of it affects the confidence and well-being of our daughters, wives, and sisters. It made real women feel better about themselves and their bodies. And the Dove Self-Esteem Fund is now working to affect the lives of 5 million girls by 2010 by creating articles and videos for girls, moms, and mentors and free workshops (with a discussion guide and DVD) that schools and other organizations (including the Girl Scouts) can use. While Dove's products work well, the marketing the company created is doing nothing less than improving the world.

"Word of Foot" Spikes Sales at Nike

Unlike Dove, Nike has never really been an underdog in its market. On the contrary, the company practically invented the premium athletic footwear category back in the 1960s, when founders Phil Knight and Bill Bowerman formed a partnership and later began using waffle irons to fashion high-performance soles for track stars. By 1980, the company owned 50 percent of the athletic shoe market in the United States, mainly thanks to "word of foot." Its first television ads did not run until 1982, but the medium seemed tailor-made for Nike, with its slick, stylish, celebrity-laden commercials. Over the next two decades, sales soared and periodic threats from competitors such as Adidas, Reebok, and L.A. Gear were easily quashed by millions in ad spending and the creation of innovative product.

By 2005, Nike, Inc., had achieved profits of $1.2 billion on revenues of $13.7 billion. But the company faced pressures it never had faced before: Adidas purchased Reebok, creating a $16 billion combined number two challenger, and the upstart Under Armour brand, with its focus on high-performance technology for high-performance athletes, came out of nowhere to hit $607 million in revenues. Many people in both the advertising and footwear industries expected Nike to fight back with a flotilla of expensive traditional advertising, and possibly even a return to the Super Bowl, from which it had been absent since 1998. But Nike did something smarter, cheaper, and more meaningful.

Instead of reviving the marketing approach it had used in the 1980s, it went back further, back to its roots, and back to generating "word of foot" by reacquainting itself with its core audience of dedicated athletes. "We're not in the business of keeping the media companies alive," Trevor Edwards, the corporate vice president for global brand and category management, says. "We're in the business of connecting with consumers."

Nike's refocus on community and its heavy use of the word *service* suggest that its new approach is a natural outgrowth of the launch of Nike+ in 2006. In a symbiotic partnership of meaningful marketing and technology, Nike joined with Apple to launch a system that combined chip-in-a-shoe and iPod sync software. This allowed for an enhanced experience for serious runners, many of whom depend on music to stay motivated. Every mile, a voice speaks over the music to provide updates on pace and miles run, and to offer words of encouragement. Placing the iPod in its cradle downloads the runner's performance into tracking software at nikeplus.com, allowing runners to compare runs, track their progress against goals, and note improvement over time. And while all this may seem tedious to most people, Nike knew that dedicated runners have been doing this for decades using pen-and-paper journals, and that offering a technology that would make this task easier, quicker, and more fun would go a long way with its target audience.

Nike+ goes even further by helping people personally connect in what is essentially the world's largest running club. The service connects runners to others around the globe in more than 13 markets—allowing friends, groups, and even entire nations to share running courses and challenge one another.

The business rationale of Nike+ is best described by Michael Tchao, general manager for Nike Techlab:

> Nike+ has been successful because it provides consumers all over the world the tools they need to become better athletes. For many users it has become an indispensable service, giving them a continued deep connection to our brand.

After only six months of sales in December 2006, Nike CEO Mark Parker reported to analysts, "Nike+ is turning out to be huge. . . . Clearly, our confidence in this concept is proving to be accurate." He credited the company's 8.1 percent rise in second-quarter profit to this line of running shoes.

In addition to boosting profits, there is no doubt that Nike+ has significantly improved the running experience for millions of athletes at all performance levels. Stefan Olander, global director for brand connections, reports that 30 percent of Nike+ users come to the site three or more times per week after an average run time of 35 minutes—and many of them have become so enamored of their Nike+ sensors that if they don't have them with them, they will actually skip running "because they want credit for their achievements."

By bringing information and entertainment to the relatively monotonous activity of running, Nike has encouraged new runners, brought lapsed runners back into the habit, and squeezed a few more miles and smiles out of those who never stopped. There may not be a

> *If we can do something to benefit our consumers and serve the needs of athletes to perform better, they will return to our brand.*
> —STEFAN OLANDER, GLOBAL DIRECTOR FOR
> BRAND CONNECTIONS, NIKE

place for Nike+ in the annual Cannes reel, but it is brilliant marketing nonetheless.

Nike is extending this concept of meaningful marketing into other sports as well, placing a breathtaking 2-minute-46-second video of Brazilian soccer star Ronaldino online, instead of on television, resulting in more than 17 million views on YouTube alone. For basketball players, Nike created the Jordan Brand Breakfast Club, an interactive online training tool featuring custom-tailored workouts from pro trainer Tim Grover that can be downloaded to a video iPod. More than 120,000 people registered on the site and spent an average of six minutes logged in.

Runners and ballers love the new marketing approach, and so do Nike's shareholders. The company's global sales have climbed from $10 billion to $16 billion in the last four years, and in February 2007, CEO Mark Parker promised Wall Street that he will grow the business another $8 billion in the next five years. His confidence, in part, comes from the fact that the company seems to have cracked the code of a new marketing model, while its archcompetitor, Adidas, is busy spending millions for the privilege of plastering its logo on Super Bowl and Olympic jerseys.

How Burger King Jump-Started Sales by Having More Fun

In 2002, historic fast-food also-ran Burger King was facing the potentially fatal combination of flat sales and a new corporate parent. Founded in 1954 by James McLamore and David Edgerton, who had visited the original McDonald's restaurant in San Bernardino, California,[1] and saw an opportunity to piggyback on the fast-food franchise model, Burger King's primary goal for almost 50 years had been to siphon off a few share points from the market leader. Unfortunately, this left the company with a poor sales base, which made it an also-ran for investors as well.[2]

Fortunately, its new owner, private equity firm TPG Capital, was more interested in reframing the brand as fresh and fun than in holding a fire sale. TPG recognized that a meaningful campaign could reposition Burger King as a brand to know and love. In January 2003, the company hired Miami-based creative agency Crispin Porter + Bogusky, which helped identify and prioritize 18- to 24-year-old males, a heavy fast-food consumer base that also helps to set trends for the rest of the population,[3] as its primary target audience. After a Crispin employee happened to purchase a 1970s oversized Burger King "head" on eBay as a source of brainstorming inspiration, the agency made the bold decision to feature the now-retro "Creepy King" character (who'd been sidelined since the 1980s) both in restaurants and in guerrilla marketing efforts. Within months, the King returned to the forefront of pop culture, as mask-wearing Kings began appearing at Halloween parties and on viral video pranks.

Separately, as part of its mandate, the team at Crispin was specifically charged with helping to increase sales of Burger King's chicken sandwiches, a task made all the more difficult by the brand's historic focus on burgers. Whereas most agencies would probably have taken the traditional approach and come up with something straightforward and predictable—say, a 30-second ad showing hungry customers (or maybe a celebrity!) designing their perfect chicken sandwich at a restaurant counter—Crispin capitalized on Burger King's decades-long reputation for being the restaurant that invited customers to "have it your way" by inviting people to issue customized orders to . . . a chicken.

On April 8, 2004, www.subservientchicken.com went live, resulting in an instant viral hit and the brand's first major breakthrough. Via a faux Webcam feed, a guy in a chicken suit responds to more than 300 commands typed into a text box, ranging from "peck ground" to "walk like an Egyptian." Joseph Jaffe, author of Life After the 30-Second Spot, reports that more than 14 million people visited subservientchicken .com in its first year, each of whom spent an average of more than seven minutes on the site. Most important, the campaign moved meals. Chicken sandwich sales were reportedly up 9 percent in the weeks immediately following the launching of the campaign, and in its October 2004 earnings report, after nine consecutive months of growth, Burger King announced that same-store sales were up 6.4 percent and total company restaurant sales rose 12.3 percent.

In addition to sales growth, Subservient Chicken guaranteed Burger King its place in the annals of pop culture. People began to see the brand as quirky, playful, and distinctive in its own right, rather than as an outdated, eternally subpar runner-up to McDonald's. More than four years later, subservientchicken.com continues to draw traffic and has spawned dozens of spoofs.

Like Dove's, Burger King's successful new marketing approach inspired the company in other meaningful ways as well. While Dove sparked a global conversation about how we should define beauty, Burger King gave its customers permission to have fun again. In late 2004, Burger King partnered with developer Blitz Games to break leadership ground in the video game business, becoming the largest distributor of advertising-related video games ("advergames"). Its three games for the Xbox—*Pocketbike Racer* (a mini-motorcycle-racing game), *Big Bumpin'* (a bumper car game with pitfalls, such as bottomless pits and ice patches), and *Sneak King* (where players become the King and sneak around neighborhoods and construction sites, surprising people with fresh sandwiches)—sold a staggering 3.2 million copies (at $3.99 apiece) in just three months, which put it in the top 10 bestselling video games of the year. More important, these games helped to increase Burger King's profits by 40 percent within a year.

As Russ Klein, president of global marketing for Burger King, says, "Interacting with our characters in the games is actually more engaging than just sitting back in your chair and watching a Super Bowl commercial." It's more meaningful, too. When we can convince people to want to interact with our marketing—or, in this case, literally play with our brand—we are onto something big, new, and different.

Burger King continues to carve a new path with advertising, including a mobile-phone-based game starring the King, and, in February 2008, a promotion that celebrated the fiftieth anniversary

> When we can convince people to want to interact with our marketing—or, in this case, literally play with our brand—we are onto something big, new, and different.

of the Whopper. Called "Whopper Freak-Out," the campaign featured television ads and online videos that caught, on camera, customers' reactions to the (completely fabricated) announcement that the Whopper had been discontinued. Visits to WhopperFreakout.com reached 250,000 in the first week. Even better, same-store sales were up 4.2 percent, sales of Whoppers grew by double-digits,[4] and the firm's stock price was up 5.8 percent, thanks to this campaign.[5]

In December 2008, the brand launched a men's fragrance called Flame that has "the scent of seduction with a hint of flame-broiled meat"—a perfect stocking-stuffer for $3.99. And the King got into Facebook in January 2009 with a promotion to support its new, spicy "Angry Whopper." Burger King offered Facebook members a free Whopper coupon if they chose to un-friend 10 people on the service. In less than a week, over 200,000 connections were severed in the name of a $3 sandwich.

Burger King proves that engaging, fun, meaningful marketing can drive a complete brand turnaround. In addition to a successful IPO in 2006, Burger King has enjoyed 20 consecutive quarters of growth in same-store sales and a 32 percent increase in its stock price in 2007. Clearly, its marketing has been meaningful for consumers and investors alike.

Partnering with Parents for a Drug-Free America

Unlike Dove and Nike, the Partnership for a Drug-Free America (PDFA) is hardly a household name. You probably remember its famous "this is your brain on drugs" egg-in-the-frying pan ads, which *USA Today* recently named as the eleventh most-recalled ad from the past 25 years. But "recall," as you probably know, does not always mean results, and in its move toward meaningful marketing, even the Partnership for a Drug-Free America has made the decision to stop scaring parents via its 30-second TV ads and instead start offering valuable educational resources on its Web site.

In the last 20 years, the PDFA's strategy has been to utilize its *one million dollars' worth of free media placement per day* to expose children and parents to antidrug messages via television and print advertising. But after years of creating memorable, award-winning ads, the PDFA decided to change course for two reasons: its mass television advertising campaign was missing its target, and its Web site, www.drugfree.org, was garnering a surprising amount of traffic (about a million new visitors each month).

The meaningful new path that the PDFA is taking is epitomized by its most recent work, an initiative called "Time to Talk" (www .timetotalk.org). In contrast to an interruptive scare tactic, Time to Talk is a "resource for parents seeking to understand drug and alcohol abuse with their children." Today's Gen X parents grew up with that very brain-frying daily dose of antidrug messages, and they saw the results (or lack thereof) on their streets, in their friends, and in themselves. Now, as parents, they are proactively seeking real solutions, and they are open to engaging with an entity such as the PDFA if it's offering genuine value-added services (which it appears to be, in such features as its Parent Talk Kit: "Top 10 Ways Teens Trick Their Parents," "How to Tell If Your Teen Is Drinking or Using Drugs," and "Answering the Question: 'Did You Do Drugs?'").

The PDFA has also partnered with Yahoo! Answers to create a destination where parents can chat directly to help one another handle the tough questions. An e-mail campaign keeps the conversation going, with regular columns such as "Teachable Moments" and Q&A from radio and TV personality Dr. Drew. A Facebook page features an active cause campaign. There is even a parent-run blog called "The Decoder" (decoder.drugfree.org), which is "breaking down teen culture, substance abuse, and parenting." While most brand managers have not personally read a blog or created a Facebook page, parents of teens have had to learn about these new technologies quickly in order to keep pace with what their kids are getting into. And now parents are using these tools to better educate themselves and one another.

The PDFA is also doing more to reach out into individual communities. Its Meth360 community mobilization program trains

> I would rather be able to reach 100,000 parents well, the way they want to be reached, than [try to] reach 10 million with a generic message.
> —STEVE PASIERB

substance abuse treatment professionals and law enforcement officials to speak at schools and town halls, and to parent groups and other civic organizations. In 2008 this program reached 12,000 individuals, and according to its recent fund-raising letter, "This powerful program was so meaningful that even after six months, over 86% of participants were still taking action and talking about the presentation to friends and families."

While this shift in marketing approach has yet to result in an Effie award, the change in what the PDFA is spending on marketing suggests that it is working; digital spending has gone from almost nothing to 10 percent of the media budget in 2007, and is expected to hit 31 percent by 2010. Its personal, grassroots programs reached 75,000 parents and teens. The PDFA still runs television ads, thanks to free media placement, but only about half as many (worth $175 million, down from $365 million). According to Steve Pasierb, president and CEO: "Our spend is down, but our effective reach is up. I would rather be able to reach 100,000 parents well, the way they want to be reached, than [try to] reach 10 million with a generic message."

By actively engaging with its target audience, the Partnership for a Drug-Free America is doing more than helping us keep our kids off drugs; it is serving as a role model to help us marketers kick the habit of destructive marketing.

Marketing with Meaning: The Model

To create meaningful marketing, you must first determine what makes people tick—what's genuinely important to them and what they aspire to. Specifically, you need to uncover which of their needs remain unmet—not just in the laundry room or at the grocery store, but in their larger lives. These are what I call "higher-level" needs. If we're honest, we all know that the detergents and deodorants we are buying now get the job done just fine. So what do people really want?

Richer experiences and deeper social connections—ways to improve themselves and to make a positive impact on the world.

People will spend $5 a cup to enjoy a Starbucks experience, $20 to personalize a Heinz ketchup bottle, and hundreds of dollars for personal carbon offset credits. A good online banking service can instill confidence in one's financial choices, even if the terms of the account and the interest rate are exactly the same as those at the bank next door. Hybrid cars offer a relatively minor improvement in gas mileage and take decades to recapture their incremental cost—yet sales of hybrids are up 500 percent in the past year alone because people *perceive* that they are better for the environment. These are the kinds of higher-level benefits that many brands aspire to provide, yet they can do so only by intimately understanding how not just their products and services but their *marketing* satisfies potential customers' unfulfilled needs and fits into the overall experience of their lives.

As a road map to help marketers meet these higher-level needs, I have created a new marketing model, the Hierarchy of Meaningful Marketing, which is the product of more than two years of research and my nearly two decades of experience both as a brand manager at Procter & Gamble and as chief marketing strategist at Bridge Worldwide.

The hierarchy presents the three tiers of meaningful marketing— *Solution, Connection,* and *Achievement*—as a tool that will help you accurately identify your customers' needs and begin thinking about how your marketing can fulfill these needs at the corresponding levels:

- Survival needs (food, shelter, safety, and clothing) = meaningful solutions

- Attachment needs (love, belonging, friendship, family) = meaningful connections

- Esteem needs (confidence, creativity, problem solving, respect for and by others) = meaningful achievements

The Hierarchy of Meaningful Marketing uniquely aligns and combines Abraham Maslow's hierarchy of needs, a brilliant 60-year-old sociological snapshot of consumers' higher-level needs, with the brand equity hierarchy, a familiar tool that marketers use every day to determine where their brand stands in the hearts and minds of consumers.

In case Maslow's theory is not top of mind, in the 1940s, the American psychologist spent time studying the healthiest 1 percent of the college population as well as exemplary figures such as Albert Einstein, Jane Addams, and Frederick Douglass. He discovered two important things. First, people are programmed to continually create new needs and strive to satisfy them. This programming is what keeps us going even after we have won a Nobel Prize or made a million dollars, and it is responsible for much of the remarkable progress in the world. Second, he found that there is a common and predictable progression of these needs among all people, starting with survival and safety and moving toward higher-level social, esteem, and achievement needs as the more basic needs are met.

In Marketing 101, we learned that strong brands stand for something more than product features and benefits. Brands like Coca-Cola and BMW are worth far more than the factories that produce them and the raw materials used to make them; their real value exists in what they stand for in the hearts and minds of consumers. Like Maslow's model, the brand equity hierarchy begins with a base level of benefits and attributes that describe what the product is and the problem it solves. It gradually ladders up to higher levels of meaning to include values, character, and a single, powerful equity statement. The pyramid shape of both models helps to connect basic needs with benefits, and so on (see Figure 2.1).

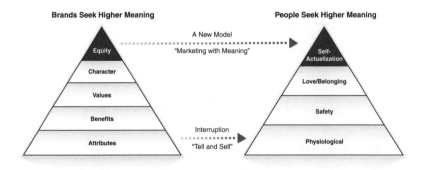

Figure 2.1 **Both Brands and People Seek Higher Meaning**

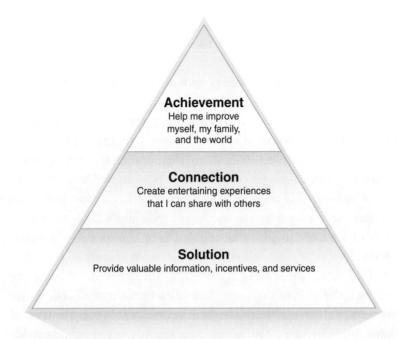

Figure 2.2 **The Hierarchy of Meaningful Marketing**

The Hierarchy of Meaningful Marketing (see Figure 2.2) marries consumers' higher-level needs with the corresponding brand features, resulting in three tiers of marketing that are increasingly meaningful to consumers:

- *Solution marketing.* Like the lower levels of Maslow's hierarchy of needs, solution marketing covers basic household needs and benefits, for example, helpful offers, money savings, and hard rewards for purchase.

- *Connection marketing.* This represents a significant step toward building a bonding relationship between people and brands. It matches closely with Maslow's love/belonging category, providing benefits beyond the basics of information and relevance to include something that is of deeper importance in the consumer's mind, i.e., social outlets and creative expression.

- *Achievement marketing.* This corresponds to Maslow's pinnacle of self-actualization by allowing people to significantly improve their lives, realize a dream, or positively change their community and their world.

Once people can feed and clothe themselves, they can focus on forging healthy relationships, and then on changing the world, because they aren't worried about where their next meal is coming from. Similarly, when you as a consumer aren't as motivated by a 50-cents-off coupon—mainly because 50 cents won't make or break you—you become more responsive to marketing that aligns itself with your goals of connecting with like-minded people, expressing yourself creatively, and/or positively influencing the community around you.

The higher the level of marketing (with achievement being the highest), the higher the need it satisfies (esteem needs being the highest), and conversely, the higher the need, the higher the level of marketing it requires. This is not to say that marketers of basic goods and services are exempt from creating marketing with meaning. For them, the opportunities to create marketing whose meaning transcends what they're selling are limitless.

The description of each of the three tiers typify the ways in which these needs tend to manifest in people and are the focus of the next three chapters (Chapter 3, "Meaningful Solutions"; Chapter 4, "Meaningful Connections"; and Chapter 5, "Meaningful Achievements"), each of which contains dozens of real-world case studies from name brands that have made great strides in their journey toward marketing with meaning—often to significantly increased sales and shareholder satisfaction.

What Meaningful Marketers Know

1. Meaningful marketers never push. They *invite* prospective customers in by creating marketing that appeals to the higher unmet needs in their overall lives.

2. Meaningful marketers know that most of our basic needs are satisfied by the products and services we already buy.

But that is not to say that the marketers of these basic products are exempt from creating marketing with meaning—on the contrary. If you sell a commodity, the need and opportunities for you to create marketing whose meaning transcends your product are limitless.

3. Marketing itself must improve consumers' lives and accomplish something of intrinsic value, independent of the product or service it aims to sell, whether or not people actually ever purchase it.

4. More meaning = more money. (The longer equation is more meaning = more loyalty = higher prices = increased sales, but the net result is the same.)

3

MEANINGFUL SOLUTIONS
PROVIDING VALUABLE INFORMATION, INCENTIVES, AND SERVICES

At the base of the Hierarchy of Meaningful Marketing lies its foundation, *Solution*. Simply put, solution marketing is relevant, appearing when and where people are receptive to receiving it. And it is helpful—aiding, rather than interrupting, the goals they are trying to achieve. Meaningful solutions meet "survival needs"—food, shelter, safety, and clothing—with straightforward benefits and information, such as useful offers, money savings, and "hard" rewards like free samples and rewards for purchase.

"Give Me Extra Incentives and Services"

Not every price promotion and Sunday coupon makes for a meaningful solution. Discounts aren't marketing—they're, well, pricing strategies, and they are neither a permanent fix nor particularly meaningful. Any brand can "rent" short-term share or sales results by slashing prices, but it has been proven time and time again in countless industries, from

computers to cars, that there is no winning the price wars—not only can your competition continually "one down" you, but lowering your prices will kill both the long-term value perception and the equity rating of your brand when it's done too frequently or too casually.

In contrast, meaningful incentives are solutions that marketers can offer to allow customers to test a new product, stay loyal to an old product, and brag about either (or both) to their friends. They can take the form of good old-fashioned free samples and/or loyalty programs. And contrary to what appears by all accounts to be a sad state of affairs in the traditional advertising realm, there are dozens of smart, forward-thinking companies and brands that are practicing this form of meaningful marketing every single day, including Maytag, General Mills, McDonald's, and the British rock band Radiohead.

Free Samples: Let the Product or Service Sell Itself

It's been said that there's "no free lunch," but in a one-day offering on May 15, 2008, McDonald's disproved the adage, giving 8 million hungry Americans in 14,000 restaurants nationwide the chance to sample both its new southern-style chicken sandwich (for lunch) and its chicken biscuit (for breakfast) with the purchase of any medium or large drink. It was the second such event of the year, following up on a two-day giveaway of 3 million McSkillet Burritos that drove same-store sales up 8 percent. McDonald's is but one of the most recent large companies to discover the magic of free sampling.

According to a survey conducted in February 2007 by the Promotion Marketing Association, nine out of ten consumers say that they would purchase a good or service if they experienced it and were satisfied with it. Six out of ten said, "If a brand wanted to convince me to buy its product or service, experiencing it firsthand would be the most effective way to get me to purchase."[1] *The most effective way.* In a sense, a higher-quality/more meaningful interaction with a brand or product allows it to virtually sell itself to the consumer.

Many brands make great new products that sell themselves when people get a chance to try them. Seth Goldman, cofounder of Honest Tea (40 percent of which is now owned by Coca-Cola), concurs: "It's the quality of impressions [that are important], if you were to look at conversions to consumers. I would trade 100 media impressions for one person-to-person, cup-to-mouth sampling impression."[2]

Free sampling becomes even more useful—and compelling—in tight economic conditions. People are generally wary of spending their hard-earned cash on new products that aren't yet tried and true, but they are naturally even more sensitive to doing so during a market or personal downturn. Sampling can help overcome this risk, and getting something for free may make people even more open to trying new products when times are tough. And while coupons aren't samples per se, the November 19, 2008, edition of the *Wall Street Journal* reports that "searches for the word 'coupon' are up 50% in the past 12 months" alone.

The Denny's chain of restaurants took this to heart when it gave away free Grand Slam breakfasts (regularly $5.99) all day on February 3, 2009. The brand had used a Super Bowl ad the week before to announce the offer and brought in extra servers and cooks to be ready for the high demand. Denny's CEO, Nelson Marchioli, signed off on the bold move to get the brand back on the relevance radar after it had completed an upgrade of its food and service quality. According to

Marchioli, "I'd rather give something away than discount it. If I've got something that I think is wonderful, I want to get it into the mouths of customers."

Free sampling becomes even more useful—and compelling—in tight economic conditions.

The Grand Slam giveaway was a very big hit for Denny's. At a cost of only $5 million, the brand brought in 2 million visitors and generated $50 million worth of PR coverage. Marchioli believes that the program paid for itself in less than one month, thanks to increased guest traffic, driven by the Free Grand Slam event.

But the campaign also connected personally with Denny's customers, coming at a time when many were struggling with the effects of a sinking economy. According to Mark Chmiel, chief marketing and innovation officer, the company received thousands of thank you calls and e-mails. One man sent a check for $300 and a note reading: "Thank you for what you did for America." A Denny's employee who went grocery shopping after her shift with her uniform on was stopped by seven people who wanted to personally thank her. These stories suggest that a single day of free meals is also building a lifetime of brand loyalty.

Aside from gaining consumers' attention and helping them experience a great product or service for themselves, sampling offers several additional benefits. First, it is completely pay-for-performance—if people don't request a sample, you don't have to pay for it. This is completely unlike traditional media buys, which cost the same whether people watch them or not. Second, sampling often generates its own free media attention in the form of word of mouth among friends and family. People are apt to share a good deal when they come across one, and today they use the Internet to share new offers with the dozens of free sample finders online. Finally, sampling often offers the chance to build up a database for future direct marketing. People who come for one offer often opt in to hear about the next one.

Sampling can work for just about any product or service at any time, but it can be especially powerful when it is linked to a situation in which people are particularly receptive. For example, Tylenol PM offered a million vacationing consumers a free chance at a good night's sleep. The brand understood that people are often weakened by the stress of travel and need a good night's sleep in order to make the most of their time away. Samples were placed on hotel guests' beds during turn-down service, accompanied by a note that said, "We know how long you've waited for this vacation, and we know how much you want to catch up on your sleep. Enjoy."

On May 21, 2008, Baskin-Robbins came up with a clever way to lure special consumers into stores in a special way—by turning a run-of-the-mill "hump" day (Wednesday) into a "bump" day, offering pregnant women a free three-ounce cup or cone. To spread the word that Philadelphia Cream Cheese's 1/3 Less Fat Soft Cream Cheese is as rich and creamy as its full-fat version, the brand kicked off its "Breakfast from Heaven" promotion in January 2008, offering free bagels and cream cheese to 500,000 passengers on morning JetBlue flights, to the tune of 50,000 hits on its mini-site and coverage on Fox News and NPR.

Sampling can work even for products and services that you might not have thought about. You can't conveniently sample a big-ticket item, like an appliance, in your own home, and consumers often end up more confused and cross-eyed when they leave a showroom than they were when they arrived. In 2004, the clever folks at Maytag created a concept store to showcase its brands and allow its significantly female target audience to "try before they buy." In stores nationwide, consumers can test-drive the latest high-end appliances—do a load of laundry, bake a sheet of cookies, or listen to a dishwasher to see whether it really is quiet—before purchasing.

Nintendo similarly gave its target audience a chance to sample its new Wii gaming console by taking an innovative approach, targeting families that are interested in gaming but are turned off by first-person shooting games and complex systems from Xbox and PlayStation. Realizing that it had to win Mom over in order to gain widespread adoption as a family gaming system, it launched a series of game night events with "Alpha Moms" in socially connected households in several major cities. They had a blast, bought their own systems, and shared their experiences on blogs and message boards, helping the Wii surpass its one-year goal in less than six months and take the lead among gaming system sales.

Car brands are also becoming clued in to the fact that their traditional sampling model—the test drive—can go farther. In the U.K., Renault has partnered with Avis to offer a free test of its new Mégane for an entire weekend. As the offer states, "We think you'll enjoy . . . the experience so much you won't want to give the car back."

> An additional benefit of sampling is that it attracts the "early adopters" who love to try new products and tell their friends about them. . . . This allows [marketers] to communicate directly with the most motivated and . . . influential audience.

Even entertainment brands are enjoying success from sampling, especially since digital media allow content to be downloaded in seconds. Growing up as I did (and maybe you did) in the era of the record album and music cassette, "sampling" music meant taping something from the radio using your radio and your cassette player. But digital downloads have facilitated flexibility of all kinds in buying and sharing music, and in October 2007, the innovative (and popular) British rock group Radiohead turned music marketing on its head, opting not only to release its latest CD, *In Rainbows*, online in addition to in stores, but also offering fans the chance to name the price *they* wanted to pay (which ranged from $5 to $8 and varied globally) instead of simply charging $15.99 across the board.

From a meaning standpoint, this so-called sampling exercise worked brilliantly in several ways. First, it served as a gift to true fans, helping to ensure future loyalty and sales of music, merchandise, and concert seats. Second, this strategy gave new listeners the opportunity to experience Radiohead's music for the first time at a low cost and at low risk (I myself did so for $5). Finally, the novelty of a "name your own price" sampling effort led to tremendous word of mouth and news coverage around the world.

From a results standpoint, the strategy broke records: *In Rainbows* made more money prior to its physical release (in January 2008) than the band's previous CD had made *in total*; in addition, the physical CD hit both the U.S. and U.K. charts at number one when it was released in stores, despite its having been freely available online since October 2007, attesting to the great value of positive word of mouth. *In*

Rainbows was also the first CD in music history to be widely hailed as "album of the year" prior to its actual physical release: the digital version topped 2007 year-end lists at NPR and at various highly influential publications such as *New York* magazine, the *New York Times*, *Entertainment Weekly, Time, People, Rolling Stone*, and others,[3] before the CD had even been made available in stores.

An additional benefit of sampling is that it attracts the "early adopters" who love to try new products and tell their friends about them. When General Mills launched its new product sampling service, pssst.generalmills.com, more than 100,000 people found the program on their own—completely independent of media—and registered for it in the first month.

This facet of sampling is also useful to marketers in that it allows them to communicate directly with the most motivated and potentially influential audience, which helps to drive initial sales, trigger word of mouth, and gain insight and input from real people outside of artificial research settings like focus groups.

How Loyalty Begets Loyalty

In 1929, at the start of the Great Depression, many companies struggled to retain their customers. Among them, General Mills saw its sales dive, and realized that it had to do something to keep up sales of its Betty Crocker flour. Instead of conducting the historical equivalent of a mass media blitz, the brand started the first modern-day loyalty program. It included stamps in bags of Betty Crocker that housewives could collect and redeem for individual pieces of flatware. By 1932, the program had become so popular that General Mills upped the ante by offering an entire set of flatware as the reward for purchase; and by 1937, the company had expanded beyond flatware to a full catalog, featuring "fine kitchen and home accessories" on which the stamps could be used for savings.

While flour is no longer considered a major branded household category, both General Mills and loyalty programs continue to flourish. Today, there are more than 1.9 billion loyalty program memberships in the United States alone—that's an average of 6 per person and 14 per household, according to Colloquy/U.S. Census. Membership in loyalty programs grew 24 percent over the past two years. But only 39 percent of people are active participants in these programs—which means that some of them work, but a lot don't.

The hope and the goal of a meaningful loyalty program are to keep customers from defecting to competitors, to win greater wallet share, and to encourage an increase in purchases. Since customers opt in, they are more willing to listen and to engage with you and your message. When done well, loyalty programs can provide marketers with both valuable data and a platform for one-to-one marketing that can significantly boost short-term profits and strengthen long-term devotion. Here's how some companies, like Neiman Marcus, Coca-Cola, and Kroger, have used loyalty programs most meaningfully and most effectively.

If you are a die-hard Dallas Cowboys fan, you might be willing to shell out $500,000 to rent the 530 square yards that make up one of the end zones at Texas Stadium—especially when the purchase includes an end-of-season party hosted by the Dallas Cowboys cheerleaders. But before you grab that checkbook, you'd better make sure that you're a member of the Neiman Marcus InCircle loyalty program.

Launched in 1984, Neiman's InCircle program works like many others, but its benefits are legendarily exclusive. While members earn one point for each dollar spent on the store's credit card, they aren't invited to join the program until they've spent a minimum of $5,000. Shoppers who earn 10,000 points achieve Platinum status, at which point they earn double points. And those lucky few who earn *1.5 million points* enter the illustrious Chairman's Circle, the rewards of which include a free cruise, an orchid of the month, and, of course, free fur storage.

What makes a program like Neiman Marcus's meaningful? Sure, it's the big rewards for purchases (and not just the cruise!) from brands like Sony and Canyon Ranch. But it's also the little things that make members feel pampered, including free gift wrapping, free coffee, double points on your birthday, and priority access to restaurants and sold-out shows.

From a marketing standpoint, a program such as this gives customers incentives to concentrate their spending and to spend more in

> Loyalty programs can provide marketers with both valuable data and a platform for one-to-one marketing, [not to mention] enhancing a brand's perceived value.

order to reach higher membership levels, resulting in over $500 million in annual neimanmarcus.com sales. Because members are allowed to bring friends to events and can send redeemed awards as gifts to others, there is a ripple effect from the program's positive word of mouth, not to mention the free PR that surrounds the company's exclusive and over-the-top annual catalog offers: while a $60,000 life-size self-portrait model made of Legos or a limited-edition BMW 7 Series plus a vacation on the French Riviera ($130,000) may not be accessible to everyone, its aspirational quality allows many Neiman Marcus customers to feel richly rewarded by their unique and legendary status in the program.[4]

Loyalty programs also provide incentives by enhancing a brand's perceived value. In early 2006, Coca-Cola kicked off a customer loyalty marketing campaign called "My Coke Rewards." Customers enter codes from specially marked packages of Coca-Cola products into a Web site; the codes are converted into virtual points, which can then be redeemed for various prizes, such as movie tickets, clothing, and music. Popular rewards range from free popcorn at the movies with the purchase of a Coca-Cola beverage (25 points) to a free 30-day Vongo movie service subscription (250 points). From February 2006 through August 2007, Coke saw more than 60 million codes entered and 100 million points redeemed; according to Carol Kruse, Global Interactive Chief, the program boasts 7 million members and growing.[5]

From a meaning standpoint, this program allows Coke to use the data culled to conduct one-to-one marketing more effectively—seeing that you consistently respond to music offers, for example, allows the company to offer you more relevant (i.e., music-oriented) promotions. In fact, the company learned that the more personalized its outreach, the more engaged its members become. And its data further show that the more engaged people are, the more Coca-Cola beverages they purchase.

Based in Cincinnati, Ohio, grocery giant Kroger offers loyal customers meaningful incentives via its Kroger Plus shopper card. By simply registering a phone number with a cashier, shoppers receive everyday discounts on Kroger products, as well as direct mail solicitations that are specifically tailored to products that they frequently buy or have shown interest in. For Kroger, the benefits are many: not only do the data collected allow for more customized marketing on a household-by-household basis, but the relevance of purchase habits data actually allows the company to predict after one week of sales whether a new product will be successful or not.

Separating the meaningful loyalty programs from the meaningless ones isn't rocket science if you concentrate on a few key rules of thumb:

Do

- Focus spending on the 20 percent of customers that drive 80 percent of profit.
- Use individual customer data to guide your efforts.
- Combine easy-to-reach and long-term rewards.
- Make programs easy to enter, understand, and engage with.
- Add visible status rewards (i.e., Platinum frequent flyer luggage tags) to encourage greater purchases and word of mouth.

Don't

- Reward the disloyal.
- Reward volume over profitability.
- Overpromise what you can deliver.
- Pull the plug without plenty of warning and chance to redeem.

• • •

By now, I hope you are convinced that interruption is not only rude but ineffective and unnecessary . . . so please allow me to introduce the concept of intelligent interruption, a key component of offering people meaningful solutions built on relevancy. Just as technology is arming today's consumers with the power and the weaponry to tune out traditional interruptive marketing, technology is also allowing marketers to provide meaningful solutions in a less interruptive manner. The key? Reaching people when and where they are receptive to your message, and knowing enough about them to ensure that your offer will, in fact, be genuinely meaningful to them. Nigel Hollis, executive vice president and chief global analyst at research company Millward Brown, says, "Personal relevance trumps context relevance. Reach people with an ad which is relevant to their circumstances and they will respond positively, whatever the context." John Stichweh, one of our client service leaders at Bridge, who came from digital leadership assignments with P&G and Coke, summarized the challenge well: "I can tell you that fishing where the fish are is necessary, but it is *not* sufficient. One must also fish where and when the fish are biting."

As a fan of the game *Rock Band* for Xbox, I can attest to the validity of both comments. Through my frequent play, Xbox knows how many (and which) songs I've downloaded in the past. So when I log in, I'm served an ad for a new song that is available for purchase. Rather than resenting the interruption, I actually appreciate that Xbox is alerting me to that song's availability—and frankly, I'd be disappointed not to know about it. Nine times out of ten, I download and pay for the Xbox suggestion within minutes of logging on, and I am soon jamming out on guitar while my daughter sings along. Similarly, 1-800-Flowers builds profiles using preferences input by its customers, many of whom like to be e-mailed once a month to be reminded of upcoming occasions. By enabling customers to register specific dates on 1800flowers.com, the site provides a free, relevant service that increases customer loyalty and saves people money. Since it began offering these personal online profiles, the company reports that customer retention has improved by more than 15 percent; access to this information in advance also reduces the amount of time operators spend on the phone, both in taking and in soliciting orders.[6]

Another interesting example of intelligent interruption centers around Alaska Airlines, a small airline that primarily serves Alaska and cities in the Pacific Northwest. Because of its narrow reach and limited clientele, AA's challenge is to specifically aim its marketing at only the people who might actually fly to these areas. Its strategy? To offer different prices to different people based on their "price sensitivity," which is gleaned from personal data, such as a person's geographic location, history with the airline, and whether and how long the person spends visiting the airline's Web site. A trip from Seattle to Portland might cost one viewer $99 and another $109. Smart, yes, but legal? You bet. Better-known commercial airlines do this all the time—consider the last-minute business flight that costs you $1,300 when you buy it the day before you need to travel, but that can be bought for $380 a couple of weeks out. The difference is that the larger airlines aren't utilizing potential customer data to proactively pitch prices, even though they could (and should).

According to Yahoo!, people who view AA's ads click on them two to three times more often than on generic ads. When asked about other marketers who are still practicing the more traditional forms of marketing, Marston Gould, director of customer relationship management and online marketing for Alaska Airlines, remarked, "I think they're very afraid of getting into the data. It's either overwhelming, or it will tell them something other than what they actually believe."[7] What's holding your organization back?

Unlike the one-sided, tell-and-sell approach of traditional ads, intelligent interruption is also considered more meaningful because of the opportunity for people to provide feedback and to tailor the messages we share with them. At Bridge Worldwide, we find that people are often very willing to take the time to provide feedback if they believe that it will improve their experience. For example, in our e-mail programs, we provide options for people to update their profiles or to complete "drip surveys" that ask one or two questions per engagement, so that we can best serve them.

Consumers today expect brands to give them tangible evidence that they want their business.
—John Gerzema, Chief Insights Officer, Y&R

The popular social networking site Facebook is desperate to attract advertisers, but it's afraid of alienating its users, causing them to defect to other growing social networks. In order to address this, the company is testing a system through which each ad it serves features a "feedback" link that enables viewers to comment on why they do or do not like the ad; it also gives members the option of blocking ads that are irrelevant or offensive to them. This technology not only engages viewers in a more meaningful exchange with advertisers but provides feedback similar to that culled and analyzed by Alaska Airlines.

Hulu.com, the online video service, provides another great example of how consumers are taking control and providing valuable feedback to marketers via intelligent interruption. Founded in March 2007 by the traditional networks NBC and Fox, Hulu.com offers TV shows, movies, and clips—from today's *Colbert Report* to 1980s episodes of *Alf*—for free, anytime. Hulu's unique advertising-supported model is fairly revolutionary compared to traditional network television. First, it shows 2 minutes of advertising for every 30 minutes of programming—that's 75 percent less than the 8 minutes of ads on broadcast TV. Second, Hulu provides advertising alternatives for viewers. It often offers visitors the option of seeing ads at the beginning or accepting a commercial break midway through. And when these limited commercial interruptions come up, a thumbs up/down button helps the site get feedback on what is most relevant to show you next time you visit. Hulu.com is still only a baby step away from the old world of traditional advertising, but it shows that the only way to win is by moving more toward consumers' desire for less interruption and more relevance.

Find New Ways to Meet People's Needs

"Meaningfully sponsored services" may be a jargony phrase that we marketers use to describe one of the new ways to meet people's needs, but is it another oxymoron? Not in the realm of marketing with meaning. There are indeed other situations in which people are glad to see advertising—like when a refurbished classic 1982 red-and-white Checker cab sporting an HSBC logo on the door stops in front of you on a rainy day in New York City and a smiling driver offers you a free ride. HSBC BankCab, the brainchild of New York City–based agency Renegade, is an example of what its founder, Drew Neisser, calls "marketing as service." This type of meaningful marketing happens when a brand succeeds in getting your attention by solving life's daily problems and frustrations—and one that has been providing free rides and invaluable PR to lucky New York City residents and HSBC customers for more than seven years.

Renegade's original mandate was, according to its site, to "increase customer loyalty . . . at a time when aggressive regional banks and more branches of entrenched leaders were popping up all over New York City." One of the most successful and cost-effective marketing programs in HSBC's history, the campaign not only won awards but, more important, increased loyalty among its existing customers, attracted new prospects, and even improved pride among HSBC employees.[8]

Charmin's restrooms in Times Square are another excellent example of a brand generating enormous buzz for a product that, let's face it, is not a common conversation piece. How many times have you skulked into a restaurant or coffee shop in a major metropolitan city like New York solely to use the facilities—only to find them locked or nonexistent? For three consecutive years, the restrooms have offered what Charmin calls its "holiday gift to New York." Open daily, these luxury restrooms are the antithesis of traditional port-a-potties—serviced by attendants after every use, and offering stroller parking, ample seating areas, and extra room for families. Providing the ultimate sampling experience, the restrooms are a unique way of helping to solve a universal and often pressing problem for locals and tourists alike at the city's busiest time of year. In 2007, more than 428,000 people frequented the restrooms, nearly double Charmin's original goal of 250,000.[9] And the brand garnered more than 465 million media impressions, 232 percent above the going-in goal.[10] Despite the brand's commitment to adding value to customers' lives independent of purchase, purchases have risen along with traffic to the Charmin restrooms; market share for the brand has increased consistently since the program was first launched.

With its charging stations for laptops and mobile phones in airports in more than 50 cities, electronics manufacturer Samsung is also providing a valuable service in exchange for the lucrative opportunity to reach business travelers—a high-income segment that buys a lot of consumer electronics for both personal and company use—in a significant and meaningful way. Unable to outspend rivals like Sony on traditional TV ads, Samsung's quiet lounges with free power and Wi-Fi position the brand as "life saver" instead of "interrupter"—engendering loyalty beyond reason for the long term.

These are but a few of the dozens of forward-thinking brands that are providing relevant messages to customers every single day. And, as Jonah Bloom, editor of *Advertising Age*, mused in his May 26, 2008, column on the proliferation of meaning in marketing today, there are countless opportunities for companies to help people resolve their daily frustrations in a meaningful way: "AT&T, how about you spare a few million from the billion you spend shoveling your bars in my face, and help the MTA fix its subway intercoms?" (While this would pose a great challenge, it would also provide a noticeable demonstration of its sound clarity!) "Or Citi, how about you take some of the hundred million a year you spend telling us how friendly you are to construct a wireless network for New York?" "BP, you really want to convince us you're green, how about putting together a borrow-a-bike system in a few U.S. cities, like the ones in Paris, Berlin, and Munich?"

"Give Me Information I'm Looking For"

People spend a tremendous amount of time doing research for purchases and life events, both large and small, providing smart marketers with the opportunity to help them find what they are looking for, while adding value on behalf of our brands. But to be meaningful, the information that brands supply must extend beyond solely the company's product or service.

David Ogilvy estimated that on average, helpful information is read by 75 percent more people than copy that deals only with the product.[11] In *Ogilvy on Advertising*, he cites a pretty compelling example. In 1949, the late Louis Engel, who published dozens of books on making money in the stock market (one as recently as 1994), wrote an informational advertisement of 6,450 words for Merrill Lynch entitled: "What Everybody Ought to Know . . . about This Stock and

Bond Business." Buried at the end was the offer of a booklet that provided more information. It pulled 10,000 responses.

> The Web offers marketers a significant opportunity to help people uncover whatever it is they want to know.

While the use of marketing as a means of providing useful information is certainly not new, up-to-the-minute technology such as the Web offers marketers a significant opportunity to help people uncover whatever it is they want to know, whenever they want to know it: answering important questions, be they about major purchases, health, or hobbies; fulfilling what seems to be an insatiable desire for specifics on available products and services; maximizing people's enjoyment of their purchases; and solving the customer's problem, *even* at the expense of your sales. (Trust me; I'll get to that.)

Providing Answers to Important Questions

When a consumer has a question—be it about a washing machine, a recently diagnosed medical condition, or a newfound passion—who better than a company that lives and breathes the subject category to answer it? Companies that provide answers to our endless information needs have a great shot at earning a steady stream of interested customers. Thanks to Google, in particular, which continues to direct searchers to the best solutions, he who provides the best information wins.

You may not have known that 70 percent of women wear the wrong bra size, but Playtex did. Capitalizing on the fact that this is not a topic that women like to talk about with their friends or with sales associates, Playtex built playtexfits.com, a site devoted to helping women find the right fit in the privacy of their own homes. Guided by the Roz, the online bra fit specialist, users enter their band size, cup size, and bra preferences or challenges; given the fact that there is no "one size fits all comfortably" in this clothing category, Playtex uses these criteria to help narrow down and identify the most satisfying product for that customer from the Playtex lineup. From a meaning standpoint, it also helps position the brand as different from competitors like Victoria's Secret, which seems to emphasize styling over sizing, and whose perfectly proportioned supermodels can be off-putting to mere mortals, who tend to respond more favorably to the real women that Playtex uses for models.

Of course, it stands to reason that the more money there is involved, the more time people spend researching their purchases. Makers of durable goods and consumer electronics will tell you that, on average, any transaction over $50 requires a spousal agreement before purchase. So your information should speak to all members of the household—increasingly including the kids.

Average Amount of Time Spent Researching (in Hours)

- A new home: 39
- Major home improvements: 10
- Car: 8
- Vacation: 5
- Mortgage: 5
- Computer: 4
- Television: 2

Source: www.reuters.com.

One major exception to the spousal agreement rule is the purchase of jewelry and diamonds, and the folks at Blue Nile have seized this opportunity to help guys overcome the key barrier of "what's the right thing to buy?" Banner ads for the site feature the main message, "Learn about Diamonds"; by clicking through to the Education and Guidance section of bluenile.com, consumers can learn not only about things like clarity, cut, and carat, but also about how to purchase jewelry to fit a woman's style and taste: "Gold looks beautiful with a darker skin tone. Platinum and silver look beautiful with pale skin." This kind of information provides a major service to guys who either don't have their own sense of style or don't feel confident assessing their significant other's, resulting in a feeling of gratitude and relief that translates into trust (to make the purchase) and loyalty (to come back for more help and additional purchases in the future). From a customized service standpoint, the availability of this information also helps to differentiate Blue Nile from the dozens of big and small online and offline jewelry sellers competing for a buyer's dime.

Beyond big-ticket items like diamonds, questions about health and health care rank high on the list of priority topics for which people seek information. Brands certainly have a right to win here, too. We're all feeling the need to take our own health, and that of our families, into our own hands as the rising costs and complexity of our health-care system put more pressure on us to be better informed, and new online tools allow people to research symptoms quickly and thoroughly, "diagnose" themselves, and gather second opinions from friends and strangers. According to Forrester, in 2006, nearly 60 percent of online consumers said that they had researched a specific medical condition online, and more than 10 million adults in the United States search online for health information each day,[12] offering health-care brands a distinct opportunity to serve the information needs of this very motivated—and very engaged—segment of the population.

And while some pharmaceutical and other health-care companies *still* insist on interrupting our football games and nightly news programs with empty pitches for their products, others—like Johnson & Johnson and Anthem Blue Cross and Blue Shield—are spending the equivalent of a fraction of a big TV budget to provide valuable information to people when and where they want it.

Ethicon Endo-Surgery is a division of Johnson & Johnson that produces surgical instruments, including those used in the growing field of laparoscopic gastric bypass surgery (sometimes called "weight loss surgery"), an effective solution for people who are morbidly obese, unable to lose significant weight through diet and exercise, and suffering from obesity-related health problems, including diabetes, sleep apnea, and knee degeneration. The results of surgery are usually dramatic—a five-year clinical study showed that 50 to 70 percent of patients experience a 50 percent loss of excess body weight. However only a fraction of the people who are eligible for the surgery choose to undergo it. Bridge Worldwide was charged with the task of growing the market.

We knew that the best way to approach this challenge meaningfully was to provide information and support for both surgeons (J&J's main customers) and patients (who might consider undergoing gastric bypass) via a Web site and nontraditional advertising. But what we didn't know until we spent months researching and talking to scores of prospective and postsurgery patients and poring over exhaustive questionnaires was that patients suffering from morbid obesity need much more than before-and-after photos of people holding out their old "big pants." They were already very knowledgeable, and they were sold on the procedure to a certain extent, having already spent hours online each day researching surgery options. What they needed was firsthand feedback from people who had been through it, who could talk frankly about both the positives and the negatives of the surgery itself and life afterward.

As a result, we created a meaningful advertising campaign that included direct-response television, targeted print/banner ads, and heavy search engine marketing that drove prospective patients to www.bariatricedge.com, a Web site that featured information on the key barriers to surgery using videos of real patients and health-care professionals who spoke of the procedure in their own words. The site also included information on risks, a surgeon discussion guide, a BMI calculator, and a glossary of medical terms.

We measured success by tracking the number of requests on a Surgeon Locator that could lead to a personal consultation with a bariatric surgeon, and only a few months after the program was launched, we could tell that it was a huge success. More than a million people visited the site in the first year, and they stayed longer, returned more often, and looked up more surgeons than we had hoped for going in. Our customers—surgeons, clinics, and hospitals—began to report an increase in appointments. But perhaps most meaningful, follow-up survey results and e-mails from individual patients showed that our marketing itself was improving people's lives. Even before going into surgery, patients said that they understood more and felt better about their decision-making process; we felt great about having created marketing that genuinely provided answers to this very significant health decision.

Headquartered in Indianapolis, Anthem Blue Cross and Blue Shield) has also made some meaningful strides with its condition management program, which is particularly notable given that most health-insurance companies are seen in a negative light for rejecting bills and limiting access to doctors and medications. Asthma is one of seven chronic diseases—the others include diabetes, hypertension, and coronary artery disease—covered by the Anthem program, which features an on-call expert 24 hours a day and periodic mailings, highlighting tools and information for better managing the diseases. From a meaningful marketing standpoint, both families and Anthem benefit from better monitoring of these diseases, which helps them all avoid an unpleasant hospital visit and a huge bill. This quality of service can be powerful when employers make their decisions on which coverage to go with each year.

Finally, there's the chance for marketers to add meaning through information concerning consumers' personal passions. Nearly everyone has some sport, game, collection, or hobby that she is addicted to. Whether it's Jimi Hendrix music, running triathlons, or knitting mittens, we define ourselves by these interests and have an insatiable need for more. Here, too, brands have a chance to add value through information. And by aiding and abetting these passions, you can easily gain consumers' attention, and just maybe anchor to this special place in their hearts.

> *The most important thing—and what the most successful brands have—is the human touch, the ability to enrich people's lives in a positive way.*
> —MARK TUTSSEL, CHIEF CREATIVE OFFICER,
> LEO BURNETT WORLDWIDE

As you may know, fantasy football is a global phenomenon, exciting the passions and imaginations of more than 20 million friends and coworkers worldwide. In case you have not experienced this phenomenon firsthand, fantasy football (which has spread to fantasy soccer, rugby, NASCAR, and any other sport you can imagine) is a game in which players "draft" a team of real-life players and win points based on those players' real-life statistics (e.g., touchdowns scored) during the week of play. Web sites like ESPN.com and CBSportsline.com compete to attract groups of fantasy football players, who pay a fee ($100 or more per team) to have their teams managed on the companies' servers. All the services essentially do the same task—help teams track their scores and the winners and losers. So how can ESPN, for example, set itself apart from its competition when it's essentially offering a basic commodity?

ESPN knew that players are constantly looking for help in strategizing and setting up their weekly lineup. So it created the Fantasy Crystal Ball, which provides an evaluation of an individual's team choices and makes specific recommendations; it's available to anyone, and it's free. This service demonstrates to users of competing services that ESPN offers more. It provides a differentiated service to existing customers, offers a unique way to educate new players, and ensures recurring accounts and loyalty over many seasons.

Don't Forget the Product Info!

While it is great to help people with their purchase or passion research, one of the most relevant topics people are continually searching to learn about is your brand! Even the most basic products and services receive enormous amounts of traffic from Internet searches. Studies show that 70 percent of consumers do Internet research on "everyday grocery items." If you don't embrace those who want to learn about your products or services, you might lose them for life.

Randy Peterson, digital innovation manager at P&G, adds that searching for information online "started in the technical world, moved to books, DVDs and travel. Now people are realizing, 'I can even look up information about coffee and laundry detergent online.' It's become a natural way people use to get information of all kinds." And people who arrive at a brand destination via search are ultimately more profitable prospects. Peterson notes, "Searchers who came to package-goods sites were much more category-involved and bigger spenders (by 20 percent) than non-searchers."

Data show that even the lowest involvement with consumer product goods Web sites can have a powerful impact on the bottom line. A December 2008 study by ForeSee Results found that highly satisfied visitors to these brands' home pages were 59 percent more likely to recommend the product and 73 percent more likely to purchase it.

Help Them Make the Right Purchase

So it doesn't much matter whether you make moisturizer or manufacture automobiles—as a marketer, you have an increasing opportunity, if not responsibility, to help people pick the right product. Barry Schwartz, author of *The Paradox of Choice*, suggests that people feel stressed when they have too many options to choose from, both in making the actual decision and, after the fact, in worrying that they made the wrong decision. In a world in which 25,000 new consumer goods products were launched in 2007 alone,[13] success is increasingly dependent on making sure that the right people can connect with the right product. Marketers who are committed to helping consumers choose the right product by arming them with essential information have a better chance of making the sale and of keeping these customers happy and loyal to their brands.

As just about any woman can tell you, skin care is a very personal and continually changing experience. Women's needs change with the seasons and with the passage of time. And women are often on the lookout for the next great ingredient or innovation that can help them maintain healthy, younger-looking skin. They also tend to spend a lot of money on these products, which means that they are wary of trying new things without research. Procter & Gamble's Olay brand, which has launched dozens of new products over the last few years, saw this need and filled it with an online product recommendation tool called Olay for You. According to a spokesperson for the brand, "The idea was largely to help Olay, and consumers, cope with a downside of the brand's success over the past eight years: a proliferation of products and product ranges has made it difficult, particularly for newcomers to the brand or category, to know what they should buy or even where they should start in making a decision."

Since January 2008, the Olay for You program has attracted more than a million visitors, 80 percent of whom completed an involved question-and-answer process and spent an average of eight minutes on the site. Following its success online, Olay took this product recommendation even further by utilizing in-store kiosks so that it could be where decisions are most difficult—and sales are most likely to occur.

Another brand that has successfully employed in-store kiosks is Dr. Scholl's, for its Custom Fit Orthotics. The process is simple (and kind of fun)—you remove your shoes and step on the mat, and its Foot Mapping Technology "identifies the areas of your feet you put the most pressure on and recommends the Dr. Scholl's Custom Fit Orthotic that is best for YOUR feet." The result is a high-quality, individualized, less expensive alternative to the custom-made orthotics ordered through your doctor's office.

The accessibility of the kiosks attracts new customers who might not have considered such a need for additional foot comfort and support until they stepped on that mat, and it ensures future loyalty from those people who were fit perfectly the first time. This tool gives potential consumers the confidence that they are making the best possible purchase and affords Dr. Scholl's valuable information about its customers' needs.

Consumer Reviews: The New Expert Opinion

Online consumer product reviews are another increasingly popular tool that people are using to research products and services prior to purchase—they're easy to find, as consumer-generated content often comes up high in Internet searches; they're plentiful, as nearly every online store asks for ratings; and they're habit-forming: people often start out using them for big purchases, like cars or appliances, and before they know it, they're scanning peer feedback on a new breakfast cereal.

An October 2007 Deloitte Consumer Business Group study found that 62 percent of consumers read online product reviews written by other consumers, more than 80 percent say that their purchase decisions are directly influenced by these reviews, and more than 70 percent share these reviews with friends, family, or colleagues, thus amplifying their impact.

Because these reviews aren't company- or agency-generated, they pack both a negative and a positive punch for brands: while marketers have virtually little to no control over what's being said about their products

> Ninety-nine percent of people say that consumer-generated online reviews are "very or somewhat credible."

and services, a positive review is viewed by consumers as having greater impact and credibility than ad copy, given that it comes from an assumedly objective source. (An eMarketer survey showed that 99 percent of people say that consumer-generated online reviews are "very or somewhat credible.") From a consumer perspective, the news is generally good: a study by Baazarvoice indicates that 70 percent of reviewers want to help companies improve the products they make and sell, 79 percent want to reward a company for good work, and 87 percent of reviews are generally positive in tone—which makes the negative ones that much more meaningful.[14]

Best of all, reviews close sales. MarketingExperiments, a research laboratory that's devoted to analyzing what really works in marketing communications, found that after the same product displayed its five-star ratings, purchasing nearly doubled.[15] That's what motivates companies to put reviews right on their sites and even in physical retail stores. At PETCO's site, shoppers who browsed the "Top Rated Products" page had a 49 percent higher conversion rate than the site average and spent 63 percent more per order than other site shoppers.[16] Burpee seeds proved that even low-rated products sell well thanks to ratings. In a test, it found that products with reviews of only two out of five stars sold more than the same product when listed without a review.

There's an even more meaningful component to consumer reviews than you might think—Sarah Welch, vice president of marketing at TripAdvisor, a company that does nothing but host travel reviews, says that people who use this site to research vacations frequently return to post reviews in gratitude to those they've learned from, and as a kind of "pay it forward" debt to those who will travel after them. This "return trip" to enter a personal review after traveling or using a product is yet another opportunity to engage with consumers.

What's next in this influential space? Look for brands to start featuring reviews in banner ads, and for consumers to start creating video reviews on sites like ExpoTV.com. Video is far more engaging than text-only reviews, and the impact of seeing a real person using a real product stands to be far greater.

The Need to "Track" Is Limitless

It seems that it's not enough to provide people with multiple sources of information about the benefits and attributes of our products and services—once they're convinced to purchase, they'll want to know as much as you do. People have grown accustomed to tracking online orders sent via FedEx and UPS, and they love to use the Web to find out where their produce was grown, when their eggs were packed, and where their delivery pizza is. Smart marketers are attracting and locking in information addicts with clever tools such as these.

Building on its pioneering efforts to equip individuals and businesses with the information they need to track the progress of their shipments online, UPS recently introduced a desktop "widget" that constantly updates shipment status, eliminating the need to log onto a Web site and enter an alphabet-length tracking number. Affording greater ease and convenience to people who frequently send and receive packages, the widget represents yet another way for UPS to ingratiate itself to its loyal customers, creating a distinct competitive advantage over its competitors, who offer similar shipping services. And while it doesn't hurt to underwrite a device that essentially serves as a free advertising knickknack on a desktop, the real goal is to provide added value—a convenient service—to the most valuable UPS customers.

It may be familiar to imagine tracking an incoming or outgoing shipment of carburetors or sweatpants or whatever it is that you sell, but bananas? In a response to the "Buy Local" and "Do you know where your food is from?" movements that are sweeping the country, Dole Organic is offering consumers the opportunity to retrace the steps of each fruit Dole produces. You can log onto Dole's Web site and, by entering a three-digit "farm code" featured on the sticker, see photos of the country in which your banana was grown and picked and learn more about its people. Similarly, through a unique code that is printed on eggshells, a Web site called MyFreshEgg.com can tell you where and when the eggs you bought at Giant or BJ's were packed.

But the product tracking system to beat them all, in my opinion, is Domino's. Launched as a Super Bowl promotion, it allows customers to see—within 40 seconds' accuracy—just where their pizza is in the "oven to box to on-its-way" cycle. Adding yet another layer of transparency and accountability to this transaction, Domino's even provides the first names of the employees who take the order and deliver the pizza, inviting customers to rate them.

Targeting the under-30 customer who is addicted to both data and pizza, the Pizza Tracker is both a value proposition for consumers and a time-saver for Domino's, whose employees have traditionally spent a considerable amount of time answering the phone and the question "Where's my pizza?!" And clearly, it's working. Within a month of its launch, Domino's logged its millionth user—and by June 2008, it was available for all 3,600 of Domino's outlets nationwide.

> *Stop creating adverts and start creating acts. It's no harder than creating ads and it's more fulfilling.*
> —TOM BERNARDIN, CEO, LEO BURNETT WORLDWIDE

Delivering on the "Second Moment of Truth"

With the myriad challenges facing marketers today, it's easy to forget that marketing means much more than just advertising your product and securing the sale. Delivering on the promise of that product is just as important as convincing people to buy it. At Procter & Gamble, we called this "the second moment of truth" (the first being the decision to purchase at the store shelf), and anyone who's ever put together a cheap piece of furniture and ended up with either too few screws or too many knows the frustration of feeling as if you've been sold a bill of goods.

Align, a new dietary supplement from P&G and a Bridge World-wide client, is an entrant in the growing probiotics category (digestive supplements that introduce helpful bacteria into your system), which is gaining mainstream acceptance for a wide range of digestive health benefits. The promise of the product is to help build and maintain a healthy, balanced digestive system, which is particularly important to people who experience episodic constipation, diarrhea, gas, and bloating.

A business school marketing professor once warned me, on the first day of class, "Habit change is really hard." Convincing people to adopt Align was no exception. With Align, there were two key challenges to overcome: it is a pill that must be taken daily, and it can take a month for the full benefits to be felt. On top of that, it's not covered by insurance, and it costs about $1 per day. People who try Align desperately need it and want it to work, but they need support to ensure that they reap the desired results.

Based on our years of work in health care, we knew that online tips and advice can significantly help people to start a new medication habit or make a major lifestyle change. So we invited people to join the My Align Advisor program upon their first purchase. It offers a digestive tracking tool to measure results, and it includes weekly e-mails to explain what people can expect to be feeling at every stage of the process. We also added a "Tell Us Your Story" feature that allows people the catharsis of sharing their own experience, while providing helpful information for others (and powerful word of mouth for the brand).

After just a few months, the My Align Advisor program test showed real results: the majority of users agreed that the program "added to the overall value of Align" and that "Align allows them to enjoy life again," convincing P&G to distribute Align not just online but in a retail test market.

The My Align Advisor program not only was a success for this single over-the-counter medication, but it serves as a model of meaningful marketing that could work anywhere a frequent habit needs to be created. Perhaps Scotts could help people kick off a healthy lawn at the start of the season, or Toyota could aid Prius buyers in their adjustment to hybrid driving. At the end of the day, habit change *is* hard, but marketing that helps people adopt habits more easily can be extremely meaningful for both consumers and businesses.

> Every single interaction between a brand and a consumer is a marketing moment of truth.
>
> **—PETE BLACKSHAW**

How Saying You're Sorry Can Equal Sales

Sometimes the only way to make sure that people know you are working to ensure their satisfaction is to apologize when they aren't happy with your product or service. Try as we may, we can't always control absolutely everything, so when people have disappointing experiences—and they inevitably do—how you handle them makes all the difference. Pete Blackshaw, executive vice president of Nielsen Online Digital Strategic Services and author of *Satisfied Customers Tell Three Friends, Angry Customers Tell 3,000*, says, "Customer service is the new marketing department." In order to communicate meaning through your marketing, you need to look at customer support postpurchase not as just a cost center but as the key to ensuring long-term satisfaction and loyalty. Blackshaw reminds us that every single interaction between a brand and a consumer is a marketing moment of truth. So it is obviously worth the effort to make this marketing impression meaningful.

New research suggests that customer service is the main reason people switch brands across every major industry; a November 2008 survey by Accenture of more than 4,000 people in eight countries across five continents found that 67 percent reported moving their business to other companies because of poor service—taking an average of $4,000 worth of business with them. And even in these tough economic times, when price competition is heaviest, customer service outweighs price as a loyalty factor; in the United States, 73 percent of people switched companies because of poor service, while only 47 percent switched because of price. And the expectations are only rising—31 percent of respondents said that their expectations are higher than they were a year ago, and 52 percent said that they are up from five years ago. Key drivers of satisfaction were polite and friendly representatives, resolution of issues in a timely manner, whether customer service agents took responsibility for resolving issues, and the convenience of service representatives' availability.

Bad stuff happens to good brands, but the moment of truth in customer service comes down to how you handle people who call, write, or text with a problem. Customer retention comes from turning a potentially angry exchange into a satisfactory and fair solution. So what does a good apology include? Here are my tips, derived from having to handle angry people as a brand manager, agency client service leader, and husband of 13 years:

- Recognize the person's disappointment.

- Agree that the situation is either less than ideal or not acceptable.

- Promise that you will learn from it, and work to make sure that it does not happen again.

- Offer some kind of remuneration.

Delta Airlines recently blew me away with its attention to my satisfaction. On a trip back to Cincinnati from New York City, I was notified by cell phone on my way to the airport that my flight had been canceled. The automated voice then confirmed that I'd been automatically booked on a flight the following morning, and I received a follow-up e-mail with the information. Was I disappointed? Of course. But I was thankful that Delta had bothered to ask for my cell phone number somewhere along the way in our relationship, so that instead of sitting at the airport, I was able to go back to the office.

My flight the next morning was fine, but somewhat uncomfortable, since I was stuck in a middle seat because of the cancellation the day before. The next day, however, I received a message from Delta in my e-mail inbox. It was addressed to me personally, and it apologized for the fact that a Gold Medallion member like me had had to be wedged into the middle seat and suffer a case of the Mondays. The note went on to credit me with 500 SkyMiles for my discomfort.

I really can't remember the last time a loyalty program was so aware of the specifics of my situation and so eager to keep me happy. I am used to expecting so little—especially from airlines that have a monopoly-like lock on my travel—that this effort, even if it was automated, made my day.

Delta seems to be making other impressive strides toward meaningful marketing as well: it's connecting with people through a very active Twitter account, and it posts a blog that takes readers "under the wing" to announce sales and promotions and to "share stories on ideas, changes and our people." Even Delta's flight safety videos are drawing attention, with a quirky flight team finger-pointing its way onto YouTube.

It's not clear why it took Delta so long to better utilize its SkyMiles loyalty program or to put a personal face on its brand, but the fact that it's doing so at all, at a time when customer satisfaction with the airlines is at an all-time low, is both meaningful and revolutionary. Maybe it's the rising cost of oil and the fact that Delta increasingly has to fight for flyers. It could also be improved software or even better management. Whatever the reason, Delta is working some magic on this frequent flyer. When I have a choice, it will be Delta all the way, and when things go wrong, I'll cut the company a bit more slack. In this specific case of the "middle seat," all it really took was for someone to write a new rule into the existing loyalty marketing database that Delta has had in place for decades. All it took was someone to notice and care, which is all we really want as human beings. This makes us feel better about the brand, which drives further positive word of mouth.

In the end, everyone wins.

Solve the Customer's Problem, Even at the Expense of Your Sales

As mentioned earlier, there are two key tests of meaningful marketing. The first is that it must be marketing that consumers choose to engage with. The second is that the marketing itself must improve consumers' lives, which means that the consumer can benefit from your brand without actually repaying you with a purchase. I know, I know; this can be a pretty big mental leap for marketers and their advertising

> **How about using marketing to improve consumers' lives in such a way that it could, in fact, *decrease* sales?**

agencies. Ready for a bigger one? How about using marketing to improve consumers' lives in such a way that it could, in fact, *decrease* sales?

Before you assume that I've completely lost my mind, consider Tylenol's recent "Feel Better" ad campaign, which appears on TV, online, in print, and outdoors. While you've probably seen the ads from this campaign dozens of times, it's more likely that you remember them because of the fairly revolutionary messages, which teach you how to avoid headaches—and, therefore, how to avoid needing to take Tylenol at all. Examples include: "Pass breakfast. You may go straight to a headache" and "Skipping meals can cause headaches." A trip to Tylenol.com leads to articles about other triggers of headaches, such as excessive noise, bright lights, and certain foods. Other Tylenol line extensions have followed suit, with Tylenol Cold formula advising that "popsicles can soothe a sore throat," and Tylenol Arthritis Pain formula suggesting that "arthritic joints need strong muscles to protect them." In the face of this revolutionary campaign, it's also important to note that Tylenol outsources its manufacturing to the same company that makes most of the generic versions of the product, further illuminating the need for Tylenol to adopt marketing with meaning.

Another brand that's doing this is Bank of America, via a campaign that teaches customers how to avoid banking fees. Banner ads advise customers to "check your balances and activity so you can prevent fees"; the landing page (the page that appears when a potential customer clicks on an advertisement or a search-engine result link) features an open discussion about avoiding fees. This might seem like a minor, counterintuitive nod to consumers, but the fact is that Bank of America knows that fees are a major source of dissatisfaction to people. Since the bank is addressing the issue up front and transparently, it feels to consumers as if Bank of America is doing the right thing, even at its own expense (half of the bank's income historically comes from fees).

It's not an entirely altruistic strategy—Bank of America knows that it can make more money overall by, say, signing up consumers for overdraft protection than by charging overdraft fees. But both Tylenol and Bank of America realize that they are much better off by looking out for the customer first, and doing it in an obvious way that builds trust, which results in higher loyalty and customer satisfaction. Bruce Hammonds, president of Bank of America Card Services, says: "Our research shows that if we equip consumers with this account information, they become more empowered to manage their finances and more satisfied with their banking experience." Ron Shevlin, author of the blog "Marketing Whims" and an analyst at Aite Group, LLC, notes: "Transparency—being open about fees and rate struc-ture—is an important component of being an advocate for the cus-tomer. Bank of America's move will help engage consumers more deeply with managing their financial lives—an important step to becoming engaged with Bank of America itself."[17]

Tylenol knows that people will still seek pain relief, despite its helpful antiheadache hints, and since its active ingredient is *exactly the same* as that in the store brand, but sold at a much higher price, this goodwill should translate to "loyalty beyond reason." And Bank of America knows that it can make a lot more money by winning long-term, cross-selling business from its customers than from screwing them on a $20 fee. Both brands are smartly using their programs to invite customers into a long-term relationship-marketing program. By providing their customers with this level of valuable information, they will keep them coming back.

Clearly, there is a wide range of opportunities for brands to deliver meaningful marketing by offering solutions. Valuable information, offers, and services position brands as helpful allies to consumers, rather than annoying interrupters. These kinds of solutions represent the initial "bar" for marketing that people choose to engage with—and while this is certainly the best way for your business to engage in a fresh approach to marketing, the next chapter will suggest a way to make an even bigger impact on consumers' lives and your sales.

4

MEANINGFUL CONNECTIONS

CREATING ENTERTAINING EXPERIENCES THAT PEOPLE CAN SHARE WITH OTHERS

Marketers who provide meaningful connections help to forge an important bond between their brands and their potential customers, going beyond providing incentives and information to create a significant value-added relationship with their target consumers. When successfully executed, meaningful connections take the product, service, or brand to a higher emotional level, tying the brand to something that is of deeper importance in the consumer's mind, usually through good old-fashioned entertainment, by creating a unique experience, by providing a creative outlet, or by building or enhancing a bond of friendship with another person or group of like-minded individuals.

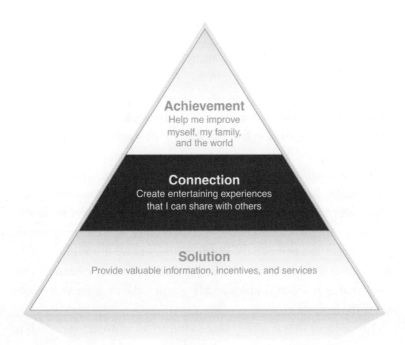

"Entertain Me"

Entertain me? Now, just hold on. I know what some of you are thinking: "Hey, *my* print ads and television commercials are funny. That means they're entertaining. And if entertainment is meaningful, then I must already be marketing with meaning. This is easier than I thought!"

In fact, there *are* lots of examples of entertaining traditional marketing—the Super Bowl is now watched as much for the commercials as for the game itself, and Times Square is filled with billboards so brilliant that tourists take pictures of them. But a funny print ad or compelling commercial on its own is not meaningful, particularly if, at its core, it's still interruptive. Recall the first principle of marketing with meaning: it's marketing that people *choose* to engage with.

There are many different ways to entertain people, depending on your business goals and your target audience, but videos and games are two of the most engaging and effective means available.

A Moving Picture Is Worth 10,000 Words

The allure of video is simple to appreciate and understand—just ask yourself which is more entertaining: a still photo of your perfectly adorable offspring (or niece, or nephew, or pet) or a video of that same person, complete with expressions, movements, and sounds. Whether people are leaning back in front of the TV or leaning forward to view a link on YouTube, video best engages an audience.

Traditionally, marketers have shied away from creating original video content because of the cost of production and broadcasting. But today, and increasingly in the years ahead, you can expect to be able to incorporate this medium into your marketing with meaning arsenal with less cost and complexity. Production costs are dropping, and the Internet—not to mention the more than 500 cable channels that exist—makes it much simpler and less expensive to share video content with the world.

Long-form film is a very successful, tried-and-true approach to video programming—for years brands have paid for product placement in movies or television series, some more subtly than others. But a handful of forward-thinking brands have seen the potential from creating original video programming that not only engages consumers in a meaningful exchange, but also puts their products in the center of the action.

BMW is one brand that embraced the long-film format very successfully and relatively early in its strategic alliance with the James Bond movie franchise. Being the official car of the movie series helped it stay top-of-mind and achieve cachet. A three-movie deal successively promoted its new Z3 (*GoldenEye*, 1995), 750i (*Tomorrow Never Dies*, 1997), and Z8 (*The World Is Not Enough*, 1999). But legend has it that after its product placement contract expired in 1999, BMW was unable to match the exorbitant bid made by Ford to renew the deal.

After your product has been endorsed over a four-year period by none other than 007, what do you do for an encore?

BMW made the smart decision to capitalize on the sexy, action-packed platform it had so carefully cultivated with the Bond placements by creating a set of eight original short films, collectively called *The Hire*, solely for Internet release, in 2001. The shorts were directed by renowned talents such as John Frankenheimer, Ang Lee, and Guy Ritchie, and they starred notable actors such as Stellan Skarsgård, Don Cheadle, and Gary Oldman. And while the plot and cast of each short differs, hero Clive Owen is the constant, playing a driver who helps people out of challenging circumstances, thanks mainly to skilled driving in—what else?—the Ultimate Driving Machine.

During the four months after their initial release, the films were viewed more than *11 million times*, which is particularly significant given that this was in 2001, long before YouTube and heavy broadband Internet penetration. As a result, BMW sales increased 12.5 percent in a single year and surpassed the 200,000 sales mark in one year for the first time in the company's history. BMW continued the series with follow-up seasons in 2002 and 2003 with similar results, to the tune of 100 million viewings over four years.[1]

> *Inferior brands, services, and marketing strategies are going to fall on deaf ears and wither away while superior brands with more relevant and meaningful ways of connecting with their customers will prevail.*
> —DAVE ARMANO, SENIOR PARTNER, DACHIS CORP.

Coca-Cola is another brand that has made history with its meaningful commitment to original video content. Earning the company's highest-ever score in TV commercial testing, "Happiness Factory" started out as a 60-second animated ad shown during the 2007 Super Bowl. It revealed a hidden fantasy world inside each Coca-Cola vending machine that comes to life when you insert your change and make a selection. Psychedelic fantasy characters like a squadron of helicopter "Chinoinks" carry a bottle to be filled, and a fuzzy, giant-lipped "Love Puppy" kisses the filled bottle farewell. Because of the ad's popular reception, the company decided later that year to reach beyond the limited medium of the television commercial and expand on the story. It developed a 3-minute, 30-second movie that was shown both with movie trailers in theaters and online.

People loved it, as did media like *Time* magazine, which wrote: "With an actual plot, cute characters, and gorgeous 3-D animation, this ambitious soda spot feels more like a Pixar short film than a commercial. We hold movie-theater ads to higher standards, but this one deserves to play alongside anything Hollywood has to offer."

Like the BMW films, "Happiness Factory" has received more than 100 million views—and counting—since December 2007. Why? Because it created a meaningful experience for viewers—especially when they *chose* to view it online or were *ready* for a movielike experience at the theater. Because they were genuinely entertained, people laughed, smiled, and developed a closer connection to the brand. When you're selling carbonated syrup water, your brand had better deliver something more; laughs and smiles are a higher-level benefit that Coca-Cola, and other brands like it, must deliver.

In addition to long-form video, there's viral video, which can earn engagement from and sharing among consumers and drive real results for marketers. In a fast-paced, low-attention-span world, we love bite-sized entertainment, and the Internet offers a boundless portal for viewing and sharing. For marketers, viral video can cost little money and time and can result in huge buzz and significant increases in sales.

But that's if it works. Every single one of us would kill to replicate the success of Dove's evolution video, which was viewed 500 million times, won the Cannes Grand Prix, and turned a diminishing brand into the cornerstone of a movement. Many marketers would even settle for a hit like Ray-Ban's viral video of a man catching sunglasses with his face. It scored 4 million YouTube views and helped make the maker of Wayfarers cool again. For every Ray-Ban- or Dove-like success, though, there are countless failures that we never see, or—worse—so-called successes that fail to deliver brand recognition and sales results.

Take Sunsilk, for example, a Unilever brand that uploaded a six-minute video entitled "Bride Has Massive Hair Wig Out" to YouTube on January 18, 2007—a presumably "candid" camcorder video of a "bridezilla" on her wedding day, freaking out and cutting off her hair in a hotel mirror. It was extremely successful in viral video terms, garnering 12 million views on YouTube and lots of speculation as to whether it was real or fake.

But most viewers had no idea that it was from Sunsilk—nor, apparently, did *Good Morning America*, as it failed to mention the brand in its recap of the actors' appearances. And even if people did know, there was no relevant tie to the product or its benefits, so its positive potential was lost.

With viral videos, it takes something truly extraordinary to succeed, and this, because of the nature of the medium, is rare. People are increasingly sensitive and cynical about videos that try to hide marketers' true agendas. And even when a marketing-related video does attract genuine attention, that doesn't mean that it will successfully build your business. Here are some rules of thumb for brand and agency teams:

1. *Don't start if you're not willing to take risks.* Every successful viral video pushes some boundary, either legal's or brand guidelines'. Get the support you need from the people you need it from beforehand.

2. *Stick to a small production budget.* Don't break the bank—remember, the odds are long. And low-cost production values add legitimacy—in other words, you'll get a better response from people if your video doesn't look, feel, and smell like a slick ad.

3. *Integrate your brand as seamlessly as possible.* If you can't work your brand into the action somehow, then it is a wasted effort. But remember to do so subtly, or you'll be stoned by the social networks for trying to infiltrate their sacred space with advertising.

A perfect example of a phenomenally successful viral is Blendtec's "Will It Blend?" videos. In the mid-2000s, Utah-based Blendtec, a small player in the high-end home blender category (with only $40 million in annual sales and *no marketing department*) needed to stand out in a stagnant and undifferentiated market. It hired George Wright as its first director of marketing in January 2006. Soon after arriving at the 186-person company, Wright was walking around the testing room and noticed some piles of sawdust in the testing lab. "I couldn't imagine why," Wright told the *Wall Street Journal*.[2] "So I asked people, 'What's going on?' And they said, 'Oh, that's just Tom [Dickson, Blendtec's CEO] testing the blenders,' like it was an everyday occurrence. And, to me, great big red flags are going off saying, 'No, this is not a normal, everyday occurrence. Blenders just don't blend two-by-twos. . . . I want to film this.'"

Blendtec spent all of $50 filming the first videos, featuring Dickson in a white lab coat and safety glasses, pulverizing objects as disparate as a rotisserie chicken, marbles, and a garden rake. Uploaded to YouTube and seeded on sites like digg.com, "Will It Blend?" received 6 million views in the first week, which has escalated to hundreds of millions since and has spawned plenty of parodies and knock-offs by others. Even more meaningfully, sales increased 43 percent in the first year alone as people became aware of the largely unknown brand and realized that if a Blendtec blender could take on a rake, it would have no problem crushing ice for margaritas.

So why did this viral work to such a great extent—while others simply do not? Blendtec did three things brilliantly. First, it made certain that the product was fully integrated into the viral—it's a product demo, after all! And while its approach was not subtle, the brand was smart enough not to take itself (or the video) too seriously. It wasn't a sales pitch, but more like a nod to a 1970s game show, complete with a retro theme song and logo. That's what people found entertaining. Second, the very low cost of the production was prudent financially and attractive to viewers in a campy way. And finally, Blendtec took risks with its product and its brand—no doubt somewhere in the company, someone said, "Hey, aren't we sending the wrong message? We don't really want people to blend golf balls in our blenders!" But Blendtec gave consumers credit for being able to see the comedic value of the viral and take away its message of durability, and it succeeded in a big way.

Clients are not saying, "Make us ads" or "Make us Web sites"; they're saying, "Create interaction between our brand and our customers."

—ROBERT RASMUSSEN, EXECUTIVE CD FOR NIKE ACCOUNT, R/GA

Beyond Pong: The Next Evolution of Games

Game playing is a diversion that is much, much older than video or other staged performances, and it represents an emerging opportunity for brands that are looking for entertaining ways to connect meaningfully. From simple word games to massively multiplayer online role-playing games (MMORPGs), we are drawn to games because they offer competitive challenges, discovery, and skill building, engaging us both mentally and physically. New data released by IGN Entertainment and Ipsos Media CT might change your perception of the stereotypical slacker-gamer-teen—their study shows that 55 percent of gamers are married and 48 percent have kids, and that gamers make an average of $79,000 per year (versus $54,000 for nongamers). And women are into video games, too—a study by the Consumer Electronics Association in April 2006 showed that 65 percent of women in the 25 to 34 age group (which so many marketers consider their sweet spot) are also actively gaming.[3]

Obviously, this is another area where digital is a big enabler. One of the most popular types of video games is what insiders deem "light diversions"—games that, for example, allow people a quick break from work. How many times have you knocked on a colleague's door, only to catch her engaged in a game of solitaire? (I use "her" deliberately, as research shows that women are particularly drawn to such diversions.)

Wrigley is one brand that has capitalized on this interest with its Candystand game site for over 10 years. A free, fun, flash-based gaming destination featuring everything from classic arcade games to sports games to billiards to card games, it furthers Wrigley's mission to "weave its brands into the fabric of everyday life," and jibes perfectly with Wrigley's products, offering a few minutes of refreshment in someone's day.

And, boy, is it woven into a lot of everyday lives. According to Wrigley, 10 million people spend an average of 30 minutes on the site every month; one case study cited by *Advertising Age*[4] shows that the site grew Life Savers more than 15 percent over two years. It's also now a media platform that Wrigley's can use to build awareness for new brands as well as promote existing products. Plus, Candystand became a new revenue stream for Wrigley, as the company offered this media property to other noncompeting entities. The site became so successful that in 2008, Wrigley sold the business to Funtank, a leading distributor of branded games. It literally had become too big for the company to handle on its own, but Wrigley remains the exclusive confectionary advertiser.

In contrast to light diversions, deep engagements offer consumers more intense, brand-focused gaming experiences, like Burger King's Xbox advergames, discussed in Chapter 2. In an unusual piggybacking of meaningful marketing and successful traditional marketing, the California Milk Processor Board (CMPB)—the folks behind "Got Milk?"—have created an immersive online game called *Get the Glass*.

While the "Got Milk?" campaign is one of the best recognized and most successful television/print campaigns, in terms of both creative output and sales results, in 2006, the CMPB saw the opportunity to connect more meaningfully with customers through immersive entertainment. *Get the Glass* is a three-dimensional online board game in which players attempt to get the Adachi family, all of whom are suffering from health problems stemming from a lack of calcium and vitamin D, around a digital game board and into Fort Fridge, where they can—at last!—secure a glass of milk.

Get the Glass presents an incredibly detailed virtual world that rivals some of the best video games available, earning rave reviews and high scores from some of the discriminating game reviewers at jayisgames.com. For these reasons, it's particularly appealing to the younger people whom the milk makers hope to win over, promising a lifetime of sales. Six weeks postlaunch, 6 million people had visited the site, with 650,000 having reached the Glass at Fort Fridge, and an additional 10 million gallons of milk had been sold, compared to sales during the same period in the previous year.[5]

Finally, other brands have found success through placement in popular games created by others. *Guitar Hero* and *Rock Band*, for example, offer free songs from new albums; new music acts that are hungry for exposure are providing game owners with free or reduced-price versions of their songs to build buzz among these passionate, connected music lovers. And it works—Ben Kuchera, a writer for the site Ars Technica, tracked the sales for new tracks from the popular bands The Strokes and Slipknot and found that "the week *Guitar Hero III* was released, [The Strokes'] 'Reptilia' sold 127 percent more digital copies than it had the week before. The following week saw another 96 percent jump in sales. That number stayed high the next week as well. . . . The story was similar for Slipknot's track 'Before I Forget.' That song jumped up 75 percent the week of the game's release, and an impressive 140 percent the week after." Kuchera concluded, "It's crystal clear that having your music included in a *Guitar Hero* game means increased sales for labels and bands."[6]

> *The agency's job is not to interrupt but to create content that's so entertaining . . . valuable and useful that [people] wouldn't want to live without it.*
> —JEFF HICKS, CEO, CRISPIN PORTER + BOGUSKY

Even Brands That Sell Entertainment Must Entertain

Some brands are simply a better fit for entertainment marketing than others, and entertainment brands are among those that fit well. Yes, even brands that sell entertainment have to think about how to, well, entertain potential customers with their marketing in order to connect with them in a meaningful way. In 2007, in the face of falling attendance and television ratings, the National Hockey League came upon a meaningful marketing idea that would raise interest and media coverage: a rare regular-season outdoor ice hockey game. On January 1, 2008, it debuted "The Winter Classic," a game between the Buffalo Sabres and the Pittsburgh Penguins played in a makeshift rink in an outdoor football stadium, complete with snow and wind. For people who grew up playing hockey, the frigid air and scratching of blades on an ice-covered pond triggered memories of the game in its pure, unbridled form. For general sports fans, the novelty of an outdoor hockey game was a welcome alternative to back-to-back football bowl games. Of course, it didn't hurt that the game went into Sudden Death overtime and a shootout, in which Penguin's superstar, Sidney Crosby, scored the winning goal.

From a results standpoint, the experiment was a huge success—the NHL enjoyed record attendance (over 70,000 people), as well as its largest TV audience since 1996. And there was significant media coverage of the event, convincing the league to schedule an encore, on January 1, 2009, between the Detroit Red Wings and the Chicago Blackhawks in the "friendly confines" of Wrigley Field. Detroit beat the Hawks 6–4 before another joyous crowd and the biggest TV audience for a regular-season hockey game in almost 13 years. It even beat the previous year's ratings by 12 percent.

Brands that are naturally linked to fun and fashion are another genre that can most easily maximize the entertainment connection. Red Bull is one excellent example. One could argue that the company has positioned itself as an events company that happens to sell a carbonated beverage—as it runs hundreds of on-location experiences around the world each year. But Red Bull is no mere sponsor in name only; instead, the company tends to take a leadership role in the events and among athletes it works with to better control the brand experience. Red Bull owns its own F-1 and NASCAR racing teams; bought pro soccer clubs in Austria, the United States, and Brazil; has created original events such as the Red Bull Flugtag and Red Bull Soap Box Derby Race; and even built a private, hidden half-pipe in Colorado for sponsored snowboarder Shaun White to work on new tricks for the 2010 Winter Olympics.

Speight's Beer provides another great example, one that illustrates how a brand can both refresh a connection with longtime fans *and* raise awareness among those who have never tried the product before. If you haven't been to New Zealand's South Island, you have probably never heard of Speight's Beer, but according to marketing legend, after the brand learned that fellow Kiwis in the U.K. missed their Speight's Beer, it launched "Speight's Great Beer Delivery," in which an actual working Speight's Alehouse was strapped to the deck of a cargo ship. About 100,000 New Zealanders applied online to accompany the vessel on a 24,000-kilometer trip to Samoa, Panama, the Bahamas, and New York City before landing in London to be greeted by thousands of thrilled—and thirsty—fans, who had tracked its progress online and in newspapers for weeks. Not only did Speight's garner millions of dollars of free PR, but it regained its leadership share in the New Zealand market and drove a "double-digit increase in Brand Adoration . . . whilst all other mainstream beers declined." Plus, it drove new distribution and sales in the U.K.

Brands that seek to connect with younger people would also be wise to consider entertainment as a means of earning these consumers' brand engagement, since things like music and movies are such a significant part of their lives.

Toyota is a brand that has long been regarded as a bellwether of safety, reliability, and sound long-term automotive investment. Perhaps as a result of this, it discovered that it was losing its appeal to young, entry-level buyers, and that the age of its average buyer had risen to 54 years old.

To counter this trend, in 2003, the company decided to launch a new entry-level car under the Scion brand. Targeting 18- to 24-year-olds—the youngest demographic a carmaker had ever targeted for its marketing—Toyota realized that because this was the first generation that "doesn't want to be marketed to," it had to work harder to help these consumers "discover" Scion on their own.

The strategy was to do absolutely no mass marketing (that's right, no TV, print, or radio), but instead to deliver its message through low-key events that were handpicked because they seemed special and mysterious. In trend-setting markets such as Los Angeles and New York, Scion sponsored, created, and handed out mix CDs at art gallery events, independent film openings, and rave parties, with great results. This modest but meaningful activity made Scion the most successful launch of a new brand in North American automotive history, ramping up from selling zero to 170,000 cars in less than four years. What's also particularly interesting to note is that the average age of a Scion buyer is 30 years old, an industry low, helping to bring Toyota's average age down, too.

Healthy Choice, a ConAgra brand and a Bridge Worldwide client, found itself faced with a challenge similar to Toyota's, in that its main users tended to be busy, health-conscious, and over 40. In fact, the brand was invented by the ConAgra CEO, Charles "Mike" Harper, who suffered a heart attack at age 58. Forced to dramatically alter his diet, he was uninspired by what he found in the supermarket and drove the company to invent the line.

Despite its success, the brand saw an opportunity to reach out to thirty-somethings who are looking for good nutrition and great taste, but are frequently eating on the go. In 2008, it launched more relevant and innovative Healthy Choice Fresh Mixers (such as Rotini & Zesty Marinara Sauce and Sweet & Sour Chicken), a line of high-quality, great-tasting meals that require no refrigeration.

In our research around this younger target, we found that many of these people work in offices and 60 percent regularly eat lunch at their desks. While eating, they allow themselves to take a short break and enjoy some "me time" online. We saw an opportunity to connect with this audience during this time. We created the world's first live improv comedy programming delivered via the Web and powered by the audience. Dubbed *Working Lunch*, this snack-sized entertainment vehicle is a cross between the television shows *The Office* and *Whose Line Is It, Anyway?* It provides visitors with unpredictable live comedy and the opportunity to interact with it directly and almost instantaneously, through polls and by proposing meeting agenda topics.

Working Lunch was developed with MSN and was aired live for two weeks in November 2008 and again for two weeks in January 2009. We extended the experience by recording all the action and creating best-of clips that can be shared easily with MSN's support. In terms of audience, we exceeded our total goal of 3 million unique visitors in only three weeks and have reached over 5 million visitors to date.

By positioning Healthy Choice Fresh Mixers as the sponsor of this entertaining concept and sprinkling a generous dose of product placement throughout the show, we've created a positive association and emotional involvement with the product that is earning attention and has helped the Fresh Mixers line achieve strong retail distribution and sales.

I see a future where advertising becomes a very different concept. It becomes a question of no longer saying, but doing. Not telling, but being.
—CINDY GALLOP, MARKETING ENTREPRENEUR

"Create an Experience"

Entertainment is just one way in which brands can create meaningful connections with customers. Creating an experience is another, and two key forces are compelling marketers to capitalize on this still-new marketing niche.

First, there is the growing need for differentiation in nearly every category. Particularly in these challenging economic times, name brands have come under greater pressure to prove their merit against high-quality, lower-priced store brands. Technology has empowered motivated consumers to do extensive research on, say, whether a Sony HDTV is really worth $500 more than a VIZIO. But by creating an experience for the consumer through their marketing, brands can deliver greater value in this flattened competitive field. Second, though it may not seem so right now, people around the globe are steadily gaining in affluence, and they are increasingly drawn to interesting experiences that enrich their lives, rather than simply filling a basic need.

In *The Experience Economy*, Joseph Pine and James Gilmore suggest that "companies stage an experience whenever they engage customers, connecting with them in a personal, memorable way." They point to the example of coffee, which has migrated from a $0.01 home brew to a $1.00 diner drink to a $5.00 mocha skim latte experience in a cozy Starbucks seat. By moving up the ladder from product to service to experience, brands can gain added profits and competitive superiority.

New research by Ryan Howell, assistant professor of psychology at San Francisco State University, suggests that the happiness created by purchasing an object fades as people become used to having it around, but experiences continue to provide happiness over a longer period of time through memories. Howell found that experiences are rated higher both because they often involve social bonding (an added source of pleasure) and because they give people a greater sense of "being alive," both during the experience and in reflection.

Some futurists say that we are nearing a "postconsumer society," in which the drive to outbuy the neighbors will be replaced by the desire to collect memorable personal experiences, ranging from a meal at a notable high-end restaurant to a flight into space. Others suggest that in a down economy, people are seeking experiences because they allow for a momentary escape from reality. Either way, the possibilities for staging experiences (and building the business through them) are practically limitless. Here are some of the most common—and most successful.

Turn Your Brand into a Tourist Attraction

In the experience economy, you stop at a store to buy, say, a roll of paper towels, but you visit a branded destination in order to enjoy *a fully immersive brand experience*. Yes, the point of a branded destination is still to make a sale, but if the experience is memorable and satisfying, the stuff essentially sells itself.

The Apple Store provides an example of a killer branded shopping experience. In 2000, Steve Jobs hired Ron Johnson, who had risen to vice president for merchandising after 16 years at Target, to create an Apple retail experience. According to the *New York Times*, when Jobs told Johnson, "Apple is one of the biggest brands in the world," Johnson said, "[Then] Apple needs stores that should be as big and spacious, a physical embodiment of the brand."[7]

"The Apple stores are selling digital experiences, not products," said Ted Schadler, an analyst at Forrester Research, in that same article. Since about half of those who are buying Macs at Apple's stores are former PC users, it makes perfect sense that "almost half of the store staff is there not to sell but to provide free help on how to use Mac computers, iPods, software and third-party accessories like digital cameras." Starting in the late spring of 2008, Apple began adding additional "concierges" to its stores to greet and direct shoppers. As Pete Blackshaw, executive vice president of Nielsen Online Digital Strategic Services, wrote of his firsthand experience at an Apple store in *Advertising Age*, "Things once considered the dark side of Apple, such as tech support, are on the verge of becoming strategic assets, with the Apple Store's geek-stocked Genius Bar able to tackle just about any issue of concern you have. And the process of planning that interaction is more akin to scheduling a haircut or spa treatment than calling those inaccessible tech-support lines."[8]

The point, clearly, is not just the sale, but the service; the personnel are not just knowledgeable, but enthusiastic, and the customers convert. And sales have certainly kept pace with satisfaction: for the financial quarter ending March 2008, Apple's store sales jumped 74 percent to nearly $1.5 billion, with average revenue per store hitting $7.1 million, up 48 percent from a year earlier, and quarterly operating profit more than doubled to $334 million.[9]

Like the flagship Apple Store, the Abercrombie & Fitch (A&F) flagship in New York City is located on Fifth Avenue alongside dozens of others, whose footprints, architecture, and decor tend to be inspired more by marketing than by actual sales. A&F, the brand long associated with low-rise jeans, distressed tees, and gangly teen models with unwashed hair and six-pack abs, is no exception. With a line for entry snaking around the block, the four-story store has the vibe of a cool loft or club, complete with loud music and a staff of beautiful people, and it was created so that customers could connect with and experience the brand's identity firsthand (yes, you can actually get your photo taken with a model). And while the aesthetics, as noted, are more marketing-driven than sales-driven, this outlet enjoys the highest sales of any store in the entire chain.

> *It's not about new media; it's about new marketing.*
> —NICK BRIEN, CEO, UNIVERSAL MCCANN

M&Ms World in Times Square; Hershey's Chocolate World in Hershey, Pennsylvania; the Crayola Factory Museum in Easton, Pennsylvania; and Kellogg's Cereal City in Battle Creek, Michigan, offer other unique store experiences. Because of the success of these kinds of destinations, many other legendary companies have turned their brands into tourist attractions. Mostly through word of mouth, the Heineken Museum in Amsterdam ranks as one of the top to-do's in that city for backpacking twenty-somethings—along with the Anne Frank House, the Sex Museum, and the Grasshopper—drawing 500,000 paying visitors per year. While its popularity may be due to the fact that several glasses of beer are included in the ticket price, the experience allows relatively new drinkers to connect personally with the brand ("I'll never forget the first time I had a Heine . . . it was on my trip to Amsterdam . . .") and naturally perpetuates word of mouth by giving them a story to treasure and share with friends for life (that is, if they remember it).[10]

You have a smaller budget than a flagship Fifth Avenue destination store will require? Or, you want to dip your toe into these branding waters before cannonballing in? Try a pop-up store. This emerging marketing concept involves creating a temporary, stand-alone retail outlet for your brand. It's a great opportunity for people to sample your product or service in a controlled, personal environment, a less expensive way of enveloping them in a deeper branded experience, and a surefire way to garner free media coverage and word of mouth.

For example, there was the Meow Mix Café, located at the corner of Fifth Avenue and 42nd Street. It was a place where people could bring their cats to sample the new Meow Mix Wet Food Pouches, play games, and socialize. While it cost $150,000, CEO Richard Thompson claims it increased sales by *$50 million* in 2005.[11]

For six weeks in the fall of 2007, Delta rented 3,500 square feet at 101 West 57th Street to create its SKY360 Lounge, a place to engage flyers directly by offering the chance to test out new all-leather coach-class seats and new menu items from Chef Todd English. To promote the space, Delta sent 400,000 e-mails to customers who live in or frequently visit New York City; those who printed the online invitation also earned a free one-day pass to visit a Crown Room Club, the airline's membership lounge. According to Delta spokesperson Andy McDill, "Delta has been making lots of changes over the last few years . . . this allows us the opportunity to show the best of the new Delta. It's an opportunity for us to engage with our customers outside of the airport."

Enhancing Consumer Satisfaction by Blurring Product Development and Marketing

Another way to create an indelible marketing experience for people is to deliberately blur the line between your product and your message— essentially, to create marketing that is so intrinsic to the consumer's enjoyment of the product and that so significantly improves the consumer's life that the marketing becomes as valuable as the purchase. As Jeff Hicks, CEO of Crispin Porter + Bogusky, put it, "We think the future of advertising is great products that have marketing embedded in them. The agency's job is not to interrupt but to create content that's entertaining. It should be content so valuable and useful that [people] wouldn't want to live without it."[12] Not only will people generally pay more for the product, but it helps to differentiate your brand from the competition, and it drives loyalty.

Nike+ offers an excellent (and literal) example of embedded marketing. Launched without significant advertising support in 2006, the Nike+ system utilizes a sensor that is placed in your shoe to relay information on your speed, time, distance, and calories burned to another sensor, which is attached to an iPod. When you sync your iPod, this information is uploaded to a Nike+ Web site. Committed runners have always loved to record their runs in a journal and look back on their progress over months and years, but people apparently *really* love seeing this information online—30 percent of Nike+ users return to the site three or more times per week, an unprecedented success for a marketing Web site. Nike encourages success by awarding 100, 500, and 1,000 miles logged with "badges" that appear on your personal home page. It offers special motivational music tracks that you can download, as well as coaching and training plans for preparing to run a 10k or a marathon. Users can even create personalized challenges for themselves and their friends to make running more rewarding. The challenge tool also allows smack talk comments, which, of course, adds to the fun.

Nick Law, chief creative officer at the agency R/GA, which built the program for Nike, says, "Where most initiatives focus on enticing consumers to complete a purchase, Nike+ continues to engage the consumer long after the transaction has occurred, keeping Nike+ runners motivated and connected with each other and with the brand. People are beginning to expect more from a brand than a witty narrative, and Nike+ redefines how a brand can reach its audience through meaningful enabling experiences."[13]

Other brands, like Adidas's miCoach, which arrived in April 2009, are looking to capitalize on Nike's success by launching similar

> *The performance of Nike and every other global company in the twenty-first century will be measured as much by their impact on the quality of life as by revenue growth and profit margins.*
> —PHIL KNIGHT, CHAIRMAN, NIKE

systems—but since Nike+ members had run over 100 million miles by the end of 2008, Nike is literally 100 million miles ahead of its competition, and it shows in its sales. Through 2008, Nike had sold 1.3 million Nike+ iPod sport kits and 500,000 Nike+ SportBands at $59 each, for a total of $56 million—not to mention the fact that Nike's piece of the running shoe pie is up from 48 percent in 2006 to 61 percent in 2008. "A significant amount of that growth comes from Nike+," says Matt Powell, an analyst at SportsOneSource, which tracks market share.[14]

Boston-based Samuel Adams provides another great example of embedded marketing. Perhaps no product category better exemplifies meaningful connections than beer, since beer brands (and alcohol brands in general) depend on forming personal bonds with the people who drink them. Great beer marketing is meaningful when it connects us more closely to the brand and to others who share the same mindset.

In February 2007, Sam Adams unveiled a beer glass that, for $30 (for a set of four), "elevates the craft beer drinking experience." Specifically designed to maximize the experience of drinking this golden ale, the concept was the brainchild of founder Jim Koch, who wondered if glassware could do for beer what it has done for wine. "We wanted to create a glass that offers beer lovers a full sensory drinking experience by fully showcasing Samuel Adams Boston Lager's complex balance of malt and hop flavors," says Koch.

After meeting with Jean-Michel Valette (who used to run Robert Mondavi's winery and now sits on Sam Adams's board), Koch gathered hundreds of glasses to sample, and initiated a 300-page analysis. Several world-renowned glassmaking companies were invited to submit prototypes, and the winner was Rastal in Germany, whose glass offered several features that add to the smell/taste experience, including an angled rim and laser etching to ensure a constant supply of bubbles. According to a marketing representative at Sam Adams, the glasses sold "far beyond expectations," proving that you can enhance consumers' satisfaction through embedded marketing to the extent that they will actually pay for the privilege of becoming an ultraloyal advocate for the brand.

It's often hard enough for marketers to sell their products and services—so imagine the challenge of not having a product or service to sell, but having to figure out how to *sell the invisible*. In the case of, say, charitable donations or political advertising, if you can connect an experience with the intangible, it can make the marketing more meaningful, thereby helping the consumer to engage more concretely with your cause, your candidate, or your perspective, each of which is largely conceptual in nature.

One of the most original cases of this is the Multiple Sclerosis of Australia's "Coin Operated Laboratory," a piece of performance art that is featured at major public events and in public spaces like malls. In a clear Lucite box, a scientist sits at a desk, working with test tubes and other pieces of lab equipment. Periodically, he stops working and slumps over on the desk until someone places a donation in a slot on the box, whereupon he perks up and continues his work. This clever embodiment of the intangible raises about $150 per hour from onlookers, but most important, through an experiential context, it concretely drives home the point that donations are essential to funding the research needed to develop a treatment for this currently incurable disease.

Blindekuh is another unusual example of this principle at work. The word is German for "blind cow," and the "product" is a restaurant that serves food at night in complete darkness. Why? To give sighted people the chance to experience what it is like not to be able to see, thus increasing our overall understanding of and respect for visually impaired people and their needs. Created in 1999, the restaurant is staffed by blind and partially sighted people and is also used for musical, theatrical, and literary events. Thirty-one thousand people per year visit Blindekuh in Zurich (the company has opened a second location in Basel); its annual budget has risen from literally nothing to $1.5 million based on donations and restaurant/event sales.

> **[Two brands] working together can create a mutual experience that benefits both brands and their joint customers.**

If You Can't Beat 'Em: Creating Meaning through Partnerships

Can you imagine two disparate brands working together in the traditional, interruptive marketing world? Say, splitting the cost and creative development of a 30-second Super Bowl ad? That would be unlikely in the old marketing world, but it's not so unusual in a world in which marketers are striving to create more meaning, and working together can create a mutual experience that benefits both brands and their joint customers. As you might expect, these experiential tie-ins seem to work best when the brands share both a common target customer and similar brand attributes.

As a vehicle to promote *The Simpsons Movie* in the summer of 2007, 20th Century Fox and 7-Eleven did just this with phenomenal results, utilizing a new concept called "reverse product placement." Together, they transformed a dozen 7-Eleven stores in the United States and Canada into Kwik-E-Marts, the convenience stores from the show. The normal 7-Eleven red, white, and green signs were replaced by yellow and tan ones; storefronts were painted yellow; and, perhaps most notably, Kwik-E-Mart products, such as Squishee frozen drinks, Sprinklicious donuts, Buzz cola, and KrustyO's cereal, were available and were hard to keep in stock: 4,000 Sprinklicious donuts were sold each day versus the usual 100, and there were continuous lines of customers waiting to get into the stores. (When was the last time you saw a line to enter your local 7-Eleven?)

Not only was this marketing merger a perfect fit to capture the interest of 7-Eleven/*Simpsons* core customers, men 18 to 34, but it also resulted in thousands of news stories within days of the store openings, and it lent a certain cachet to 7-Eleven that it hasn't enjoyed in a long while. As Bob Garfield wrote in his *Advertising Age* column, "The real credit goes to 7-Eleven for taking such an astonishing risk."[15] The truth is, 7-Eleven at first resisted the idea. According to Rita Bargerhuff, vice president of marketing for the company: "Reverse product placement had sprung up in previous conversations, but the hierarchy at 7-Eleven . . . never quite embraced the concept. This time, however, 7-Eleven marketers vowed to erase internal doubt and inspire consumers to take a fresh look at their brand." Clearly, the gamble paid off for 7-Eleven. According to Bargerhuff, "It made our brand relevant again. We'd lost some of that over time." And thanks in part to this meaningful connection, *The Simpsons Movie* raked in an impressive $74 million in its opening weekend.

TiVo and Domino's have partnered in a similarly innovative experience, offering viewers the opportunity to order a pizza and track its delivery on their television. This is one of those smart services that helps TiVo to differentiate itself from (often free) cable DVRs, and it helps to explain why TiVo loyalty ranks above 90 percent. Instead of passing the cost on to its customers, TiVo charges Domino's for the right to offer this feature to its users; Domino's benefits in that it is able to increase its share among TiVo households, who are likely to be heavy pizza delivery consumers, given their affinity for convenience. This novelty makes ordering pizza fun, and so easy that customers tend to order more food, more often.

Of course, both brands benefited from the significant free PR coverage of this announcement, in outlets ranging from the *Wall Street Journal* to the Gizmodo technology blog. And both brands are seen as forward-thinking and forward-acting, which results in a valuable bump in their equity scores.

When you can't beat 'em, you can often join 'em—think about other relevant brands in your customers' lives and consider the synergies that lie in a partnership. Then pick up that BlackBerry and reach out. Chances are there will be other marketers out there who are also looking for ideas to create a new and meaningful experience by which to connect with their customers.

"Give Me a Creative Outlet"

Picasso once said, "All children are born artists; the problem is to remain artists as we grow up."

Whether as the master of an audience at a TED conference or leading a U.K. government task force on education, Sir Ken Robinson agrees, and he is on a mission to transform our society for the better by encouraging us to teach our children—and ourselves—how to further develop our innate power of creative thinking. He believes that "creativity is not exclusive to particular activities; it's possible whenever human intelligence is actively engaged."[16]

What's this got to do with meaningful marketing? Well, marketers that can help people unleash their latent creativity can forge powerful connections to their brands and earn the loyalty beyond reason that is critical to long-term profitability. Once you recognize that people have an innate desire to create and to invent, you might also see that this is a genuine way to bring greater meaning to their lives.

Do-It-Themselves Advertising

One of the more popular ways in which marketers are encouraging people to tap their creative energies on behalf of a brand is to let them try their hand at doing the marketers' jobs for them. Both Doritos and Pringles, for example, have invited fans to submit original commercials or songs on video; sneaker maker Converse received more than 1,500 commercial contest entries in two years; Sony asked its customers to send in video ads for its Walkman and Handycam products. Even the Pretzel Dog brand ran a $5,000 commercial film contest.

Such activities can generate strong engagement, buzz, and sales. The problem with turning TV production over to the masses is that only a small handful of fans actually have the time and the skill to create a decent piece of video. To truly involve one's target audience, brands must extend and expand beyond consumer-created commercials.

> *The ad industry has got to understand that it's no longer in the ad business.*
> —BOB SCHMETTERER, CHAIRMAN AND CEO,
> EURO RSCG WORLDWIDE

One of the promotions that Bridge created for grocery giant Kroger was the Design a Reusable Shopping Bag Contest. Launched around Earth Day 2008 to promote the idea that small changes can make a big difference in helping to reduce waste, we took the idea of simply reusing any old shopping bag a step further by inviting Kroger loyalty card holders to design their own ideas for a reusable cloth grocery bag. Within minutes, visitors could upload a photo or draw a design, modify its shape and colors, add words, and publish it to the world.

By inviting shoppers to use their creativity, we inspired them to engage with the brand, offering people the chance to show off just how artistic they could be, and also allowing them the opportunity to showcase their work to their friends and family. And there were added incentives—everyone who submitted a design received a credit on his Kroger loyalty card for a free reusable bag. Even those who didn't win the $500 prize were invited to print their designs on a bag online, for an extra fee.

The promotion received a huge amount of participation—more than 36,000 original designs—in a very short time, with little media support. And not only did it position Kroger as an environmentally friendly brand—a competitive advantage in swaying shoppers who can virtually go anywhere to buy groceries—but it also provided a means of introducing customers to the redesigned Kroger.com site and gathering e-mail addresses, a component that is lacking in many other loyalty card promotions.

Among the many brilliant marketing tactics created to support the release of *The Simpsons Movie* in the summer of 2007 was "Simpsonize Me," a Web site that helped people turn themselves into *Simpsons* characters. Just upload a photo and pick your body size, hairstyle and color, eyebrow shape, and even your favorite shade of yellow (for your complexion, of course). Voila, you're a Springfield inhabitant.

Did Fox *need* to dream up an outlet where *Simpsons* fans could go to personally interact with the brand in order to drive traffic into movie theaters? Probably not, given that the *Simpsons* franchise was already so successful. But did it create a novel way of connecting with its already loyal fan base, encouraging them to spread the word about the Web site (and, by association, the movie) to their friends and coworkers? Absolutely. Six million fans spent an average of 30 minutes each creating avatars of themselves that soon infiltrated Flickr, YouTube, MySpace, and Facebook. Whole classrooms and companies banded together to put themselves alongside Homer, Bart, and Marge, serving as highly motivated proponents of the brand and testifying to the effectiveness of social networking.

This tool was actually an extension of Burger King's support of the movie. Instead of just relying on traditional signage, collectors' cups, or in-movie placement, Burger King again employed its brilliant strategy of enabling fun—and having it *their* way.

But did this meaningful connection influence Fox's bottom line? Did it ever. More than 40 million photos have been uploaded at Simpsonizeme.com, and, as noted in the Kwik-E-Mart example, *The Simpsons Movie* earned just over $30 million on its opening day and $74 million in its opening weekend, putting it at the top of the box office, and nearly doubling Fox's $40 million goal.[17]

Tips for Maximizing Success in Participatory Marketing Programs

- Make participating simple.

- Make it easy to share.

- Attract and keep people with contests and daily voting. (This gets the competitive juices going and makes people more intent on sharing.)

- Allow people to engage more deeply at a price. (They just might fall in love with their creation, so feed it by letting them turn it into T-shirts, mugs, hats, and so on.)

How Personalization Inspires Motivation

People absolutely love to personalize the products and services that they buy, mainly because the concept tickles both sides of the brain. The rational left side believes that there is a perfect package of features that will maximize the utility of a given purchase. Meanwhile, the right side loves to create something and show it off to others. More and more marketers have discovered the power of product personalization, and how it leads to great sales results.

M&Ms, a brand that has been in the personalization game for some time now, lets people log onto a Web site and create a personalized message to print on their M&Ms candy. After starting in 2005 with simple messages of a few words, the company's manufacturing process has evolved to allow faces, sports logos, and pretty much anything else a customer can imagine. When people create a bowl of M&Ms with their wedding date on it, or buy a package of M&Ms with the Phillies 2008 World Series logo, they enjoy an experience that connects them deeply to the M&Ms brand. The result is a permanent bond with the brand that drives loyalty beyond reason.

For M&Ms, the business benefits of personalization are just as powerful as the customer payoff. For example, one 7-oz. pack of Kyle Busch–themed candy sells for $12.99, which adds up to $38.97 (plus shipping) for the three-bag minimum order. Compare that to less than a dollar for regular M&Ms at the checkout lane. Personalized products also enjoy a strong word-of-mouth factor, as people often give them as gifts or can't wait to show off their creations to their friends and family. Ryan Bowling, PR manager for Mars North America, credits the MyM&Ms program with "nothing less than revitalizing the brand."

More and more companies are getting the message that personalized products represent a model of meaningful marketing and strong business results, including:

- *NIKEiD*, which allows consumers the chance to pick the perfect shoe fit in a range of colors and styles.

- *Jones Soda*, which will add your photo to the label of your favorite flavor for only $29.99 per 12-pack (plus shipping).

- *Pringles Pop Art*, which allows snackers to create a personalized label, print it, and tape it onto the iconic can. With barely any media support, thousands of people created and shared personal labels (including one of the senior Pringles executives, who created eight cans!).

Product personalization offers huge prospects for meaningful marketing and business success. If you are not at least experimenting here, your brand—and its most loyal customers—is missing out.

Enlist a Crack Team of Designers—for Free!

A final way to tap the collective creativity of fans of your brand is to invite them into the process of product development itself. There are two ways in which companies are reducing development costs and building meaningful marketing connections with their most loyal consumers—through new product or service ideas, and through beta testing.

Beginning in 2006, Häagen-Dazs ice cream partnered with *Gourmet* magazine to invite ice cream lovers nationwide to create what they thought should be the newest flavor of Häagen-Dazs ice cream. The Häagen-Dazs Flavor Search allowed eight weeks, from December 15, 2006, through February 9, 2007, for contestants to dream, test, and invent an idea for a tempting new flavor. Five thousand consumers entered the contest, submitting video clips, photos, and letters.

The winning flavor was Sticky Toffee Pudding ice cream, a mix of creamy vanilla ice cream, chunks of moist, brown, sugary cake, and swirls of gooey toffee sauce, based on a well-loved British dessert. It was promoted in *Gourmet* magazine and sold in 2007 as a limited edition in the Häagen-Dazs ice cream lineup in grocery stores and Häagen-Dazs shops nationwide. (In fact, Sticky Toffee Pudding was so successful that it was added to the regular roster of Häagen-Dazs ice creams available year-round). To further sweeten the prize, the winner, Judiaann Woo, was flown to *Gourmet*'s headquarters in New York City to launch the new flavor with television show host, cookbook author, and executive chef Sara Moulton.

No doubt Judiaann Woo felt an important connection to Häagen-Dazs once her flavor was selected. After all, she had literally contributed to enhancing the brand. But Häagen-Dazs was just as smart to involve countless others who voted on the top three flavor ideas and taste-tested them at select Häagen-Dazs shops and events around the country. All of them played a role and contributed to building the brand. That kind of connection lasts a long time, and it is sure to win over someone who is debating between Häagen-Dazs and the other superpremium ice cream brands featured in the frozen foods aisle.

It's not just our computers that are being reprogrammed, it's customers themselves.

—Jerry Wing, Wharton Business School

This approach can also apply to services, as evidenced by "My Starbucks Idea." In late 2007–early 2008, Starbucks was experiencing a negative turn in sales and customer experience. As an antidote, founder Howard Schultz returned as CEO, and one of his first initiatives, in March 2008, was to launch "My Starbucks Idea," a Web site where passionate fans could help turn the company around by contributing and responding to ideas to improve the customer experience. More than 200,000 votes were cast in the first month alone, and one of the first—and best—ideas that the company acted on was the creation of "splash sticks," a plastic plug that slips into the sip hole in the cup to prevent spills while you're walking or driving with a full cup of joe. Starbucks remains in turnaround mode, but this effort helped it gain a burst of very positive media coverage and word of mouth.

Beta testing is the other way in which some brands are capitalizing on the currency of consumers' creativity. For years, software developers have invited small groups of people to preview an advanced version of upcoming programs for free. Developers benefited from getting valuable feedback from the users, who understood that bugs came with the territory, and beta testers valued the chance to run cutting-edge software and felt a sense of pride and ownership in being one of a handful who helped to bring the product to market.

Today, one could argue that "product research is the new marketing," as beta testing has become a major brand-building tool that is not limited to software insiders. Google is one of the most frequent users of beta testing on a mass scale; in fact, it launched its e-mail service, Gmail, as an invitation-only beta test on April 1, 2004. Over time, it allowed beta testers to invite others into the service, providing a handful of coded links that could be forwarded to friends; adding to the allure, it didn't take long for these codes to be sold on eBay.

Gmail's advanced, more intuitive features—and the exclusivity of an invitation-only list—powered the service to expand with no traditional marketing campaign. On February 7, 2007, Gmail opened up to the uninvited, and it now has tens of millions of users.

Call of Duty 4: Modern Warfare provides another glimpse of successful beta testing. The fourth installment of this first-person-shooter video game for Xbox 360, PlayStation 3, and PC was scheduled to launch in November 2007 against *Halo 3*, another first-person-shooter with huge hype from its previous success. Like movie releases, video games need an enormous amount of buzz on their opening weekend to drive word of mouth, especially when they're released only weeks before the end of the critical holiday season.

So in August 2007, Activision, the publisher of *Call of Duty 4*, released a free beta version of its multiplayer game on Xbox 360, presumably to test that "settings on the multiplayer levels were balanced, and to ensure that there were no bugs in the final version of the game." Only a handful of codes were distributed to the first people to register in advance on the game's Web site. Eventually, more beta invitations were distributed, and additional levels and weapons were unlocked; the beta test concluded on September 30, 2007, about a month after its start, leaving players salivating for the game's release in stores on November 9.

This beta testing resulted not only in big interest—the first few thousand beta invitations were gone in minutes, and the initial buzz was very strong, as players loved the game and began to rave about it on blogs and message boards—but also big sales. It became the best-selling game in the world in 2007 with only two months on the market, beating its main competitor, *Halo 3*, and selling the most first-person-shooter games ever. To date, it has sold 11 million units in less than a year; at $60 a copy, that's over half a billion dollars.

"Help Me Connect Socially"

I've wanted to mention my great passion for playing *Guitar Hero* a couple of times already in this book, but, until now, I've shown restraint. I've not yet raved about my experience in moving from the "Easy" to the "Expert" level; about how I won a *Guitar Hero* contest at a marketing conference in Greece, playing before 300 awestruck people; or about how smart this game is at connecting me socially with others who share my enthusiasm.

You see, very few of my closest friends share my *Guitar Hero* passion. They spend their "geek time" on things like golf and fantasy football; my passion for punching colored buttons on a small plastic toy is more of a source of laughter and derision among my friends than a shared bond. So whenever I want to connect with fellow rockers, I simply go to my favorite forum on GuitarHero.com.

With the launch of *Guitar Hero 3* in the fall of 2007, the marketing team behind it at Activision launched an online community that is directly linked to the game itself. Like the Nike+ system, it uploads high scores automatically, and players can get together to form Tour Groups among themselves. Within days of the new site launch, hundreds of groups had formed—for every country, every university, and every sports team.

> *People seek to create meaning for themselves, and what better way to do it than to join an online community that lets you define yourself to the world, write and blog your thoughts, link up with friends, and decorate the walls of your profile page with the artifacts of your existence.*[18]
>
> —JOHN GERZEMA AND EDWARD LEBAR

It didn't take long for many fans to discover the group that most appealed to their interests; people who were considered oddballs in their offices and neighborhoods jumped at the chance to "get together" online with people with similar tastes.

Specialized groups became private discussion forums where fans could find people to jam with online and create weekend tournaments. Having met through this common passion, groups connect in other ways as well, talking "off topic" about everything from global politics to strategies for dealing with their kids.

By creating this ingenious Tour Group feature, *Guitar Hero* has added value to the lives of millions of players. We get more out of the game by working and playing together. And this keeps us loyal to the *Guitar Hero* franchise, buying more than $1 billion in game sequels and song downloads.

The lesson: any brand that is tied to a strong personal interest or hobby must create a means by which to connect its consumers with one another.

• • •

The human need for connection dates as far back as, well, humanity itself. Primitive people banded together for all sorts of reasons related to physical survival, but also for emotional closeness—friendship, companionship, and procreation. We are, in fact, hardwired to join forces and share perspectives, knowing inherently that our whole is more valuable than the sum of our parts.

These days, consumers are increasingly embracing technology to make social connection a more accessible and convenient part of our daily lives. From e-mail and texting to social networks like Facebook, most of us have a variety of tools at our disposal that allow for constant communication, and businesses are learning that marketing through social connections can drive results. Beinggirl.com, a program created by the Always and Tampax brands at P&G, targets developing girls with advice from their peers and a physician. Two million girls worldwide visit the site each month, with traffic in 2007 up 150 percent over the previous year; the program offers *four* times the ROI of TV advertising, and it has recently been expanded to reach 29 countries in Europe, Asia, and South America.[19]

If a tampon brand can realize a quadruple return on its marketing spending, surely your brand can find a way to succeed in the social space. Here are five ways that companies of all kinds can benefit from creating social connections between their brands and their customers.

1. IMPROVE THE VALUE EQUATION FOR YOUR PRODUCT OR SERVICE

The combination of low cost and high stickiness makes technologically enabled social connections practically a no-brainer. Some setup and maintenance are required at the start, but services like Facebook and Ning offer free platforms, and companies like LiveWorld make it easy for organizations to create their own social networks. Once you're up and running, member interaction and consumer-generated content happen with little incremental investment from you—and the more people who join, the more valuable the site becomes for both the members and your brand. People will tend to return often in order to stay in touch with the friends they have made, and if your brand does something that makes them mad, they are more likely to forgive you than to abandon ship.

For example, through its "Cruise Connections" Web site, Carnival Cruises offers a handy way for small groups to plan trips (invite your friends and plan activities in advance) and to share videos, photos, experiences, reviews, and comments afterward; within five months of Carnival's adding this social networking feature to its Web site, 1.5 million people had visited the site, posting more than 2,000 reviews.

In the spring of 2008, GM's Saturn brand launched its own social networking site, ImSaturn, on which members can read Saturn news, share photos, upload videos, chat with other members, play games, and post music recommendations. Given the fact that the brand was founded on the principle of community, ImSaturn is a logical extension of its equity/identity and provides a clear differentiator in the automotive market. Visitors can form or join subgroups based on their interests and geographic location, and Saturn is using the site in a variety of interesting and valuable ways: to promote new products; to lower marketing expenses by capitalizing on the ability to speak directly to current fans; to reinforce the connection between the brand and the customer, leading to deeper and longer-lasting loyalty; and even to gauge reactions to new advertising. Saturn's original hope was that it would attract 1,000 people in the first six months—at the end of three weeks, it had 1,200 members and counting.[20]

2. BUILD LOYALTY WITH A NICHE FAN BASE

Produced in Barbados since 1703, Mount Gay Rum holds the esteemed position of being the oldest rum brand in the world, with historically close ties to sailing. According to legend (or the modern equivalent, Wikipedia), "Tales were told of sailors returning home with a barrel of Mount Gay in order to prove that they had reached Barbados—considered one of the most difficult islands in the Caribbean to reach."

More than 300 years later, the brand continues to actively foster a strong link to sailing, both as a main sponsor of the United States Sailing Association and as a supporter of more than 110 regatta events worldwide each year. At each regatta, Mount Gay hosts parties where the rum flows freely and the brand gives away red hats with the name and date of the event stitched on them. While the hats are an obvious memento of the specific sailing race, on land they are used by sailors as a way of identifying others who share the same passion. The scarcity of the swag and the fact that the brand has come to signify good times on the high seas have made it quite a phenomenon in the sailboat racing community (wear your Mount Gay hat through the airport and you'll no doubt be approached by a fellow sailor!). Despite very limited marketing spending on a niche audience, the brand is growing at double-digit rates in the United States and U.K.

Similarly, the Harley Owners Group (H.O.G.), started by Harley-Davidson in 1983 in response to a growing desire by owners to share their experiences with others, now boasts one million members in 49 local chapters. For $45 a year, members receive a magazine, a touring handbook, and commemorative pins and patches, but the pride in being a member is priceless.

3. Provide Better Service at a Lower Cost

As any manager knows, one of the most critical yet often underfunded departments within a company is customer service. Because customer service represents the front line, where real customers engage with real company representatives over really big problems, it is essential to the health and lifeblood of any organization. But because it is typically viewed as a cost center (with a $6 to $7 average cost per call) rather than as a critical piece of the marketing model, it often fails to get the resources and the respect it deserves. As a result, most companies are notoriously slow to invest in this department, either by adding staff or by adopting new communications technologies like online chatting or blog mining. But customers themselves are increasingly banding together, in a community effort, to help solve one another's problems. And smart companies are encouraging and rewarding this kind of self-help.

The TiVo users forum is one example; as of September 2007, it included more than 161,000 registered users. Soon after the launch of the first TiVo in 1999, brand fans banded together to create the TiVo Community Forum (TCF), which quickly became a critical way for new users to get assistance from seasoned pros. While TiVo did not fund the organization directly, it did provide a link to the TCF from its home page, which encouraged the group to keep up the good work and provided the brand with a highly motivated, low-cost venue for customer service.

4. SPREAD POSITIVE WORD OF MOUTH

Every marketer knows that positive word of mouth is the holy grail, in that it is powerful, authentic, and cheap (if not free). The value of the following cases is self-evident.

When the Coca-Cola Company was launching its Vault brand of energy sodas, a group of rabid fans created a Web site called "I Found Vault," on which they flagged stores in cities and towns across the country where Vault was in stock. Currently, there are more than 1,500 members of this spontaneous social network.

Amazon's "See a Kindle in Your City" demonstrates how a brand can tap satisfied customers as passionate advocates. Kindle, the new digital book reader from Amazon priced at $359, is not available in stores and is not supported by any advertising.

Its sole marketing "push" consists of a message board where current owners can (presumably enthusiastically) volunteer to show their Kindles to people who are considering buying the device but want to test it for themselves.

This "social experiment" seems to be moving product, as Citigroup analysts projected that Kindle will sell out its 380,000 available units in 2008, up from an earlier estimate of 240,000. With 4,200 customer reviews on Amazon.com—the vast majority of which are positive—the Kindle has garnered the most reviews of any product in the company's electronics category.[21]

5. Gain Insights for Upgrading Current Products
and Launching New Ones

Launched in the summer of 2008, Mercedes's "Generation Benz" online community uses questionnaires, polls, and live chats to gather feedback on product designs and advertising concepts, as well as open forum discussions on hot topics like sustainability; its 800 Gen Y members (19- to 32-year-olds) provide the brand with insights that it would be hard-pressed to gather in any other way. Steve Cannon, vice president of marketing, says, "[We have learned that] we have a generation that actually likes their parents and would definitely drive what their parents drove." That's meaningful! And because of this success, the brand will be launching another community targeting boomers in 2009.[22]

• • •

To forge a genuine connection with your customers, you have to be one of your own biggest fans, and it helps to be vocal about it. Contrary to what you might have learned in business school, today's successful marketers aren't staying behind the scenes—customers are responding positively to this human-to-human outreach, which often adds a memorable face or personality to the brand.

Zappos.com is creating a brand from scratch with a new marketing model that draws heavily on personal connections between employees and customers. CEO Tony Hsiech and more than 450 of his employees keep active Twitter accounts, where they talk about their jobs, new fashions, and what is going on at the company.[23] The company makes 75 percent of its sales to repeat customers who have fallen in love with the brand. This has helped the less than 10-year-old online shoe company reach over $1 billion in sales.[24]

Even advertising agencies can get in on the act. Plaid, an agency based in Danbury, Connecticut, decided in the spring of 2007 to change its name from Visual Intelligence Agency (which sounds like a new secret DARPA project). After many brainstorms about how to get its new name out there, the team decided to drive around the country (in a Plaid van) in what became the first Plaid Nation tour. In addition to showcasing its new name, the agency wanted to demonstrate its knowledge of social media, how they could be used, and how they could benefit a brand and help it connect with the public. Plaid spent three weeks visiting its current clients (such as Sony and Iron Horse bikes), other agencies it admired (Martin and Digitas), and brands that it thought were cool (Segway, Hanes, and Alltel). Some of these firms knew that people from the firm were coming; others, they simply dropped in on.

Plaid toured the country to promote itself, but by creating meaningful moments and conversations with those it met along the way, the tour resulted in new business, clients, and partners. Its success is further proven by the fact that Plaid is in the middle of its next annual tour.

By building powerful connections between people and brands (and the people behind them), marketing can make a product more interesting and more valuable, and seed long-term loyalty. Creating meaningful connections is an approach that can certainly be more effective than solutions—yet there is another, even higher level of marketing that fewer brands have followed to even greater success.

5

MEANINGFUL ACHIEVEMENTS

HELPING PEOPLE IMPROVE THEMSELVES, THEIR FAMILIES, AND THE WORLD

While *connection* marketing represents a significant step up in building a more meaningful relationship between people and brands, there is a way to go even further to meet consumers' highest goals and expectations. The highest tier of the hierarchy, meaningful *achievement*, fulfills this promise; marketers who aspire to the highest level of meaning will create marketing that significantly improves their customers' lives, helps people realize their dreams, or enables them to positively change their community and their world.

Most of humankind's greatest achievements have taken place because, after satisfying the basic needs for food, shelter, love, and belonging, someone was driven to "self-actualize" (as the psychologist Abraham Maslow would say) or to "make a dent in the universe" (as Steve Jobs would say). From local neighborhood watch patrols to advances in global technology or in economics and government in

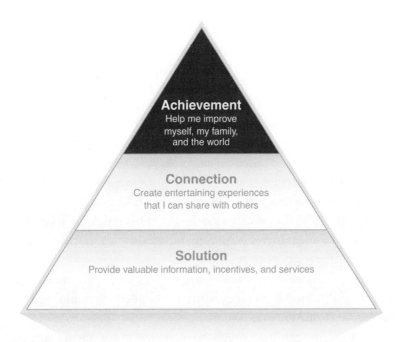

less-developed nations, millions of people are acting on their innate drive to improve not only themselves but the world around them.

Self-actualized, achievement-oriented consumers pose a particular challenge to marketers, as many of them have discovered that simply collecting material possessions does not satisfy their highest-level needs. Instead of flaunting Rolex watches, they're sporting Live Strong bracelets; instead of running up the charge card, they're raising funds for the breast cancer walkathon. A study of the brands that have reached this summit suggests possible paths for those that dare to make the ascent; those that succeed will be rewarded with the highest levels of loyalty and the greatest return on their marketing dollars.

"Improve Me"

Help Support Meaningful Lifestyle Goals

One of the richest areas in which marketers can hope to help people improve themselves is that of personal wellness. Driven by expanding waistbands and soaring health-care costs, more and more individuals have decided to take the responsibility for changing their lifestyles and improving their health. "Lose weight," "Eat better," and "Get more exercise" are probably the top three New Year's resolutions for millions of people, year in and year out. Why? Because, given the stress of a job and the demands of a family, losing weight is hard. Making more healthful food choices is hard. And finding the time and motivation to get moving is *hard*. What some marketers have realized is that if you can help potential customers achieve goals of this kind by getting them started, helping them make the right decisions along the way, and measuring their progress, they'll feel supported, they'll feel grateful, and they won't soon forget. This type of marketing is considered a meaningful achievement because it truly can change someone's life for the better—for good.

Several brands have found ways to help their customers make meaningful personal changes while simultaneously building their businesses. ConAgra Foods is one.

In 2007, the company sought to capitalize on consumers' increasing interest in healthier food options; after studying successful brands like Weight Watchers and eDiets, we identified an opportunity to use the Web as the center of a meaningful marketing program built around healthy foods and healthy living. By marrying multiple brands from within the company, rather than focusing on just one, we saw a way to make the campaign even more efficient and more relevant.

In January 2008, we launched Start Making Choices, an online resource to help people achieve better balance in their lives. The focus of the program is the Balanced Life Index (BLI), a tool that dynamically rates an individual's wellness. Upon joining, members are asked to complete a detailed survey, and the BLI uses the results to make personalized recommendations in the areas of nutrition, activity, and well-being.

Personal planning tools enable members to log their weekly meals and exercise; when they stay on track, their BLI score is automatically updated—either on the Web site or on their Facebook pages. Articles, blogs, podcasts, and expert advice are also available on the site, as are recipes and healthy snack/meal ideas featuring ConAgra Foods brands such as Hunt's, Egg Beaters, PAM, and SmartPop! popcorn. For potential customers—200,000 of whom have joined the program, and more than 2 million of whom have visited the site since it went live—this program demonstrates how healthful foods can fit into an overall approach to wellness that is enjoyable, practical, and achievable. For ConAgra Foods, it embodies the firm's commitment to "help our consumers enjoy happier, healthier lives," as well as marry disparate brands in the minds of consumers.

> *The market for something to believe in is infinite.*
> —HUGH MACLEOD, MARKETING CARTOONIST

Just dropping a few pounds may be one person's definition of a major life accomplishment; for another, it's running a marathon. Clif Bar is a brand of energy bar that is designed to deliver concentrated, palatable calories that you can eat while you're literally on the run. A small, private company with sales increasing past the $100 million mark, it continues to grow even though large companies have been entering the "energy bar" market with more marketing money and better-known names. Why? Marathon runners are very heavy consumers of specialized products like Clif, and Clif works hard to maintain a generous presence in the actual races, employing "pace runners" as billboards for the brand in a genuinely helpful way. If you register with Clif for a free marathon training kit, you'll receive guidance from the pace runners, both online and in races. They are available for questions, to offer guidance on topics like training, eating, and what shoes to buy. Here is the profile of one of many pace leaders, Theo, a former Peace Corps member from San Diego:

> Why run with Theo? I take this seriously, so you can relax a bit and enjoy the experience. I'll do my absolute best to keep you on pace and help you reach whatever goal you are striving for. We're in this together!

Anyone who has ever completed a marathon will agree that it is a major life accomplishment. An energy bar that helps people achieve this dream forges a special place in its customers' hearts for life.

Teach a Skill, Change a Life

Going beyond physical improvement, marketing that facilitates inner self-improvement can trigger a deeper change in someone's self-image, driving a kind of reciprocal loyalty; much as we feel grateful when we receive a gift, we are programmed to want to return the favor, which can benefit brands in the form of higher consumer demands for their products and services.

Perhaps no company in the world has done more to educate its customers than Home Depot, whose current tagline summarizes its position in the very competitive home improvement market: "You can do it. We can help." When you walk into a Home Depot, you immediately notice a chalkboard with listings of upcoming free courses on topics such as "Build an outdoor deck" and "Install a shower." Television ads and mailed flyers specifically mention the training programs and upcoming classes, often more prominently than the advertisements for the products themselves.

After research revealed that many consumers looked at ads featuring major do-it-yourself projects skeptically, Home Depot started offering these free single-subject "how-to" classes in all 1,967 of its stores, as well as online. Jack Aaronson, CEO of the Aaronson Group, which advises companies on customer conversion, retention, and loyalty, says, "If your sales cycle involves lots of customer education, think about creative ways to become a 'learning center.'"[1]

Home Depot made this investment in consumer education from the beginning, as often as possible staffing its first stores with men and women who were experienced in doing home improvement projects for a living. It was the company's desire to help people achieve success in projects that motivated the brand. Home Depot understands that if it helps its customers hone their home improvement skills, they will gain the confidence to do more projects themselves and revel in the satisfaction of a job well done. As Roger W. Adams, senior vice president and chief marketing officer for Home Depot, said, "The underlying component of the emotional connection to the brand is the power of 'I did it.'"[2]

Since the inception of the store clinics, the brand has continued to improve on the original concept, with extensions including

"Do-It-HERself" workshops that are more female-friendly; classes for contractors—both in-store and online—that teach skills such as marketing and time management; and even workshops for kids aged 5 to 12, which "teach children do-it-yourself skills and tool safety, while at the same time helping to instill a sense of accomplishment."[3] In addition to receiving a completed project, kids get a Home Depot apron and an achievement pin.

Do these classes help to sell drills and hammers? Of course they do. They also help to differentiate Home Depot from Lowe's and other retail alternatives, which is critical in a market in which the competitor is often located across the street. But most important, these classes teach skills that instill pride and can create loyal customers for life.

Sony is another brand, perhaps somewhat surprisingly, that takes educating its consumers very seriously. While it still does tons of traditional advertising, the company noticed in 2004 that it needed to reach consumers at a specific, critical point of product consideration—i.e., when someone is ready to buy and is starting to compare brand or product benefits and attributes.

Consumer electronics is a very competitive category; Sony has a premium-priced product line, and many of its products include features and functions that are basically identical to those of significantly lower-priced brands. So it takes something more meaningful to earn a sale.

The company created an online learning center, called Sony 101, to provide potential buyers with education on a wide variety of technology topics, including digital photography and HDTVs. Online discussion boards with experts added to its credibility, particularly since the courses didn't push people to Sony products in particular. On average, "students" spent two hours per course on the site, resulting in 94 percent user satisfaction and 87 percent being willing to recommend Sony 101 to a friend. Of those users, 20 percent purchased a Sony product, which is impressive, considering that many of Sony's products are priced at $1,000 or more.[4]

Monster.com is one of the top job-search Web sites and a perennial Super Bowl advertiser, and yet a significant part of its strategy for positioning itself as a one-stop employment resource is to offer

---

Other Branded Learning Opportunities

- *Land Rover and BMW:* driving school

- *Hewlett-Packard:* free online courses for technology professionals (e.g., Linux 201)

- *Kendall-Jackson:* free wine-tasting classes to students enrolled at major business schools

- *Fender guitars:* four-day seminar with individual instruction from noted musicians

- *Viking cooking appliances:* local cooking classes

- *Nikon:* photography schools

---

value-added career advice, such as salary negotiating tips from experts, top 10 most-asked interview questions, and résumé building advice, as part of its meaningful marketing

This added dimension is a great way for Monster.com to differentiate itself in a very competitive job-posting market. While it can be argued that large rivals like CareerBuilder and niche sites like PracticeLink.com (which is specifically geared toward physicians) offer a similar commodity, Monster's advice keeps people coming back to the site for benefits beyond mere job listings. This advice also actually makes a discernible difference in job seekers' ability to land a job, helping people get a leg up on the competition in interviews and salary negotiations. And clearly it's working: Monster.com's traffic was up over 40 percent in 2008, while CareerBuilder.com was flat, despite the challenging economy and lots of folks looking for work.

"Improve My Family"

Once they have their own lives reasonably under control, people are compelled to look after their family members in hopes of protecting them from harm and maximizing the potential of their lives. Thus, brands have an opportunity to help us reach achievement through programs that directly target the members of our family.

As the father of two young girls who are still comfortably far from the age of 16, I can only speculate about something that many of you dear readers may have already experienced: the fear of teenage children behind the wheel of our automobiles.

And there's good reason for this fear. Every year in the United States, 6,000 teenagers die and 300,000 are injured in automobile accidents. But one brand is helping our kids be safer out there. Allstate Insurance has created resources to help parents teach their teens safe driving skills. For example, it offers courses at local high schools (called Allstate Drive Crew) in which kids are asked to navigate an obstacle course while the radio blares and they send text messages; they quickly (and safely) learn that these devices can cause trouble in an instant. The brand also created the Allstate Parent-Teen Driving Contract, a downloadable PDF that features eye-opening and lifesaving statistics on such hot-button issues as speeding, cell phone talking, and drinking and driving; both parties are required to sign the document, acknowledging their mutual awareness of these crucial issues and agreeing to certain consequences if the contract is breached. Through all of these efforts, Allstate is helping parents to begin this all-important safety conversation in a way that is neither confrontational nor accusatory.

In addition to parent-child interaction, Allstate learned through its research that peer-to-peer communication is also key to helping kids learn safe-driving skills. In a report conducted by the company in 2005, it found that more than half (53 percent) of teens surveyed said that friends would be the most effective influence in getting them to drive more safely,[5] so Allstate launched Teen Safe Driving Summits in 14 cities across the country, through which students learn how to become safe-driving activists in their schools and positively influence their peers.

The business benefits to Allstate are clear: in addition to attracting new insurance business from parents of teens, by teaching and encouraging safer driving and thus saving lives, Allstate reduces claims and increases its profits, resulting in a genuine win-win all around. Allstate even won a corporate citizenship award from the U.S. Chamber of Commerce in 2008.

> *The risk is not being useful to this generation of kids and parents
> . . . if we're still doing in 2012 what we're doing now, then we
> won't deserve to be around because we won't be relevant to our
> consumers.*
> —STEVE PASIERB, PRESIDENT AND CHIEF EXECUTIVE,
> PARTNERSHIP FOR A DRUG-FREE AMERICA

Canon is another brand that is helping to improve families' lives in a meaningful way. In partnership with the National Center for Missing & Exploited Children, Canon's Canon4Kids program capitalizes on its unique position as a leader in the photography industry to drive awareness and prevention of child abduction. Canon shares statistics and tips on its Web site (e.g., the first three hours after a child is missing are the most critical, and be sure to have a recent digital photo and a 5- by 7-inch printout on hand), and each year it donates digital cameras, printers, and scanners to help authorities disseminate photos and information quickly when children go missing. To date, more than 1,600 pieces of equipment have been distributed to agencies in 47 states.

From the print ad featuring color photos of missing children that Canon ran in the front section of *USA Today* in January 2008 to its Canon4Kids Van Tour, which promotes child safety awareness in public forums, Canon is working to connect personally with parents in a meaningful way and provide some peace of mind.

"Improve My World"

Once we've worked to ensure our own health, safety, and relative happiness and those of our family members, many of us are compelled to achieve success by making a positive impact on our communities, our nations, and the world we live in. It is little wonder that cause-related marketing is a growing tool for brands around the world—and a fitting example of meaningful marketing. And yet the origins of the modern cause campaign reach only as far back as 1983, the year that Jerry Welsh, worldwide marketing leader for American Express, thought it would be a good idea to sponsor a drive to support the restoration of the Statue of Liberty.

The idea was simple, and the results dramatic: for every dollar spent on transactions using an American Express card, the company contributed a penny to the restoration cause. During the campaign, card usage increased 27 percent, new card applications rose 45 percent, and American Express succeeded in raising $1.7 million. The Statue of Liberty was rededicated in time for its centennial in 1986.[6]

While this program was new and different at the time, it made sense, according to Welsh, because it "was based on a clear business vision. We saw that a clever, informative, positive promotion of an underappreciated cause or a misunderstood problem could spark both the interest and the commercial patronage of customers, contributing to the good reputation and the profits of the company."[7]

In a way, it could be argued that this campaign not only kickstarted the concept of cause marketing, but also signaled the beginning of a shift toward people—and brand marketing—working to change the world, little by little, in their everyday lives.

How Doing Good Makes for Good Business

"The internet has politicized everything and created a newly informed consumer," wrote Jonah Bloom in his October 8, 2007, *Advertising Age* column. "To be successful in such an environment, a lot of brand managers . . . will also have to learn to stand for something bigger and more complex than a brand position."[8]

There are lots of compelling reasons why doing good makes good business sense, starting with an increase in sales. A 2008 Cone/Duke University Behavioral Cause Study showed that a whopping 87 percent of consumers will switch from one brand to another that's comparable based on its association with a good cause—that's up 31 percent since 1993. When, for example, a particular shampoo was associated with a cause, the brand saw a 74 percent increase in actual purchases. That's 74 percent!

Significant—and meaningful—media coverage is another benefit of cause-related marketing. There is simply no better advertisement than the free coverage that a trusted media source can impart.

That's why your PR agency continues to look for cause-related tie-ins for your marketing initiatives—these professionals know that the media cover what they believe their readers, viewers, and listeners want to hear, not what we marketers want to promote. Whatever we might hope for, Oprah and Salma Hayek are not going to spend 10 minutes on national television talking about a new and improved Pampers diaper. But they *will* (and did) talk about how Pampers is donating vaccinations to benefit children in Africa for each package of Pampers purchased—a program that has distributed 135 million vaccinations and helped prevent 87,000 newborn deaths from tetanus in one year.[9]

> *Moms and Dads need to believe that Pampers is the best choice for their babies. They want brands that are not only good values, but that support their values.*
>
> —JODI ALLEN, VICE PRESIDENT OF BABY CARE,
> PROCTER & GAMBLE

Even during economic downturns like the present, the majority (71 percent) of consumers globally say that they are giving as much (or more) time and money to causes they deem worthy, and more than half of them will continue to buy brands that support causes, even at a premium price.[10]

But it's not enough to do good for goodness' sake; as with any other form of marketing, cause-related marketing must be done right and executed well. There are three basic "musts" that ensure good cause marketing:

1. *Your target must believe in the cause.* Start by understanding what causes are near and dear to your core customer's heart. If you're looking to reach a large, general market, choose something with broad appeal, such as the Red Cross or the United Way; if your target is smaller and more focused, chances are that you already know the causes that the people in it value most. If you're not sure, why not solicit input through a communications tool like e-mail?

The fact that you are looking for customer input will only draw people closer to your brand.

2. *Your brand must fit the cause.* You'll fail to win business or fans for your brand if there doesn't seem to be an organic link between what your brand stands for and the cause you're investing in. Everything you do on behalf of your brand reflects on its equity, for good or for ill. It makes sense for Pampers to donate vaccinations to children in Africa because it's a brand that's focused on improving child development; likewise, it makes sense for Pantene to encourage its customers to cut and donate their hair to make wigs for cancer victims. In cause marketing, relevance equals meaning.

3. *Your investment must be meaningful.* This may seem to be common sense, but it bears repeating: consumers will not support a program that does not hit some meaningful, minimum threshold of giving back—and they will increasingly use the Internet to protest any perceived tightfistedness. That's not to say that you need to give all of your profits to charity, or that consumers will find, say, a nickel per purchase insignificant. Remember, AmEx donated only a penny per dollar transaction to the Statue of Liberty's makeover fund, and that campaign was a huge success. Ultimately, you need to figure out for yourself and for your brand what amount is meaningful. Start by looking at the size of your brand. The fact is, people expect big brands to be bigger spenders. But before you cringe at that prospect, know that it is perfectly acceptable to base most programs on a "pay-for-performance" model—meaning that you give only when a purchase is made.

PEDIGREE is one brand that has embraced cause marketing by covering all of these fundamentals. It draws motivation from the sad fact that "over 4 million dogs enter shelters every year. And each one deserves a loving home." Through the use of television, print, and online marketing, the brand has succeeded in educating people on the desperate need for homes for all unwanted dogs, even going so far as to write an open letter to U.S. President Obama, in an ad in major newspapers, asking him to adopt a shelter dog as First Pet (which succeeded in creating a national dialogue during a slow news period).

Through donations that the brand has made with each purchase of PEDIGREE foods, it created the PEDIGREE Foundation, a private 501(c)(3) organization "dedicated to helping dogs in need find loving homes by supporting the good work of shelters and breed rescue organizations throughout the country," complete with valuable online resources, such as links to local shelters, where visitors can get information about volunteering, and heartwarming video clips of individual dogs adapting to their adoptive families.

To date, PEDIGREE has contributed $250,000 to the foundation, and consumers have contributed an additional (and impressive) $1.38 million. PEDIGREE saw a substantial bump in sales as a result of the campaign—a 10 percent increase from the previous year, which boosted sales to over $1 billion for the first time in the company's history. And it earned recognition by taking home the $100,000 grand prize in the Kelly Awards for magazine advertising, which agency TBWA\Chiat\Day aptly donated to PEDIGREE's charity. Perhaps most importantly, the lives of more than 100,000 dogs were saved.[11]

It makes perfect sense for a brand like PEDIGREE to channel its enthusiasm and its charitable dollars into saving dogs, but what's a beauty brand to do? For the cultish cosmetics company MAC, whose brand embraces both women and men with the motto "All ages, all races, all sexes," supporting men, women, and children affected by HIV/AIDS was, according to Nancy Mahon, senior vice president of MAC Cosmetics, "integral to the business model and the philosophy of who we are." Fourteen years after the brand created its Viva Glam program, with 100 percent of the $14 lipstick's sale price going to the charity (yes, even retailers are expected to forgo their margin), MAC Cosmetics has provided over $128 million in donations to date. And Viva Glam remains the only product in MAC's lineup that is advertised—a fact that's even more impressive when you consider that the brand is wholly owned by the monster cosmetics conglomerate Estee Lauder. But MAC's numbers show why Lauder is apparently so supportive of it—in its 2008 annual report, Lauder cited MAC as a significant reason for the parent company's 10.6 percent increase in sales in its $3 billion makeup business, proving that marketing with meaning can make a difference both in people's lives and in a company's bottom line.

Graduating to Greatness

While the PEDIGREE and MAC programs are different, they both succeed in bringing value to people's lives and generating the highest business return on their investments because they go beyond the basics of cause-related marketing. The best, most meaningful achievement campaigns have several other distinct features in common.

1. The Cause Supports the Brand Back

The best cause-related marketing is reciprocal; that is, the target cause organization itself works to promote your brand. Twenty-five years after the company invented modern cause marketing with the Statue of Liberty renovation, the American Express Members Project provides a good example of this reciprocity. First launched in the summer of 2007, the American Express Members Project invited cardmembers to submit ideas for making a real impact in the areas of arts and culture, community development, education, health, or the environment. Sample ideas included reading lessons for the illiterate, small business loans, clean water initiatives, free vaccinations for poor children, and efforts to rebuild deserving communities. As the American Express Web site boasts, "Your ideas. Your decision. Our money."

After an advisory panel narrowed down the submissions, cardmembers were encouraged to vote for the ideas that they believed American Express should support. This brought a vast surge of awareness and engagement from the people and organizations behind the suggested causes—they literally did the marketing for American Express. In 2007, the winner of the $2 million contest was the Children's Safe Drinking Water project, a cause submitted by Greg Allgood, a public health specialist who works with the PUR water filter brand at Procter & Gamble. By promoting its own cause in hopes of receiving added financial support, Procter & Gamble itself was investing in the American Express brand!

The year 2008 saw a total of 8,000 project ideas being submitted, 400,000 people registered to participate, and 1.8 million unique visitors to American Express's Web site, up 20 percent from 2007. Based on feedback that a single "winner take all" contest left too many worthy causes (and passionate cardholders) on the sidelines, American Express upped the ante in 2008, increasing the total funding to $2.5 million and dividing it among five different projects, including an Alzheimer's early detection education project and an effort to provide school supplies to low-income communities.

Whole Foods has followed a similar path befitting its unique brand. The company maintains a strong belief in supporting the little guy—in its case, local producers and local causes. Its "wooden nickel" program works in two ways: first by encouraging shoppers to use reusable grocery bags, and then by rewarding this environmentally sound activity with a charitable contribution. When you bring your bags into the store, the Whole Foods cashier gives you a "wooden nickel" token for each bag, which you then deposit in one of three boxes representing local charities; Whole Foods then makes a cash donation to each charity based on the number of nickels that are collected.

Giving back to the community is a wonderful way to end a shopping experience, and because each store selects the local causes it wants to support, these charitable organizations return the favor by "marketing" to get their supporters to shop at Whole Foods. By choosing multiple causes, Whole Foods multiplies the reciprocal support it receives from the charities, creating multiple avenues for meaningful word of mouth. For example, the Web site of my local Cincinnati Parks Foundation encourages supporters to shop at Whole Foods and drop their wooden nickels in its marked box. It's hard to find a better kind of advertisement than that.

When launching its Green Works line of natural cleaning products in January 2008, Clorox knew that it needed to overcome doubts about the true "green" nature of its formula. So it worked with the Sierra Club to earn its support for the line. According to Katherine Hagan, marketing director for environmental sustainability for Clorox, the Sierra Club rigorously tested the Green Works line before allowing Clorox to feature its name and logo on the product labels. As part of this relationship, the Sierra Club receives a fee from Clorox based on part on a percentage of product sales.

This support from a trusted, mainstream environmental group helped Clorox Green Works quickly become the leading brand and doubled the size of the natural cleaning category. For the Sierra Club, this not only drove brand awareness and $470,000 in contributions from Clorox in the first year, but it has helped the group achieve its goal of driving natural cleaning products into the mainstream of the marketplace.

2. Commit for the Long Haul

As no doubt you're aware, far too many marketing programs overall are short-term affairs. Whether it's a new product launch or a cause-marketing effort, the three-month "launch and leave" mentality is pervasive in our industry . . . you work on the new, new thing as soon as the current new thing is out the door, and you keep working on it until that new, new thing becomes the current new thing—and so on.

One of the most compelling benefits of cause marketing is that it can build lasting long-term equity for your brand. While a short-term program might well boost sales temporarily, it has little chance of generating ongoing "loyalty beyond reason" among your target audience. In fact, today's consumer is more cynical in general, and more skeptical of marketing in particular, and might well view your new, short-term cause-marketing program as an insincere effort.

Sustained support over time builds awareness of the link between your brand and your chosen cause, which is worth noting, since raising awareness is typically the number one way to improve the impact of any kind of marketing. An ongoing commitment also helps you to continually learn and improve your efforts, as each year gives you an opportunity to test new ideas and compare this year's results to last year's. In fact, continuous change is important, as people require fresh news to keep them engaged and talking to their friends about your brand, and the media will not cover the same story this year that they did last year.

When it comes to cause marketing, the best advice is to go long and go deep. It'll pay dividends, as those brands that are launching their cause-related marketing campaigns and leveraging them into long-term commitments have seen. General Mills's Yoplait brand provides a great example of long-term meaning and business building through continuous cause support.

When 6,000 people from the United States, the United Kingdom, Brazil, Canada, France, Italy, Germany, India, China, and Japan were asked, in the second annual Edelman goodpurpose study, to name a brand they associated with a good cause, they said: Yoplait. And, in the modern equivalent of best media coverage, Yoplait's 10-year commitment to funding the Susan G. Komen Foundation for breast cancer research is the first example listed under "cause marketing" by none other than Wikipedia.

Since 1998, Yoplait has contributed 10 cents to the foundation for every specially marked lid sent in by its buyers. Those who take the time to collect and return the lids feel good about themselves and about the positive impact they are having on a still-incurable disease, but they also feel good about the role that Yoplait plays in facilitating this support. Those who don't send in lids—heck, even those who don't even buy the yogurt, but who see the bright pink packaging as they scan the dairy aisle in the grocery store—are also influenced, as the advertising raises awareness of the issue and encourages self-exams.

And despite Yoplait's long-running commitment, it hasn't rested on its meaningful laurels. In 2001, it became the primary sponsor of Race for the Cure, a marathon that's held every year to raise additional research money for breast cancer, and in 2008, the brand added a Web site where friends could create running teams and organize lid-gathering efforts. To date, the company has contributed over $19 million to the cause.

3. Provide Benefit Even without Purchase

Recall one of the basic precepts of marketing with meaning: *the brand's marketing provides value to a consumer's life, whether or not he ever even buys what you are selling.* Now apply that thinking to cause marketing, and you get Tide's "Loads of Hope" program.

A few years ago, during a period of unrest in Venezuela, Procter & Gamble's Ariel brand set up complimentary washing centers in that country to provide a safe, clean place for women to do their family's laundry. Now, clean laundry may not seem like it would be a priority in a country in turmoil, but it is, and a brand that comes to the rescue at a stressful time—while literally ensuring that consumers can continue to use its products with minimal interruption—has an excellent chance of creating deep, long-lasting loyalty.

In November 2005, in the wake of Hurricane Katrina, the Tide brand in North America took this example to heart, providing free access to 30 washers and driers and unlimited quantities of laundry products, including Tide, Downy, and Bounce, to the residents of New Orleans who didn't have electricity—or, sometimes, even a home—to enable them to wash wet, moldy clothes. As the Tide Web site says, in the wake of disasters, small comforts make a big difference, and 35,000 loads of laundry—and sales of 25,000 vintage Tide T-shirts (with the proceeds being used to build homes for people in Louisiana)—later, consumers say that they feel that the brand "speaks to me" and "helps me feel that I'm spending my money wisely."

> *Loads of Hope is a key pillar for the Tide brand going forward. It's the number one driver of traffic to Tide.com and the number one source of positive consumer verbatim and testimonials in our consumer relations group. A key part of what we're doing is to connect with consumers.*[12]
>
> —KASH SHAIKH, P&G FABRIC CARE CONSUMER
> RELATIONS MANAGER

According to P&G's former global marketing officer, Jim Stengel, Tide saw a lift in key equity measures, and marketing mix modeling (an ROI measure that compares all spending equally) revealed that this program resulted in a "far greater lift than traditional advertising." Those results came despite a direct (required) link between product purchase and the brand's cause.

4. MAKE THE CAUSE A PART OF YOUR COMPANY CULTURE

What happens when an organization makes a personal investment in a cause? If you're genuine in your enthusiasm for and commitment to that cause, your passion will come through, loud and clear, to your audience in the big ways and small ways your marketing is executed. In many ways, the time that you and your employees contribute is more powerful than any cash contribution.

Lauren Clark is a wedding photographer operating in Lubbock, Texas, who has a killer Web site and blog at www.laurenclarkpho tography.com. Since she's a sole proprietor, her time is limited, but each year she gives away one complete wedding photography session for people with a special need, using her blog to solicit requests and share the stories. So, what's in it for Lauren? She clearly loves what she does, and, as you can see from her site, she's great at it. Her desire to share her gift selflessly is genuine and, in terms of cause marketing, speaks volumes to couples who are searching for a wedding photographer. People are looking for someone extraordinary to chronicle their special day, and Lauren's effort demonstrates to potential clients that she has heart to spare.

Another clever cause-related program can be found across the pond at a company called Innocent Drinks, a new, growing bottled juice brand in the United Kingdom. A few years ago, company management was shocked to learn that every winter, more than 25,000 older people in the United Kingdom die from cold-related illnesses. In 2003, Innocent began a promotion called "The Big Knit," in which small knitted hats—donated by fans of the brand and other do-gooders—are placed on bottles in stores. For each bottle sold, Innocent donates 50 pence (about $1) to the Age Concern, an organization that provides hats, hot meals, blankets, and other supplies to keep older people warm. The more hats the company receives, the more bottles that get capped, and the more donations Innocent makes to Age Concern.

What's really remarkable is how all Innocent employees seem to get behind the cause as well. They join together to knit—and elderly women even visit to teach them—and they share people's submissions and stories on the company's blog and Flickr account. But it's not just the employees' involvement that makes a difference—it's their attitude. As Innocent's Web site (www.innocentdrinks.uk.co) makes clear:

> And for all of you that sent in hats this year, we thank you. The road to 500,000 hats was a treacherous one, filled with numerous brews and hours of needle clacking but we got there in the

end. Thank you is a funny old thing to say, people chuck it around willy nilly, but we just want you all to know how much we mean it. We really couldn't have done it without your support. You all rock. Big time.

In 2007, Innocent raised an impressive £200,000; even more important, each pound raised was felt personally by the people who work at this great, growing company. Culture investments like this help to retain and attract the best employees in the market. In some ways company culture is the new marketing.

5. The Brand Creates a Cause, or the Brand Becomes a Cause

It's not hard for a brand to link to an existing cause, but truly remarkable cause marketing happens when a brand identifies an issue and acts to create the critical mass of support on its own.

Häagen-Dazs is one such company that has executed this brilliantly with Vanilla Honey Bee, a new flavor launched in February 2008, that was created expressly to support actions to arrest and reverse the sudden decline of the honeybee population, which, because of the importance of pollination for flowering plants, is a direct risk to the production of all food brands, including Häagen-Dazs.

The brand did a number of things right in creating a cause behind this issue—from designing a Web site that increased awareness of the issue to donating a portion of its sales from all honeybee-dependent flavors to research. In the "well beyond the call of duty" category, Häagen-Dazs created the first plantable, flower seed–embedded magazine insert; and the brand director, Katty Pien, went so far as to take her personal passion for the cause all the way to Capitol Hill, testifying before Congress to advocate funding for further research into the bees' demise.

According to Christine Chen at Gooby, Silverstein & Partners, the agency behind the program: "We felt like this was something that allowed us to stay very true to who we are and it presented a clear case to consumers as to what kind of skin we have in the game. It was something that probably came as a surprise to consumers because it was a way they never really thought about the brand before."[13]

And Häagen-Dazs's devotion to the cause is a key differentiator in a tightly competitive market, where people now have many options in the superpremium ice cream category alone. This is also a unique way for Häagen-Dazs to close the "cause" gap with rival Ben & Jerry's. Clearly, consumers responded enthusiastically, as the brand fulfilled its *full-year* PR goal of 125 million media impressions in just the first two weeks, despite spending only $1 million on the program. Brand advocacy for Häagen-Dazs among consumers reached 69 percent, the highest among 19 brands tracked, unaided brand awareness grew from 29 to 36 percent, and overall sales increased by 16 percent for the brand in 2008.[14]

It's one thing for a brand to create a cause—*becoming* a cause is quite another. As Carol Cane says in the *Harvard Business Review*, "Some companies are taking CRM to a new level, [creating] 'cause branding.' More than a one-time promotion, a cause-branding program is a core component of a company's corporate identity and overall strategy. Cause branders reach deep into their company's history, values and culture to develop comprehensive programs that are uniquely theirs and cannot be easily duplicated."[15]

Newman's Own is a perfect example of a brand that was created solely out of Paul Newman's desire to provide great food to benefit great causes. Since its launch in 1982, Newman's Own has donated 100 percent of its after-tax profits to what it calls "progressive causes" in the United States and abroad—to the tune of $250 million. Fueled by Newman's personal mission statement for the company—"shameless exploitation in pursuit of the common good"—the lineup of products continues to grow, along with the brand's charitable giving, under the leadership of Paul Newman's daughter Nell, despite Newman's passing.

Perhaps no single company better embodies the "brand as cause" than California-based Patagonia. Founded in 1972 by Yvon Chouinard, Patagonia is more than just a favorite clothing company among outdoor enthusiasts. With a mission statement like "Build the best product, cause no unnecessary harm, use business to inspire, and implement solutions to the environmental crisis," this company sets its standards high and appears to live up to them, both from a meaning standpoint and from a financial one. While customers buy

Patagonia products to better enjoy the outdoors and minimize their footprint on the planet (curious browsers can track the impact of 10 Patagonia products from design through delivery on www.patagonia .com), Patagonia's marketing aims to improve the world by concentrating on environmental issues *and* enrolling its customers to join like-minded causes. The goal of a recent marketing campaign, for example, was to permanently protect the 1.5-million-acre Coastal Plain of the Arctic National Wildlife Refuge. The Patagonia "Heart of Winter 2008" catalog featured, on the first two pages, highlights of its "Freedom to Roam" campaign, a long-term initiative dedicated to establishing migration wildways for animals between protected areas.

If Burger King made it into the annals of meaningful marketing for its pioneering efforts in advergames, it can be said that Patagonia earns its stripes for its excellence in *adverlogs*. The Patagonia catalog rivals *National Geographic* in its beauty and its content—action photographs appear on one side of the book, with product information on the other. A URL under each photo invites the reader to go online to read more about the people in the pictures. Patagonia's message comes across in every piece of marketing material that the brand puts out. Founder Chouinard writes, "We have come upon a balance we find just about ideal: 55% product content and 45% devoted to message—essays, stories, and image photos. Whenever we have edged that content toward increased product presentation, we have actually experienced a decrease in sales."[16] And, as you would expect, the confirmation page of the catalog reads: "When you're finished with it, please pass it on to a friend or recycle it." (Attesting to their desirability, back issues of the catalogs are available for sale on eBay.)

In the book *Marketing That Matters*, authors Chip Conley and Eric Friedenwald-Fishman point to three guidelines that inform Patagonia's marketing strategy: (1) to inspire and educate rather than to promote, (2) to earn credibility before buying it—"the best resources for us are the word-of-mouth recommendations from a friend or favorable comments in the press," and (3) to advertise only as a last resort. Patagonia estimates that it receives press coverage that would be comparable to about $7 million in annual advertising costs.[17]

These efforts would qualify Patagonia as a meaningful marketer even if it didn't sell anything—but it does, and plenty. Revenues have steadily grown 5 to 7 percent per year, and operating margins are at the high end of the 12 to 15 percent industry average—and that's after donating 1 percent of total sales (or 10 percent of profits, whichever is higher) to environmental groups. Since 1985, when Chouinard cofounded the nonprofit One Percent for the Planet, Patagonia has donated $25 million to more than 1,000 organizations.

Now *that's* a meaningful move toward saving the planet and changing the world.

Prepare for the Worst When You're Doing Your Best

There's an old saying, "No good deed goes unpunished," and if you pursue this highest form of achievement marketing, you must be willing and able to defend your position from those inevitable few who will try to take you down a rung or two. Here are some things to watch out for and risk areas that you should be prepared for in any cause-marketing program.

1. *Keep your promises.* If you don't, the crowd will pull you down to a place worse than where you started from and probably will never trust your brand again. British Petroleum (BP) is a case in point. In the last several years, it has focused its advertising on positioning itself as a "green brand." But this positive message took a big hit when the company recently applied for—and was granted—approval to dump 54 percent more ammonia and 35 percent more suspended solids from its Whiting, Indiana, refinery into Lake Michigan. The company later cut its investment in alternative energy and abandoned a proposed carbon capture and storage project in Scotland.[18]

2. *Actions speak louder than words.* The BP example also reminds us that companies cannot win by just talking about their commitment to a cause; they must take real actions

that show a meaningful impact on the world. Instead of spending millions of dollars in television advertising talking green, BP could have created some valuable new service to prove its commitment. Take PickupPal, self-described as a "global eco-friendly transportation revolution that connects drivers, passengers, and packages with the places they need to go." It's basically the digital equivalent of the college bulletin board. BP could have (actually still can!) picked up on this idea first to actually help its customers save some gas while doing something for the environment. Similarly, one of many large, global bank brands should have invented Kiva, the world's first person-to-person microlending Web site, through which people can finance specific projects by entrepreneurs in the developing world. It is receiving numerous awards and recognition around the world from people like Bill Clinton and Oprah Winfrey.

3. *Don't jump on a crowded bandwagon.* October is National Breast Cancer Awareness Month, and a ton of brands (admirably) line up every year to support this worthy cause. But this can backfire and lead to cause overload. Last year, I was served a banner ad for a special-edition Oreck pink vacuum that offered a donation to the Susan G. Komen for the Cure program. The promotional Web page is titled "One Powerful Cause. One Powerful Vacuum," and while the site includes some copy about the charity, it is mainly focused on product features and performance claims such as, "Strong enough to pick up a 16-lb bowling ball."

I'm sure the hearts of the people at Oreck are in the right place. It is a worthy cause and a novel way to sell vacuums, but it left me doubtful about the true meaning and marketing results of such a program. The ad certainly got my attention, but more because it seemed odd than because it seemed sincere. The lesson is, don't jump on a crowded bandwagon just because it seems like the right thing to do—people can see through a thinly veiled agenda and will hold it against you.

4. *Expect backlash but keep the high ground.* No good cause
   is immune from negative sentiment and cynicism.
   Greenpeace parodies Dove campaigns in protest against its
   use of palm oil, as farming has been linked to deaths of
   Indonesian orangutans; and Pampers' efforts to donate
   vaccinations to babies in Africa have been protested by
   people who believe that vaccinations are linked to autism.

What to do in these situations? First, realize that your opponents are
leaning on your platform. Listen carefully and demonstrate thought-
fulness and empathy, then let your consumers defend you. If your
heart and actions are in the right place, they will cast the naysayers
aside.

PART II

HOW TO IMPLEMENT MARKETING WITH MEANING IN YOUR BUSINESS

At this point in the book, you may have questions. Sure, meaningful marketing sounds great on paper, and seeing a few examples of companies that are shifting their strategies is interesting, but you may feel that you've seen this movie before. Marketing gurus are famous for platitudes that look great on the bookshelf, but fall far short of providing an approach that brand managers can employ come Monday morning. They offer novel nuggets and examples, but they rarely lay out a framework that you can use to sell your boss on a new approach. As in too much of today's advertising, there's plenty of sizzle, but not enough steak.

The standard approach that these books take is to present a concept, share several examples, and end with a call to get back to work and make it happen. In this book, the purpose of Part I was to convince you that you need to embrace marketing with meaning if your brand is to survive the fundamental changes in consumer habits that are taking place, and to show you a new strategy for success that is supported by a logical model and dozens of case studies. Now that you understand the concept of marketing with meaning, and you have been exposed to a wide range of examples, it's time for you to roll up your sleeves and figure out how to make fundamental changes in your own brand's marketing process.

The number one objective of this book is to help you, dear marketer, personally make the shift to this new paradigm. And so in Part II, I will lay out a road map that you can consult in order to successfully follow the trailblazers who were featured in Part I.

From my personal experience as a brand manager, I understand just how hard it is to change an organization. Reading a compelling book and advocating a strategy is about 1 percent of the work. Actually selling a new strategy to your bosses and executing it successfully is the other 99 percent. The forces of resistance within a company can be high: legal isn't sure what the rules are in new spaces, senior management is more comfortable with TV copy and GRPs, and your advertising agency is embarrassed to admit that it isn't really expert on what's new or next.

I also understand that an even bigger barrier to change is the lack of a process for making the change happen. No matter where you work, you probably have an existing marketing planning and execution process, and this process has probably become ingrained in your mind and engraved on an 18-month calendar. Your company has probably refined this process so that it drives costs down and keeps wasted time to an absolute minimum. Your retail customers, franchisees, and shareholders are used to seeing the usual ads and media plans. And if you believe in marketing with meaning enough to make the leap, you're probably wondering just where to begin.

Part II will take you, step by step, through one approach to implementing this organizational shift; it's more of an evolution than a revolution relative to what you are doing today. The steps are:

- Establish business objectives.

- Gather relevant consumer insights.

- Develop and launch the marketing plan.

- Measure results and continue evolving.

You will probably want to use this suggested path as a starting point for creating the process that works best for your organization. I encourage you to share this book with as many people on your team as possible in order to begin enrolling them in the process. After all, you will need a strong team of fellow believers to bring an entirely new marketing model to life.

6

START AT THE END
WHAT DO YOU HOPE
TO ACCOMPLISH?

Whether your aim is to move cases of laundry detergent or to convince people to carpool, all marketing begins by establishing objectives—the results you hope to achieve. Before you can begin to create marketing with any meaning, before you can even begin to think about how to improve the lives of your customers, you've got to focus on the best ways to improve the lives of your shareholders. If you want to hit your numbers in the short term and boost loyalty-beyond-reason in the long term, you must uncover the fundamental business drivers and opportunities that have the greatest chance of boosting sales and profits, select the right business goals for your meaningful marketing program, and successfully sell the approach to senior management. This chapter will show you how to do just that.

Don't Waste Your Money Pitching Engagement Rings to a Married Man

For Sears Holding Corporation (SHC), the spark to create marketing with meaning didn't come from a daylong brainstorming session in the company's Chicago-area headquarters—it came, instead, on an

> Acquiring a new customer costs about five to seven times as much as maintaining a profitable relationship with an existing customer.
> —MARC FLEISHHACKER

ordinary day, as CEO Eddie Lampert was riffling through his family's mail. Weeding through the catalogs and solicitations, Lampert came across a flyer—from Sears—advertising engagement rings. A married man and father of three, Lampert was suddenly aware that his company didn't know its customers very well.

Lampert, the investor who had purchased Kmart in 2003 (after it had filed for bankruptcy in 2002) and added Sears to the chain in 2004, had been in search of a powerful new way to grow the business for some time. After focusing on closing unprofitable stores, merging the two large corporations, and following the same formula that had been used for years—frequent sale events, big TV campaigns, and droves of identical direct mail to every household in the nation—Lampert realized that getting to know Sears' customers and using this information to create customized marketing would give the company an edge against competitors (Wal-Mart, Target, and Best Buy) who were selling similar products.

"Acquiring a new customer costs about five to seven times as much as maintaining a profitable relationship with an existing customer," says Marc Fleishhacker, managing director at Ogilvy Consulting,[1] the firm that designed Sears' new marketing approach, including its all-important objective: increase share and profitability by improving marketing to existing customers. With this objective in mind, the marketing team launched Sears' meaningful makeover by dramatically cutting back on its one-size-fits-all TV ads and—perhaps somewhat counterintuitively—deliberately *expanding* its direct marketing. Utilizing its rich database of information on online and in-store purchases to predict consumer interest, the company was able to offer relevant e-mail/online promotions (for example, those who purchased an appliance at Sears received a follow-up offer for an extended warranty). SHC was also able to create customized discount offers based on the historical long-term value of each individual customer.

SHC also created an online community, MySears.com, and encouraged consumers to build their own profiles on the site, not only to help the company do better, more focused direct marketing, but also to enable its customers to take advantage of the collective wisdom of the SHC community and make better, more informed purchases. After indicating their interests on the initial registration form, customers receive free information on those topics that matter most to them, including how-to guides (how to buy a space heater, what to look for when buying a mattress) and relevant product reviews from other members (including videos and photos). And as an added bonus, the site affords members the opportunity to build a list of friends from people with similar interests, which SHC can mine for future events and promotions.

According to Rob Harles, senior vice president of SHC and owner of the program, the Sears and Kmart communities allow the company to go back in time to the days when a friendly shopkeeper could make appropriate recommendations to neighborhood guests: "By getting to know its individual customers better, we can offer better product assortment and pricing." And by using digital social media tools, SHC is also allowing its customers to help each other.

Having homed in on a very specific objective that, if successfully implemented, has a strong likelihood of delivering bottom-line results *and* creating long-term customer loyalty and differentiation in a very competitive retail marketplace, Sears provides an excellent model for what your company or brand must first do if it is to create meaningful marketing and solid business results: choose a business objective that will serve as a core guide for the campaign you will create.

How Near-Term Objectives Promise Long-Term Results

A simple, useful way to start the process of establishing short-term business objectives is to use the classic "purchase funnel." I know there are several marketing gurus out there who claim either that the purchase funnel is dead or that it is more like a matrix than a funnel, which may or may not be true, but I find that it is still a good place to begin.

A purchase funnel can be broken down into several areas. Start by performing a thorough analysis of how your product or service stands in each of these areas. Estimate what percentage of your target

audience is at each level, and look into the reasons why these percent-
ages are high or low. The areas used in a purchase funnel can vary, but
for this purpose, the basic form suffices:

- *Awareness.* This is the starting point in the purchase
  process. It is achieved when a customer learns that your
  product, service, or message exists and why it exists. It can
  be measured with pre/post surveys, and it can be further
  divided between aided awareness ("Have you heard of
  Brand X?") and unaided awareness ("What brands are you
  familiar with?"). Typically, this is where we marketers spend
  the bulk of our dollars when we're launching a new product.
  We pour funds into awareness in hopes that a large group
  comes into the funnel.

  But awareness can come at a huge cost and often
  requires repeated messages to gain the initial attention of
  the target group. Increasingly, brands are working to solve
  awareness issues by defining their target audience(s) more
  narrowly, or by being present when customers are changing
  their habits or entering new categories (a topic called the
  market entry point, which will be described further in
  Chapter 7). In general, the more focused your target
  audience, the easier it is to uncover a meaningful place to
  reach them.

- *Consideration.* In the consideration phase, the customer is
  in the thick of evaluating purchase options, weighing the
  pros and cons of trying the product. You can figure out
  where your product stands by asking the classic purchase
  intent question, "Would you buy this?" This is usually asked
  with options for the answer, such as "Definitely would buy,"
  "Probably would buy," "Might or might not buy," "Probably
  wouldn't buy," and "Definitely wouldn't buy." To make a
  general prediction, most marketers divide the "Definitely
  would buy" percentage by two and the "Probably would
  buy" percentage by four, then add the two results together to
  estimate what percentage of people will end up buying over
  the course of a year.

It's important to note that your target consumer evaluates your product or service both rationally (intellectually considering its benefits and attributes) and emotionally (noting the feelings that the brand provokes). This means you have the opportunity to win her over on both fronts by both providing deep product information and product reviews and connecting with her in a more personal context. Furthermore, remember that you're not the only brand she's considering—she's probably comparing you to one or more of your competitors and weighing what value your product or service holds. So there are opportunities to increase both purchase intent and market share by offering something unique and valuable through marketing that is different from your competition.

- *Trial.* The trial phase is triggered when—you guessed it—the customer uses the product or service for the first time. This is a critical point in the process, as your customer is judging your performance against the expectations you set forth in your marketing. While it is mainly the quality of your product or service that's on the line, there are several ways in which meaningful marketing can maximize the trial experience. For example, you can offer helpful information, customer support and service, valuable experiences (as discussed in Chapter 4), and even free samples (covered in Chapter 3) that allow a customer to try the product at low risk.

- *Loyalty.* Broadly, loyalty measures the consistent purchase of your product or service, but loyalty can also be divided into three important subcategories: the measure of *market share* for your brand, as compared to your competition, within an individual household; how much of your product or service each consumer buys over the course of a year (*consumption*); and how often an actual transaction occurs (*purchase frequency*). Each of these can be measured individually, and focusing on each can provide useful targets for meaningful marketing.

In contrast to awareness, which, as I noted, tends to receive the majority of our marketing dollars, I would argue

> [There is no] reference to the classic, traditional-model measures such as reach, frequency, and recall. These measures are used only for evaluating the old interruptive media, and they are associated only with attempts to drive awareness, consideration, and trial.

that loyalty deserves much more attention (and resources). After all, the majority of a brand's sales are increasingly driven by a very small percentage of its buyers. A recent study by Catalina and the CMO Council showed that even for broadly purchased consumer product goods brands, an average of 80 percent of sales come from only *2.5 percent* of buyers (so much for that old 80/20 principle).

Unfortunately, I would bet that most brands don't spend anywhere near 80 percent of their budgets on loyalty and relationship-marketing programs that home in on this proven 2.5 percent.

- *Advocacy.* While it is not always included in a typical purchase funnel, advocacy is an increasingly important measure of success. Because consumers are less trustful than ever of advertising and are more actively avoiding it, marketers have to depend more than ever on raving fans to spread positive word of mouth. We can measure this by asking about consumers' willingness to recommend our products and services, and whether or not they have "told a friend" about our brand. In addition to improving the quality of our wares, which makes them worth talking about, marketers can conduct specific, meaningful activities to encourage advocacy, and thus generate awareness that brings new consumers into the purchase funnel.

In evaluating these potential marketing objectives, notice what is not here. You will not see any reference to the classic, traditional-model measures such as reach, frequency, and recall. These measures are used only for evaluating the old interruptive media, and they are associated only with attempts to drive awareness, consideration, and trial. You also won't see any "new media" measures such as time on site, open rate, or content downloads. While some of these measures can be important to the marketing with meaning analytics, which will be discussed in Chapter 9, they are merely measures of the strategies and tactics that *result* from strong marketing objectives.

Designing Strong Marketing Objectives

The purpose of any type of marketing plan is to change consumer behavior in a way that helps your company or your brand meet its goals. And while goals will vary from organization to organization, there are three common characteristics that all meaningful marketing objectives must have in order to drive business success.

First, your objective must be *measurable*. This may seem elementary, but it's often ignored. Worse, marketers commonly set an objective that relates to an *activity* rather than a result. For example, a pharmaceutical company could set an objective to "provide information to consumers who are researching diabetes drugs." Well, that's not a hard goal to meet, if you can find the folks who are looking and give them something of interest to read. But doing so, in and of itself, is not likely to improve your bottom line in any significant way. Each marketing objective should be assigned a clear, numbers-oriented goal; if the objective is to increase trial of a new product, choose a target percentage that you will aim to achieve by the end of the program. If the goal is to increase repeat use, determine the current rate of repeat use and set a numerical goal for its increase as a result of your campaign.

Second, a strong marketing objective is *achievable*; it is realistic and something that might well happen without a pig taking flight or a snowball traveling unscathed through hell and back. What's an unrealistic objective? A modest Web site redesign that "generates a 50 percent increase in loyalty." That's not likely to happen, despite your best intentions. When you're assessing what is genuinely achievable, make sure that you can realize these results in the near future, when the business needs them most—anywhere between the first week and the first year, depending on your particular business and sales cycle.

Finally, be sure to *prioritize* your marketing objectives. There is the constant temptation to slip several objectives into a single marketing

> **Commit to one or two key objectives for the campaign. . . . If your marketing objectives are measurable, achievable, prioritized, and focused on key business drivers, you are well on your way toward developing marketing with meaning.**

plan, but this serves only to dilute the marketing you produce and decrease the likelihood that you can actually achieve any single goal. Instead, commit to one or two key objectives for the campaign, and list them in priority order. This not only will help to clarify what is most important for both your management and your agency partners, but also will ensure that the objectives you set are really the most important if your business is to succeed.

If your marketing objectives are measurable, achievable, prioritized, and focused on key business drivers, you are well on your way toward developing marketing with meaning. Here are a few illustrations of organizations that found success in part by starting at the end and being clear about just what it was they wanted to accomplish.

Founded in 1916, the Professional Golfers Association (PGA) is the world's largest working sports organization, made up of 28,000 professionals who are committed to growing, teaching, and managing the game of golf through spectator events, education, and training programs.[2] The challenge the PGA was facing was a decline in actual rounds played—with today's families being increasingly pressed for time, even on weekends, golfers were having a harder time rationalizing spending five hours on the course. In addition, fewer kids—in particular, fewer girls—were getting into the game at an early age.

The PGA arrived at a measurable, achievable, focused business objective: increase repeat play by current players and trial by kids. This helped lead the organization to kick off an annual "Take Your Daughter to the Course Week." Participating courses promoted the idea and offered incentives such as free lessons and discounted greens fees. This gave girls a taste of the game and helped to get golf-loving dads and moms onto the course guilt-free, since they were spending quality family time with their daughters. The short-term results showed that participating courses enjoyed an increase in rounds played and lessons purchased; long term, if "Take Your Daughter to the Course Week" gets girls to play more golf, it could result in a huge upside for the PGA and the entire golf industry, creating new, lifelong fans of the sport and more opportunities for whole families to play together.

Eight years after its launch, Netflix, the leading provider of DVD movie rental services, was confronted with a different kind of marketing dilemma. The company entered the market in 1999 with a unique service: a monthly subscription model paired with the novel offering of mailing movies to customers' homes. Powered by a strong online management tool, Netflix succeeded by winning over people who were tired of paying late fees, having to leave their homes at 11 p.m. to return movies, and not being able to find the DVDs they wanted when they wanted them at stores like Blockbuster. Despite these strengths, Netflix foresaw an issue. The company realized that its monthly subscription business model would suffer if customers ran out of movies that they wanted to watch. After all, a monthly fee is easy to cut when the service goes unused, and Netflix was worried that membership would tail off once the novelty of convenience wore off and people were "caught up" on new releases.

Its business objective was to maintain customer loyalty by maximizing their use of the Netflix service. Using this objective as a guide, Netflix created a powerful recommendation engine—a tool that constantly asks members to rate the movies they have watched and provides recommendations based on their ratings. Once the data have been input, a powerful predictive software algorithm uses the information—along with the collected history of all of the service's members—to make new recommendations. The service also reveals which specific previous rentals and reviews guided the recommendations.

Netflix is further driving this advantage by getting others to help. It launched the Netflix Prize, a $1 million incentive to be awarded to the first person or group that achieves a 10 percent improvement in the accuracy of movie recommendations. Netflix has motivated 2,000 teams worldwide to work on improving its service! (The closest contender at the time this book was going to press was at 9.63 percent.)

And its efforts are paying real dividends; Netflix has enjoyed 10 straight years of subscriber growth, from 107,000 in 1999 to 9.4 million in 2008. Furthermore, 94 percent of its subscribers recommend it. An e-commerce satisfaction survey by ForeSee Results puts Netflix as number one in customer satisfaction for the seventh survey in a row. This tool has become a major strategic advantage for Netflix. Because its customers have invested the time and goodwill in sharing their information and are receiving a constant flow of valuable recommendations as a result, the company has "locked in" its customers at a time when movie downloads are rapidly replacing mailed DVDs. This has provided Netflix with the leverage to cut deals with brands like TiVo and Xbox, becoming the movie service of choice for these platforms.[3]

Finally, here's a cautionary tale regarding the topic of setting clear, definable, achievable marketing objectives. Have you ever "Elfed Yourself"? Chances are that you are one of the more than 30 million people who have spent the equivalent of more than *3,000 years* collectively on this Web site, turning yourself and your friends into Santa's festive little helpers. This incredibly viral online toy has attracted a huge amount of interest in the past three holiday shopping seasons.

These numbers prove that Elf Yourself is meaningful—falling into the category of building connections through entertainment, which we addressed in Chapter 4. Surely the marketing results match the incredible engagement rate, right?

Well, let me ask you this: what company created Elf Yourself? Whenever I ask an audience this question, the results look something like this:

Office Depot: 30 percent

OfficeMax: 30 percent

Staples: 30 percent

Other: 10 percent

That's the start of the problem—there is no clear link between the Elf Yourself tool and the company that produces it (which, by the way, is OfficeMax). And despite enormous buzz and traffic, Elf Yourself does not seem to have helped OfficeMax's bottom line. During its first launch in the fourth quarter of 2006, sales *decreased* by $7 million—*despite 11 million Elf visitors.* Robert Gorrell, managing editor at GrokDotCom, a marketing optimization blog, suggests that OfficeMax "elfed itself" out of millions of dollars of potential sales

by selecting the wrong business objective for its campaign. He points to
a comment by OfficeMax's vice president of marketing and advertising,
Bob Thacker, who said: "We were
looking to build the brand, warm up
our image. We weren't looking for

> **Always double-check that your marketing objective will truly have an impact on your bottom line.**

sales. We are third-place players in our industry, so we are trying to
differentiate ourselves through humor and humanization."

We weren't looking for sales?

The fact that OfficeMax is struggling with the perception that it is
"just another" one of the big three big-box office supply chains is
understandable. And differentiating itself from its competition is certainly a keen and worthy goal. But differentiating itself without paying
any attention to bottom-line results is just bad business practice—and
poor marketing planning. OfficeMax could have succeeded at both
goals by establishing a more robust objective that included bottom-
line results, such as, "Drive holiday-season sales growth by differentiating ourselves in the market." Gorrell suggests adding a promotional
sales offer to the tool, say: "Elf Yourself and save 10 percent on last-
minute holiday treats when at OfficeMax.com." Personally, I would
love to see the brand use a value-added end result to the Elfing
process that drives traffic into physical stores—perhaps an offer for a
free printing of an 8½- by 11-inch photo of your Elf Self (or, better
yet, of one of your loved ones), which would provide plenty of fun,
conversation, and brand relevance during the holiday season.

The moral of the story is: always double-check that your marketing objective will truly have an impact on your bottom line. You
should expect a lot from your meaningful marketing plan, as small
expectations have a way of leading to small business results, even
when the buzz is big.

Aim for Long-Term Equity Building

You may have noticed that throughout this book, I have often referred
to the potential for marketing with meaning to drive "loyalty-
beyond-reason." As extreme as that phrase might sound, what it

means is that, in addition to securing your near-term business results, the path of meaningful marketing can also pay long-term dividends in the form of repeat sales that can span lifetimes, or even generations. Investing $1 in such a program might return $2 next year and $200 over the next 10 years.

There are essentially three key ways to think about building long-term loyalty: equity, trust, and brand identification. Each of them would make a good secondary objective for a meaningful marketing program, and all of them can be measured over both the short and the long term.

The first key way is *equity*. Broadly defined, equity is the measure of what the brand stands for in your customers' minds. As marketers, we often identify key equities that we want to "own" in the minds of our target audience. They can be basic—for example, Dawn detergent owns "tough on grease," while Palmolive owns "soft on hands." They can also be more aspirational. Pampers has evolved from owning functional equities like "dryness" and "comfort" to owning more enlightened qualities like "promoting child development." Its recent program of offering vaccinations for children in Africa is a great example of a marketing program that delivers on this higher equity. Equity works like a bank account—a brand hopes that it is putting equity "in the bank" with individual customers with each marketing or product interaction, and benefiting from a return in the form of positive brand associations and long-term loyalty. If a brand fails to meet customer expectations, this equity account is drained down to nothing, along with future sales.

Equity can be measured over time and against the competition, and various organizations have created models that literally measure the value of brand equity in dollars and cents. In its annual equity survey, Millward Brown, one of the world's leading research agencies, claims that Google is the most valuable brand in the world, with an equity worth $86 billion.[4] Another survey with different assumptions by Interbrand claims that Coca-Cola is number one, with an equity value of $66 billion.

It's important that you ask: What's *your* brand equity? And is your marketing adding to its value? We find that the more meaningful the marketing, the more the equity value adds up.

The second way to think about building long-term loyalty is in terms of *trust*. In these cynical times, trust is rapidly gaining mind share as an important driver of a brand's business. Because consumers are growing tired of products and services that fail to live up to their (advertised) promises,

> There are essentially three key ways to think about building long-term loyalty: equity, trust, and brand identification.

they are limiting their purchases to a close set of brands, and looking to one another for truthful recommendations. (It's no accident that Jim Stengel, former global marketing officer for Procter & Gamble, reported that the P&G brands with the most trust have the highest market share.) Trust has also become increasingly important in a world where a consumer's personal information can be laid bare with a simple Web search or sales transaction; from credit card and social security numbers to Web site visits, sensitive information is more exposed than ever before. Consumers appreciate personal, customized offers, but only from brands that they trust.

Last, there's *brand identification*, which is the extent to which people feel that your brand in some way defines who they are. Think of the Mac users, who place stickers on the windows of their hybrids, or the NASCAR fans who fly Budweiser flags on their RVs. People who assimilate a brand into their lives in such a way that they believe it helps to define them show off their "loyalty-beyond-reason" and represent the ultimate bond between company and consumer. While only a small percentage of your customers will go to such an extent for your brand, there are ways you can develop your marketing that will inspire people to become walking, talking representatives of your brand, some examples of which follow.

Did you know that Vicks is a brand that actually encompasses multiple cold and flu treatment and prevention subbrands, including Formula 44, NyQuil, DayQuil, and VapoRub? Probably not; most consumers didn't either, until we took steps to let them know it, like redesigning Vicks.com to be a one-stop information resource for people who are looking to manage their cold and flu symptoms.

Historically, there was no clear link among these disparate products, like DayQuil and VapoRub, but we realized that there was a huge upside in cost savings and cross-selling if we could educate people on our broad lineup. Simply put, we saw the equity opportunity for Vicks as: present Vicks as a trusted ally offering solutions across multiple needs.

But it wasn't enough for us just to talk about how all the subbrands were "now" under the Vicks branding umbrella; the consumer couldn't have cared less. What people were interested in—which is not surprising, considering how much time we spend online on health Web sites "diagnosing" ourselves and our loved ones—were valuable tips for identifying what ailed them, and solutions and product recommendations that would help them to feel better fast.

Knowing this provided us with an opportunity to connect with consumers in a meaningful way. Two key features on Vicks.com are the Symptom Analyzer, in which you rank, on a sliding scale, your discomfort level for seven common symptoms (such as head congestion, cough, sore throat, and fever) in order to receive tips on how to treat yourself without medication (e.g., "drink chamomile tea") as well as suggestions for products, from cough medicines to humidifiers, courtesy of Vicks. Another popular tool is an online cold- and flu-tracking tool, which provides a forecast of sickness according to zip code and indicates what percentage of people in your area have a cold or the flu. Naturally, it is also available as a mobile phone service.

While these tools will certainly help short-term sales, as we expect that a high percentage of visitors will purchase more Vicks products in response to this valuable information, you can also see how this program will build brand equity, long-term trust, and category identification, positioning Vicks as a partner in treating and preventing these common illnesses.

Intel is another company whose strong short-term business goal also has the potential to improve its long-term equity. The brand had increasingly been losing its cachet as a cool technology company, as was evident from a 26 percent fall in its brand equity value estimate. The goal? Restore its status as a cutting-edge technology brand.

Fortunately, Intel understood that the way to regain its hipness factor was to focus on winning over the small group of technology thought leaders who help define what is cool for the rest of the marketplace. You may have come across a tool called "digg.com," an online listing of news items that have been flagged by a small, influential community of heavy-duty tech geeks. These people are both incredibly vocal and incredibly influential in terms of determining which technology stories catch the attention of major media outlets, which also use digg to see what stories are breaking. As a way of repositioning itself and building "geek cred," Intel created a visualization tool called "Digg Arc" that allows digg users to see stories appear dynamically in a cool, colorful pie-chart format. This graphical application made a boring news feed more engaging and useful. Because it was a unique, valuable technology, it helped Intel prove its software design chops, drawing attention and excitement from digg users—who, of course, gave it more than 1,000 "diggs" in the first day, a positive endorsement that trickled out to the rest of the general media, effectively altering Intel's perception in the marketplace in a very short period of time.[5]

The success of the Digg Arc helped Intel to recognize that, as a brand, it had to be fluent in "geek speak" if it wanted to win over the true opinion leaders in the technology sector. Around this same time, it also realized that it already had a treasure trove of geek-speaking engineers in its company who could hold their own with the most sophisticated technology insiders around. So in 2007, Intel put its in-house talent to work in marketing. It brought a few of its engineers into a question-and-answer session with the audience on Slashdot, another technology-focused Web site that is often the first to break stories and that encourages forum-style comments on its articles. Because Slashdot's audience was so excited by the direct access to Intel's engineers (to the point that the Slashdot Q&A system was overwhelmed), Intel went on to create ITopia (a sufficiently geeky merger of "IT" and "Utopia"), a section on the company's Web site that hosts ongoing chats with its engineers, adding a deeper level of credibility to what is now considered the mass Intel behemoth.

While it is difficult to tease out whether these small efforts targeted at a narrow technology audience made a direct difference in Intel's brand equity, the fact is that the value of its brand equity rose 18 percent, from $18.7 billion to $22 billion, from 2007 to 2008, suggesting that the brand is on the rise again in the minds of both the influential insiders and the general market that they tend to sway.

Selling Marketing with Meaning to Your Organization

> Selling your management and your stakeholder team on the significance of marketing with meaning before you begin any real work is essential to your ultimate success.

While this is obviously a chapter on the importance of marketing objectives and how best to meet or formulate yours, selling your management and your stakeholder team on the significance of marketing with meaning before you begin any real work is essential to your ultimate success. As you have probably found, making changes of any size or magnitude can be very difficult. You will have to go beyond simply aligning your management and your stakeholders on a meaningful business objective in order to drive marketing with meaning throughout your organization.

The good news is that your company probably already recognizes that a somewhat radical change in how it goes about marketing and advertising is needed. In addition, you are holding a book full of tried-and-true examples of how large and small companies alike have successfully made the move to meaning—possibly including a few of your competitors. Such examples from others (especially if they're competitors!) can help your team see that success is, in fact, possible. Here are some additional tips for meeting and defeating the organizational resistance you are likely to encounter.

Enlist Upper Management's Support First

Thankfully, somewhere along the way in my career, the phrase "that's not my job" was purged from daily business discourse (if, however, you still hear this in your office, leave now!). I would nominate the phrase "we've never done that before" to be the next to go. Despite the fact that in today's marketplace, any organization that stands in the way of change will fail to exist for long, there are probably still people in your company who are afraid of betting their careers on a new marketing model.

Perhaps the easiest way to counter this is from the top down. Enlist the support of a strong senior manager—the higher up the better—who can both deliver the marketing budget you need and lend the political power you will require within the organization to rally other resources and overcome as-yet-unforeseen barriers.

Eddie Lampert's enthusiastic push to improve marketing at Kmart and Sears is a good example. Another is ConAgra Foods, where Gary Rodkin, the CEO, and Joan Chow, the CMO, were totally invested in the company's efforts to create the Start Making Choices platform described in Chapter 5. They provided funding, pulled multiple brands together, and personally oversaw the strategy, creative, and business results.

Bring the Customer into the Room

Regardless of general organizational resistance and specific personal agendas, there is nothing more powerful than reminding your organization that you are all ultimately in the business of serving customers. If you understand your target audience better than anyone else in the organization—as you should—you probably have the currency to convince the powers that be that the customer is doing nothing less than demanding marketing with meaning.

Symbolically, some brands "create" a personality, based on research and other firsthand consumer information, for use in key meetings. While you may not choose to go this far, I have actually seen brands create a cardboard cutout of their typical customer, which is given a suitable first name like "Gwen." Gwen is brought into the conference room during important decision-making discussions, and a team member will periodically look over at the cutout and ask, "What would Gwen think about this?"

"What If They Say Something Negative?"

It may seem counterintuitive, but negative feedback about your brand actually provides you with excellent intelligence and adds credibility to whatever it is you are trying to sell or do. For example, when I built an online community for Tide, we knew that if we tried to somehow keep people from talking about their negative experiences with Tide or their preferences for our competition, we would fail at our goal of becoming the center for solving stain emergencies. Also, it pays to have faith in your consumer—on its own, the community often keeps the noisiest people down by ignoring or discounting those perspectives that seem too extreme or that seem to lack real merit.

"What If They Do Something Offensive?"

This is more of an academic concern than a reality. Not only are today's language filters quite sensitive, but you can also opt to review consumer content before posting or displaying it. In our "Design Your Own Reusable Bag" contest for Kroger, the company's consumer relations team personally inspected each of the 30,000-plus entries; for other campaigns, such as our "Pringles Can Creator," we let the community self-police by offering a "Do you find this offensive?" button. If someone sees a questionable posting, we automatically sequester it. But in both cases, very, very few entries were flagged.

"What If They Make a Claim We Cannot Support?"

The beauty of letting people speak for themselves is that they will often say things that you cannot. Consider the comment "I think Chiquita bananas taste better." If this was a claim that the marketing department wanted to make, Chiquita's legal team would probably mandate that the brand spend thousands of dollars to prove that it was technically true.

But the courts don't regulate the words that consumers use on their own, so if someone posts this on a brand message board, it's fair game. To benefit from such consumer comments, you must allow an open, largely unmonitored conversation (which may include comments like "I don't like Chiquita" or "Dole tastes better"). It's not for the faint of heart, but it can be worth it.

Bet Your Career If You Have To

Sometimes, in order to get the support you need to do what is right for your brand, you need to put your reputation and/or your career on the line. Now, I certainly wouldn't recommend doing this in every situation, and no, I haven't completely lost my mind, but occasionally this endgame conviction is necessary, especially when you are already responsible for the brand's ultimate success.

> Sometimes, in order to get the support you need to do what is right for your brand, you need to put your reputation and/or your career on the line.

As the P&G brand manager for Mr. Clean AutoDry Carwash, I was in charge of launching this new product, an innovative new system for washing your car at home and the company's first foray into auto-care products (and only its second foray into marketing to men—after Old Spice). The product's unique selling proposition was that it utilized a special soap and a filtered rinse setting to allow the car to dry spotlessly on its own. Unfortunately the auto-care aisle had seen decades' worth of "spot-free" soaps and "streak-free" shines that underperformed, so our number one challenge was countering car guys' disbelief of our claims. Our other challenge was timing; sales in the car-wash category are concentrated in the spring—that "first nice day of the year" when guys rush out and buy their car-washing supplies for the entire summer. If we didn't have a lot of them using and talking about our products early in the season, our word of mouth wouldn't hit until the fall, when they were packing their products away for the year.

I was convinced that we had to build buzz months prior to our launch, so we put together a plan to give away our device to hundreds of discussion forum moderators and car club leaders across the country. We would spend less than 5 percent of the total launch budget to do so. It wasn't easy, but I was able to rally my delivery team to make enough product for this effort nearly six months before the launch. My team believed in the strategy and worked incredible hours to deliver.

But I still had one big barrier to clear. My global president—who was three levels above me—hated the idea of putting the product into the market before launch. He was very concerned that doing so would give the competition a head start in producing a product that could challenge ours. (This worry was valid, given that we had been similarly burned on another recent new product launch.) He also thought that even 5 percent of our budget was too much to spend ahead of our spring launch plan.

I was clear in my conviction, and so I persisted in trying to convince him to accept our plan. Sometimes it was in meetings with 25 other functional leaders; other times it was one-on-one, when he would stop by my office to check on the progress of this, his favorite new product.

Eventually, though, I needed his final approval to release the funding and the sample product. So I went into his office and made my last appeal. I said that I had lived and breathed this product for months, and that I knew that prelaunch sampling was the right way to go. I started with my main rationale—that it wasn't worth worrying about the competition if our launch failed out of the gate—and I finished by saying that since he had chosen me as the leader of this product, as the leader I needed the freedom to make this call in the best way I saw fit.

I didn't have to hand him my resignation, but it was understood that I was putting myself on the line. He studied me for what seemed like 10 minutes and finally said, "OK, Bob, it's your business—go for it."

Go for it we did, and it succeeded wildly. As I'd anticipated, once the auto opinion leaders were receiving the free devices and falling in love with them, they were providing long, detailed reviews, complete with dozens of photos. The buzz built up through the winter, and when we hit the stores in March 2004, there were thousands of eager buyers ready. On the day before our official launch, our 5 percent budget investment had created 25 percent general marketing awareness and 45 percent awareness among the car aficionados that we most coveted. Mr. Clean AutoDry went on to be the number one product in auto care in its first year. One day in the hallway, my president even patted me on the back and said that I had made the right call. That's priceless.

•   •   •

The journey to marketing with meaning depends on knowing where you want to go, mapping out your objectives, and rallying your team to the challenge. In my experience, if you can make it this far, you are halfway there, and well on your way to achieving success.

Once your team is ready to roll, it's time to take another step back and reevaluate what you really know about your customers and what you can do to improve their lives through your marketing—perhaps for the very first time.

7

JUST ASK

DISCOVERING WHAT KEEPS PEOPLE UP AT NIGHT AND GETS THEM OUT OF BED IN THE MORNING

Once you have put together a strong objective, it's time for the hard part—actually figuring out how to market to your target consumer with meaning. When I say "the hard part," I really mean it. These are not the good old days when we put the marketing objectives in a creative brief and let the advertising agency start drawing pictures. Nope. Today, we have to roll up our sleeves, think deeply, and learn about our customers anew. But do not despair; this is not necessarily about deep psychology and complicated spider charts, but rather about putting ourselves in the kitchen-logic mindset of the people we hope to reach. Once you have homed in on a discrete target audience, performed relevant research, and isolated a meaningful insight, the rest will fall into place. Remember, all we're trying to do is create marketing that our customers find valuable.

> Today, we have to roll up our sleeves, think deeply, and learn about our customers anew. But ... remember, all we're trying to do is create marketing that our customers find valuable.

In his defining book *Truth, Lies and Advertising*, Jon Steel summarizes the purpose of this chapter in one sentence:

The aim of the best advertising research is to embrace consumers; reach a deeper level of understanding of the way they think, feel, and behave; and then use those observations and discoveries to kick start the creative process and begin to build a relationship with them through the advertising itself.

Steel wrote these words in 1998, after spending decades creating print ads, television commercials, and radio spots, which should reassure you that shifting to marketing with meaning does not mean that you must categorically dump everything you have learned in your career. Rather, Steel's words should serve as a reminder that our real strengths and passions do not rest on perfecting TV copy or coupon redemption rates, but on understanding how people operate and figuring out the best way to meet their needs.

The next step in creating marketing with meaning is to think about your target audience as people first and consumers second. Only this mindset will enable you to ask the right people the right questions and help you to achieve the business objectives that you are looking for.

For many readers, the concept of "consumer understanding" is nothing new. You have probably spent countless hours in focus-group facilities munching on M&Ms and watching your target consumers react to your product and your advertising concepts. You may have dissected $200,000 quantitative surveys to such an extent that you really do understand why second-generation Hispanic females in Oklahoma prefer chunky peanut butter to smooth. Maybe you have had consumers cut out photos from magazines to describe how your product makes them feel. If you are really on top of the latest research trend, you are increasingly going into consumers' homes and observing how they really use your product in their natural environments.

All of these kinds of research can help you improve your product and your marketing, but it is likely that the *questions* you are asking today will not arm you to create meaningful marketing. Sure, they all help you refine the packaging, price, and positioning of your product or service, but they do little to help you design marketing programs with your strategic objective in mind.

Instead of asking questions that reveal the consumer's "scent preference" and "intent to purchase," we must uncover what type of marketing is likely to break through the clutter and be regarded as genuinely valuable by the people we are hoping to win over. We have found that there are two broad questions that can help us get to where we need to be: "What do you want in life?" and "How do you respond to marketing?"

What Does She Want in Life? (or: "True Love, Thin Thighs, and World Peace")

If we want to connect meaningfully with people, we must get back to the very basics of human nature. We must understand what makes people tick and how our marketing (that's right, not just our products and services, but our marketing) can improve their lives. This means using our training to uncover unmet needs in product categories, then taking the results to a higher level to understand what unmet needs these people have in their overall lives.

Many brands offer products that can move up the ladder to provide a higher-level benefit. A good online banking service can make people feel more confident about their financial choices. A reliable, comfortable diaper can help new mothers feel that they are doing the right thing for their newborns. Really good food and service at a fine restaurant can kindle romance (and maybe another newborn). These are the higher-level benefits that many of our brands aspire to reach, but we can hope to reach them only if we understand how our products and marketing fit into the overall experience of people's lives.

One of the best illustrations of this comes from the Fairy dish detergent brand in Israel. I know the dish detergent category probably doesn't seem like it would offer the richest source of new insights, but it is a great example of how, by starting from scratch and really

> If we want to connect meaningfully with people, we must . . . understand what makes [them] tick and how our marketing . . . can improve their lives.

getting inside our consumer's head (and life), we can uncover now-obvious insights that inspire a new, meaningful marketing approach.

The Fairy brand entered the Israel market only a few years ago in 2002, coming into a market dominated by Palmolive for 25 years. Although late to the game, Fairy expected to gain a following rapidly, thanks to its superior grease-cutting formula. While the brand gradually grew, traditional advertising and performance demos were far from enough to significantly cut into Palmolive's lead.

In early 2007, the Fairy team began three months of new research, focusing on the higher-level needs of dish detergent users, and the moments of truth where important times of their lives intersected with a sink full of dirty dishes. The brand specifically focused on the 20 percent of consumers who drive 80 percent of revenue: traditional mothers who do the cooking and cleaning for the family. These traditional mothers were skeptical of the claims of new brands like Fairy and tended to trust historic leaders like Palmolive.

In spending time with these women, the brand discovered that they are continually torn between their desire to keep a clean, tidy home—a way they show their love for their families—and actually spending quality time with their husbands and children. They feel guilty if either responsibility is neglected. And a moment of truth emerged around the traditional Friday night Sabbath, as the family all comes together and Mom shows her love with a large meal. It is the best time to be with the family, including children who return for the weekend from other cities and military bases. However a big meal and Mother's desire for a tidy house mean that she has to spend too much of her few quality family hours in the kitchen cleaning up.

This insight became a powerful way for the brand to present Fairy as a solution for traditional mothers. Because the product is a high-quality grease-cutting cleaner, it actually can help women complete their dishwashing faster and allow them to spend more time with the family at this special weekly event. Fairy and its agency, Mediacom, began work on a campaign that it dubbed "Come sit with us!"—itself an oft-repeated Hebrew expression—which launched in October 2007.

But instead of simply airing television commercials that claimed Fairy worked faster, the brand chose to bring this benefit to life through meaningful marketing related directly to this insight. The focus of the campaign was a unique sampling program that targeted college students and soldiers as they were returning home for the weekend. The brand team set up shop at train stations and handed full-bottle samples of Fairy to these young travelers as they walked by, each sample packed with a letter asking moms to spend more time with them while they're home. Thousands of children gave their mothers a valuable sample at a meaningful moment. Skeptical mothers had the opportunity to try the product without risk, experienced excellent results, and felt special about the Fairy brand liquid dish detergent.

As a result of this powerful, higher-level insight and meaningful marketing, the Fairy brand in Israel finally ended Palmolive's 25-year reign, becoming the market share leader within four months of the start of this campaign. Awareness, purchase intent, and "top of mind" scores achieved all-time highs. Months later, Fairy's lead in the market grew further, and it continues to lead the market through May 2009. And Fairy has become the *new* tradition in many Israeli homes.

Further Defining Your Target

It probably goes without saying that a primary role of a marketer is to define a target customer for your advertising efforts. But while you're in the process of shifting your efforts to a new model of marketing with meaning, it is probably a good time to reevaluate this part of the process as well.

The main error that most brands make at this stage is that they fail to tightly narrow down their definition of their target customer. Just as we love to put five objectives into a creative brief, we often cannot help but find some way to work as many people as possible into our core customer profile. We tend to think along the lines of the purchase funnel—the more people we can put in the top, the more will buy our products in the end. And we fear that if we narrow our pool too finely, we will have too small a base to achieve success.

It's psychographics—differences in things like habits, attitudes, personality, and values—that help us to develop the most meaningful marketing.

The second common error that brands make is to rely primarily on demographics to define their target, either because demographic information—like age, gender, income, and household size—is easy to define or because demographic groups are easy for media buyers to reach. But just because people are the same age or even live in the same neighborhood doesn't mean that they have much in common. It's psychographics—differences in things like habits, attitudes, personality, and values—that help us to develop the most meaningful marketing plans, providing real insights and meaningful connections to specific brands.

Microtrends, one of the most talked about business books in recent times, suggests that the world's consumers are rapidly segmenting themselves further and further into one or more small but significant-sized psychographic profiles, each with at least 1 percent of the U.S. population. Author Mark Penn, who coined the term "Soccer Moms," unveils new groups such as "Video Game Grown-Ups" and "Young Knitters." Such narrow but well-defined groupings offer clear opportunities for marketers (i.e., game makers and yarn suppliers).

There are two broad approaches that we have found that can help brands dive into a well-defined target market fairly quickly. First, you can focus on the 20 percent (or, as you know from Chapter 6, 2.5 percent) of customers who are driving 80 percent of your sales today. While tracking down this 2.5 percent for local focus-group recruiting may be difficult, quantitative research services such as the Kantar Group and Nielsen can help you pull together enough people to tease out their common psychographic traits. Or, you can simply invite the people in this 2.5 percent to interact directly with your brand by mining your e-mail database and inviting your existing customers to participate.

This approach can be adapted even for new product marketing. When we were launching Mr. Clean AutoDry Carwash, my team and I spent a great deal of time in driveways talking with men who loved the product. We asked them why they spent so much time washing their cars, and they often replied that they thought their cars actually "ran faster when they are clean." This unusual and repeated comment revealed that our product would appeal to people because it "brought out the best" in their cars, rather than just because it helped them finish a chore faster. This became a guiding principle of our launch marketing, and it was directly related to the product's success.

> Identify people who are at the market entry point for your product or service. Reaching consumers at the moment of entry is one of the oldest tricks in the marketing playbook.

Another great example is what the Dockers brand team did back in 1994 when it was launching a line of men's casual wear. Rick Miller, who then headed up the San Francisco office of public relations firm Burson-Marsteller, described how the concept of "business casual" dress was still new at the time. His team saw an opportunity to grow sales by communicating directly with human resources directors at large companies nationwide. They were struggling with defining appropriate work dress; so Rick's team shared guidelines and suggested that business casual dress was a great, no-cost benefit and productivity booster for employees at a time when a recession was winding down.

A second approach, which can be executed as a separate marketing effort entirely, is to identify people who are at the market entry point for your product or service. Reaching consumers at the moment of entry is one of the oldest tricks in the marketing playbook: the Welcome Wagon has brought samples and discounts to new homeowners since 1928; Gillette provides a free razor to young men after they register for the draft at age 18; Similac provides formula samples and a handy diaper bag for nearly every woman who delivers a baby in the United States. Tide, Downy, and Bounce samples accompany new washing machines, and new computers come with a free month of virus protection and Internet access.

Chances are there's one or more typical, very specific occasion(s) when people enter your product or service's category, and by identifying these situations and stepping into the shoes of the people who are going through these life changes, you will find a priceless opportunity to start adding value to their lives.

General Mills is a good example of a company that has put several of these lessons together and redefined the process of aligning on a target audience. Each of the dozens of brands at General Mills has created a target "brand champion," defined by Mark Addicks, CMO of General Mills, as "people who have found that the brand plays a meaningful role in their lives." General Mills isn't worried that its brand champions are too small a group to focus on. In fact, by marketing specifically to this core group, the firm has found others who identify with that group and end up coming along for the ride.

In the case of Lucky Charms, the brand identified its champions as kids who love to use their imagination. You probably remember the brand merely for the marshmallow shapes included in the cereal ("pink hearts, yellow moons, orange stars, and green clovers"). While this might have been compelling enough to our generation(s), basic shapes are not impressive to kids who learn to log on to computers at age five.

After 43 years of marketing this cereal straightforwardly, General Mills has taken its cue from its new brand champions, shifting its focus to "powering childhood imagination," and it now imbues each shape with special powers: hearts make things come alive, shooting stars facilitate flight, horseshoes speed things up, clovers bring luck, blue moons offer invisibility, rainbows allow instant travel from place to place, and balloons help make things float, not to mention the new hourglass shape, which has the power to control time!

Following the lead of its brand champions, Lucky Charms has also added more entertainment-oriented, immersive marketing experiences that power the imagination, including digital Webisodes of Lucky the Leprechaun's adventures and an online game called "Quest for the New Charm" that challenges kids to solve problems and riddles in order to win.[1]

How Does Your Target Consumer Respond to Marketing? (or: "Sorry, I Don't Watch Your Commercials")

This is the second question you need to ask in order to better understand what you can do differently to make your marketing more effective. Simply put, what you really need to know is: Does your target consumer watch ads? What is her response? What does she love, hate, and ignore? You won't be surprised to find that there's plenty of cynicism and negativity out there, and some of it will be justified; after all, the pent-up frustration caused by the antics of traditional marketing has to

> Consumers will usually tell you honestly that they do appreciate some forms of marketing. The key is to find out which ones.

come out sometime. But after the initial onslaught, consumers will usually tell you honestly that they do appreciate some forms of marketing. The key is to find out which ones.

Don't limit yourself to questions focusing on your own category: Instead, look across the entire spectrum of product and service marketing that your consumer is exposed to 3,000 times per day. Ask him what types of marketing he finds most and least effective. If you don't already, spend time reading case studies in *Advertising Age* and *Brandweek*. Think about how the lessons from other categories might be effective in your world. Remember, a lot of the best ideas are already out there—you just have to find them and make them relevant for your use.

These kinds of insights alone can often drive meaningful consumer marketing. Remember Dove? The brand's research unearthed the fact that most beauty advertising actually makes women feel inadequate and depressed about their bodies. Home Depot found that many consumers looked at the ads that featured smiling people building decks and finishing basements and said to themselves, "Yeah, right. Like I could do that on my own." Many brands have discovered that tourists visiting midtown Manhattan are willing to become immersed in a brand environment; hence, they set up branded destinations like M&M's World in Times Square and Abercrombie & Fitch on Fifth Avenue. These are the kinds of marketing insights that can fuel your team's imagination and your business results.

Blatantly asking consumers what they think of your marketing can be tough, as we marketers usually don't like to hear people tell us how ineffective they think the ad we spent six months perfecting is. By tackling this tough question, though, you can start to solve your business challenges and begin to see the power of marketing with meaning.

I had to learn this lesson the hard way. In 2000, while conducting research on Tide, I was surprised to find that in nearly every single consumer interview, women would look me right in the face and tell me that they never watched television commercials. At first, I just laughed along with them and moved on to my next question without fear. After all, I had beautiful color-coded bar charts showing that, in fact, 85 percent of my target audience had been exposed to my commercials more than three times per week for the last six months. My target consumers also said that they didn't believe it when brands like mine claimed that a formula was "New and Improved!" Again, I was confident this was simply a research recruiting issue, since I had *data* that showed a significant improvement in stain removal and purchase intent from my research team's in-home trials.

Boy, was I arrogant—and boy, was I wrong. A few months into just such a "New and Improved!" launch, I learned that maybe there was some truth to their words. Our most recent initiative was not doing well, and it was my job to fix it. My team and I went back to the drawing board and thought long and hard about the types of marketing tools and tactics that our target consumers actually said they liked and paid attention to, like free samples and coupons. It turned out that our target customers *were* always looking for better results and *did* like to try new products—but given all the empty claims of the past, they weren't about to take the financial risk of buying a whole new bottle, only to have to stash it at the back of the laundry room shelf.

For the second round of our product upgrade initiative, we chose to focus our spending on a device called Tide Kick, which people could fill with Tide liquid and use to pretreat stains before tossing clothes into the wash. This gave them something truly new and different that they could experiment with at home. We used an online request sampling program to provide a free Tide Kick and a $0.50 coupon to anyone who came to our Web site, along with lots of online and offline media to promote this offer. Through the online sampling registration, we were able to walk our visitors through product instructions and superiority data.

In six months, nearly 3 million people had requested and received a free Tide Kick, and more than 2 million of them had also signed up for our monthly newsletter. Further research showed that these people were seeing great results and buying more Tide than ever before. Loyalty and brand equity measures were also up, allowing us to achieve a record share of the liquid subcategory. By finally listening to how consumers really felt about our marketing, we were able to achieve a breakthrough.

> In terms of conducting research, the right question is: why should we conduct research at all?

There are many tools you can use to help bring this meaningful understanding to life. My agency and others often use a "persona design" process to capture the goals of a brand's target consumer, which reach far beyond product performance. As mentioned previously, some brand teams actually have cardboard cutouts of their target consumer that they bring to meetings. When they have to make a tough decision, they look over at the cutout and ask, "What would Susan want?" Yes, "Susan" is just a literal representation of the consumer, who should be top of mind anyhow, but the point is that you and your team must internalize the mentality of your consumer—not just in the laundry room, the bank teller line, or the grocery store, but in how she interacts with our marketing ecosystem and the world at large. Of course, it takes research to truly understand what "Susan" wants.

Conducting the Right Research

By now you know the importance of asking the right questions. In terms of conducting research, the right question is: why should we conduct research at all? It is heretical to suggest this, I know. For many of us, research is the default stage of any new marketing campaign. Unfortunately, though, we often perform research for the wrong reasons.

In my experience, research is too often a step we take to overcome our fears. We may know what the right decision is and conduct research in order to gather the proof to support it, but the fact is, all the precious resources (time and money) that you spend doing research won't change the fact that your consumers are actively tuning out your interruptive marketing.

The reality is that you may already have at least some, if not all, of the information you need. By the time you get to the research step in the process, you have probably spent months or years living and breathing your product, your category, and your customers. Jon Steel often asks his account planners to imagine that they must make a decision without conducting any research at all. Many of them discount the first answer that comes to mind because it seems too obvious, but it's often very close to the final mark. Steel goes further to say, "Almost all of the best advertising campaigns with which I have been associated are based on ideas so obvious that it's almost embarrassing to be paid for coming up with them."

If your gut isn't providing the solution immediately, don't pick up the phone and start scheduling a focus group yet. Instead, spend time digging into the masses of historical research that is probably sitting on your company's shelves and network drives. With some distance, a fresh perspective, and the new mission of creating marketing with meaning, these "old" data (which have already been paid for and nicely summarized) can lead you to the insights you are seeking with a fraction of the time and effort that would be required to begin anew. In the worst-case scenario, relying on your gut and reexamining old research will help prime your mind for the task at hand and help you uncover the unasked questions that you need to focus on going forward. And these two tasks can be accomplished in one week, if not in a handful of hours.

If you do choose to forge ahead with new research, the next question to ask is: why conduct the typical forms of research? Most traditional marketers are familiar with the classic pattern of consumer research. X number of people fitting the target consumer profile are recruited to engage in a research project. They are brought to a research office building or steered to an online survey with the promise of receiving some reward for their effort. Participants are asked a plethora of questions about life insurance or computers or pet food, collect their modest remuneration, and then go back to their homes and lives. While this process is straightforward and designed to glean the information that's needed, it also leaves a lot to be desired.

Most people don't know this about me, but I actually love to participate in research as a subject. Long ago, in my first year or so as a marketer, a mentor advised me to volunteer myself as a research subject in order to better conduct my own research on the other side of the mirror. His advice was to leave my marketing hat at the door and experience the process the way a consumer does.

So for years I have taken any opportunity I have had to assume that role. I jump at the chance to fill out surveys on Internet sites, or to join in-person focus groups for business publications. Unfortunately, I'm honest about my occupation as a marketer, so I get kicked off a lot of lists. But I have been the subject of more than enough research to have learned a thing or two. The biggest lesson? Traditional research is problematic. While we think that the typical process is the most efficient and effective way of prying out the answers we need from complete strangers, it's not. Here are a few of the things that your subjects are really thinking while your expensive research is under way:

- "I really don't care about this product that much."

- "I'm too embarrassed to talk about this in front of others."

- "I wonder what those people behind the glass are thinking right now."

- "Why won't the guy next to me shut up?"

- "This isn't worth the $50."

- "Let's answer quickly so that we can get out of here."

Sorry, folks, but this is the way people work—and you would feel and think the same things in their shoes. The reality is that real people in their real lives are complex, and forcing them into an oversimplified, artificial setting yields oversimplified, artificial results. In science, there's something called the Heisenberg uncertainty principle, which states that *the act of measuring something has an impact on what is being measured.* In science labs, for example, even the act of placing a thermometer into a liquid causes a minuscule amount of incremental heat—tiny as it may be, this heat raises the temperature of the liquid itself, thereby skewing the results. In conducting market research, we don't just discreetly dip the proverbial thermometer into the mix— we swirl it around, throw it in the air, stick our fingers in, and expose it to radiation, leaching whatever natural insights might have existed right out of the work.

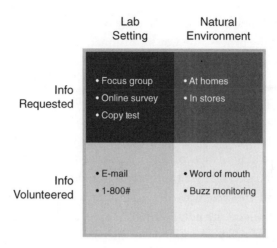

Figure 7.1 **Categorizing Research Alternatives**

If you find that you need to continue conducting research in your quest to make your marketing more meaningful, reevaluate its biases and prioritize those tools that provide the right insights. Therefore, I created a simple way of categorizing research alternatives to show the level of external bias on the results (see Figure 7.1).

Research can be broadly broken down across two variables. First, it can be handled in a research environment ("Lab Setting"), where activity is controlled and people understand that their actions are under the microscope, or it can happen in more of a "Natural Environment," where people have more control over the experience and are more comfortable in their surroundings. Second, most research can be divided along the variable of how the subjects provide information. It can be conducted with formal surveys and direct guidance by the researchers themselves ("Info Requested"), or it can be spontaneously provided at the initiative of the research subjects, who are allowed to do and say whatever they want ("Info Volunteered").

I have populated Figure 7.1 with several of the most common forms of research in the quadrants where they best fit. As you might expect, the forms that come with the least bias fall into the slot of Natural Environment + Info Volunteered. By monitoring word of mouth about their products and observing the lives of their customers without directly engaging them, marketers can gain truly valuable insights.

Word of mouth has existed since the birth of human communication, but traditionally, marketing insights from this source have been limited to whatever happens to come our way via our friends and family. Fortunately for us, digital communication has made private word-of-mouth conversations public; marketers who crave real, raw feedback can simply surf over to relevant message boards, examine product reviews and ratings on Amazon, search blogs on Google, and even set up alerts to see what Twitter users are telling one another about their brands. Best of all, this information can be delivered right to your inbox while you sleep.

And if there's just too much raw information coming your way, there is a group of companies that for a modest fee will monitor the buzz and help identify issues and opportunities. Nielsen BuzzMetrics, Cymfony, and MotiveQuest will report on your brand, your competitors, and any other relevant topics and issues that you wish to track. But while these companies offer many benefits, sometimes you need to get into the mix yourself in order to uncover the insights you require, bringing me to my second favorite source for insights, the category Natural Environment + Info Requested.

Sure, the act of asking questions brings risk into the equation, but by keeping your subjects in a natural setting—the homes they live in, the bars they drink in, or the cars they drive—you have a greater chance of keeping things real. Jon Steel believes in keeping research subjects in their natural habitat—to create "an environment for respondents that replicates as closely as possible the place and mood that they will be in when they have contact with a brand or a piece of advertising, so that the amount of post-rationalizing they are tempted to do about their opinions and preferences is kept to a minimum."

Steel's planners have eaten pizza with consumers for Pizza Hut research, held a dinner party at a martini bar for a gin brand, and brought prospective vacationers onto a ship for Norwegian Cruise Line. Aside from being a heck of a lot more fun than staring at stiff subjects through a two-way mirror, these experiences also helped his team gain "a broader perspective to understand where a product or category fits in the context of people's lives, and the other way around."

Jim Stengel, former global marketing officer of P&G, says that most of the company's research has moved from focus groups into

> **Spend quality time with consumers, not just asking how they use your products, but how they live their lives.**
>
> **—JIM STENGEL**

consumers' homes, primarily to let marketers observe when, where, and how people really use their products. That's why the company has even gone to the trouble and expense of building a full-scale grocery store for research purposes, and has installed cameras in consumers' showers (with their knowledge, of course). Many of the same research companies that arrange focus groups are happy to arrange this kind of "more natural" study instead. This up-close research also offers deeper insight into people's broader lives. You don't just get to observe how a mom pretreats stains before putting her kids' laundry into the machine, you also get the chance to see her list of chores, what Web sites she is surfing, and what time her kids get home from school—all of which are relevant to developing a more complete understanding of what her higher-level needs might be. Stengel directed his organization to "spend quality time with consumers, not just asking how they use your products, but how they live their lives, and figure out how you can positively impact [them]."

Further insight can be gained from the category Lab Setting + Info Volunteered. Here, obviously, lies information like the e-mail and customer service phone calls that brands receive on a daily basis. Earlier I quoted Pete Blackshaw as saying, "Customer service is the new marketing department," but I would add that customer service should also serve as the new research department. The people who reach out to your company by phone, e-mail, instant message, and even the plain old letter provide a free, immediate source of information. And while the messages you receive tend to be polarizing (typically, only the angriest or happiest people take the time to reach out), this is still a good place to start, and it's a reliable way to monitor responsiveness to your brand over time.

A trend that is taking hold in this category of research is the use of company-managed communities. Unlike broad, open communities like the TiVo forum mentioned in Chapter 4, these communities are inhabited by anywhere from a few dozen to a few thousand members; the topics are free-flowing and the discussions self-generated, allowing members to feel as if they own and run the community. Again, we have digital technology to thank for making it easy and cheap to set up a private research community. In their social media marketing manifesto *Groundswell*, authors Charlene Li and Josh Bernoff call private communities "a continuously running, huge, engaged focus-group—a natural interaction in a setting where you can listen in." In basic terms, these are online discussion groups hosted by companies that are password-protected and limited in membership. Li and Bernoff describe how the Axe brand set up a private community where guys uploaded photos of their rooms and talked with one another about everything from music to girls. Charles Schwab also set up a private community to learn about Gen X investors—influencing its growth in this segment by 32 percent.

Throughout the 1990s, long before the advent of Facebook and Second Life, General Motors invited a small group of owners into its Saturn Brand Character Studio to test new product and advertising ideas on them. Its design and marketing team took panel members to the Detroit auto show and asked them which cars they liked and why. As one Saturn manager said, "It's easy to forget or ignore a meeting. . . . But you can't ignore dozens of emotionally saturated episodes with real people—people you know personally and can easily picture in your mind's eye and hear in your mind's ear."[2]

At the end of the day, there will be times when you will need to tap into the Lab Setting + Info Volunteered section of research. When it's done well, this, too, can reveal valuable insights. But here, again, it's important to ask, "Why?"

Aside from inertia, the main reason that focus groups remain a default research format is that they are easy to execute. We hire a moderator and sit behind the glass watching several people chat while we take a few notes and check our e-mail. But for the focus group to be meaningful, it's got to be rethought—we've got to roll up our sleeves and spend real quality time with our consumers.

In my experience, the best way to perform this kind of research is through personal, one-on-one interviews, a model perhaps best described by Harvard's Gerald Zaltman in his must-read book *How Customers Think: Essential Insights into the Mind of the Market*. Zaltman has found that as much as 95 percent of consumer thought

> I have always felt that there's an inverse relationship between the degree of order and control that one might have over any research project and the quality of the information it yields.
> —JON STEEL

is unconscious, and that emotions are closely interwoven with the reasoning process. As a result, he favors one-on-one discussions—as much as three hours per person. This quality time allows researchers to build trust with their subjects and dig deeper into the unconscious. Similarly, research by Abbie Griffin and John R. Hauser shows that eight one-on-one interviews are as effective as eight focus groups (which could comprise as many as 60 to 80 people),[3] proving that one-on-ones provide a significant time and cost savings, too.

Instead of sitting behind the glass, every member of your team should be interviewing a consumer. Start by asking broad questions and talking about your subject's life, only gradually narrowing your focus to the category and product that you represent. Make frequent use of open-ended "why?" questions rather than closed-ended "yes or no" questions; these questions force people to rethink their assumptions and tap into that 95 percent of their decision-making process that is unconscious. And don't be afraid of long (even uncomfortable) silences, as that's usually a (good) sign that people are processing deeply.

Also, don't feel compelled to stick to the script that you and your team agreed on in advance. Once you're in a conversation with someone, allow the conversation to take its own unique direction. Jon Steel remarks, "I have always felt that there's an inverse relationship between the degree of order and control that one might have over any research project and the quality of the information it yields."

After the session is over, gather your team members together and share the real insights that you uncovered, preferably off-site, over dinner and drinks, where you're more apt to share spontaneous recollections. Rather than recounting the same one-dimensional experience that you would all have had if you were behind the focus-group glass, each person on your team will have his or her own unique research recollections to relate. And while your discussions will be diverse, chances are that you will uncover common insights that will infuse your approach to marketing with deeper meaning.

To this day, I remember a conversation I had with a woman nearly a decade ago about her experience with Tide. After an hour of discussion, she revealed that Tide was important to her because it had removed a stain from her daughter's first communion dress—a dress she had hoped to save for her daughter's daughter to wear one day. By saving the dress, Tide had earned a special place in this consumer's heart.

This is just one story from one person, but it got me thinking about other ways in which Tide could connect personally with others. Just as mothers pass meaningful garments and other heirlooms down to their children, they also pass down lessons on how they do laundry and the products they favor.

There's little doubt: consumer insights can indeed lead directly to powerful, meaningful marketing strategies. You just need to know the best ways to find them.

Nailing the Insight for Meaningful Marketing

Throughout our work at Bridge Worldwide, we have found that uncovering relevant insights is the number one driver for creating meaningful consumer marketing. Unfortunately, nailing just what an insight is isn't easy, although *Encyclopedia Britannica* offers up a simple, succinct definition: "Insight occurs when people recognize relationships or make associations between objects and actions that can help them solve new problems." It's important to note that this definition hits on the fact that an insight is goal-oriented, and that it occurs when there is a discovery of a previously unnoticed but existing relationship.

Great insights are not necessarily obvious, but when they are shared, they make perfect sense, connecting us to one another and to our universal experiences and values. Counterintuitively, great insights often invoke the paradoxes that populate our lives—for example, we *say* that we want a safe, reliable car, but our pulses pound when we hear a Porsche drive by; we *think* that anything healthy can't taste very good; and we are *convinced* that an environmentally friendly cleanser can't do the job on tough grime. But the most important

> Great insights are not necessarily obvious, but when they are shared, they make perfect sense, connecting us to one another and to our universal experiences and values.

ingredient of any insight is that it can trigger action in the form of marketing with meaning.

Judging an insight to be worthy is something that tends to happen deep down in your gut; it takes exposure to many insights—and to the resulting marketing strategies—to develop this instinct. In the cases that follow, take a look at how meaningful marketing flowed instinctively from a variety of brands' relevant insights, and where you might find inspiration for your own.

Palomino is a "drop-in downtown restaurant" chain with about 10 locations nationwide. At the end of each meal, the server provides a feedback card with an offer to join an e-mail list for special events and promotions. That's not unusual. What *is* special is that Palomino asks a single question on the registration form: "When's your birthday?"

Palomino wants to be top of mind for this kind of occasion. Knowing that people often go out for dinner on their birthdays, and that they're inclined to spend a little more, and maybe even dine with friends, on this special night, Palomino sends an e-mail to its customers about two weeks before the big day (when people start to make plans, line up a babysitter, and so on), wishing them a happy birthday and attaching a $20 discount voucher.

Palomino knows that people value the fact that someone—a restaurant, even!—has remembered their birthday, not to mention the generous gift (the cost of which is negligible for Palomino, and the results of which can be tracked through e-mail clicks and voucher redemptions). It also knows that people feel more inclined to repay the gesture by choosing Palomino for their birthday celebration. This simple insight concerning birthday dining powers a unique and effective marketing strategy for this restaurant chain.

If the folks at Avis Rent-A-Car lived in a city with a Palomino restaurant, they might have learned the lesson about gathering meaningful insights even earlier. In Avis's case, the company sought to understand how it could improve its customer experience overall, as well as how it could better connect emotionally with its customers.

Using Newark (New Jersey) Airport, one of the company's largest locations and a major travel hub, Avis decided to conduct deep research with its target travelers, and it asked more granular questions about their overall experiences and needs. Avis was surprised to discover that its customers' main emotional need was to reduce the stress associated with traveling, and that they cared more about that than about other features—like speed of service, cleanliness of cars, and location.

So Avis began to focus on what it could do to lessen the anxiety that surrounds travel. It installed video monitors of flight departure times and gate numbers in its storefront areas, created business centers that customers could use to make calls and recharge their laptops, and provided better training for its customer service representatives— including how to give better directions. The results were astonishing: Avis's Newark location moved from last place to first in customer satisfaction (among 60 offices).

The "Newark model" was rolled out across the company, leading Avis to claim first place in the industry in customer satisfaction and loyalty.[4]

Even Sears, which you'd be hard pressed to think of as a leader in technology, developed a strategic use for the social network Facebook, based on consumer insights. After realizing that high school girls often seek approval from their friends before choosing their prom gowns, Sears created a Facebook app that lets girls share photos of prom dresses worn by models, accompanied by a description, in order to gather opinions from their circle of friends.[5] By using the insight into how teen girls shop, Sears was able to create a service that helped it meaningfully reach out to the 2.4 million 15- to 17-year-old Millennials using Facebook, driving both immediate sales and word of mouth.

Speaking of connecting with Millennials in new ways, the Doritos brand at Frito-Lay presents a compelling case for how an entire marketing strategy can shift as a result of uncovering specific insights about this group. As is typical in business, the first sign of change was a decline in key indicators for the brand. In late 2005, Doritos began to see its household penetration declining from 50 percent to 48 percent, a clear sign that the brand was losing relevance among its buyers. Doritos already knew that its audience, which it dubs "Hyper-Lifers" (the Millennial generation of young people between the ages of 16 and 24), drove the majority of its sales; what it found, when it asked the right questions, was that the members of this group not only were exceptionally comfortable with digital technology, but liked to use it to create their own entertainment—including cocreating the brands that they buy into. They are creators, not consumers. Doritos seized upon their willingness and skill—a unique psychographic attribute—as a means of cementing the brand bond with consumers, creating more meaningful marketing, and increasing its market share.[6]

In the campaign's first year, Doritos began to populate its brand team with independent marketing managers who mirrored the target audience more closely, and gave them the freedom to make their own calls. They launched the "Crash the Super Bowl" ad contest, a four-month-long promotion that invited consumers to create Doritos' Super Bowl ad for the chance to achieve world fame and win $10,000 during the January 2007 event. Given the cost of a Super Bowl media buy—$2.6 million at the time—Doritos was taking a huge risk in handing the creative reins over to its 16- to 24-year-old target consumers, yet the leap clearly paid off. More than 1,000 commercials were submitted, and 1 million visitors each spent an average of five minutes on the brand's Web site. Not only did the winning ad earn the fourth-most-liked spot in the USA Today Ad Meter and generate $30 million in PR value, but Doritos' volume was up 12 percent over the previous year.[7]

Given its success, Doritos followed up this contest with another customer-driven challenge. For its "Crash the Super Bowl Song Contest," the brand asked aspiring musical acts to submit MP3s of original songs (not necessarily Doritos-related). Visitors to the Doritos Web site cast their votes and chose Kina Grannis's "Message from Your Heart" as the winner. A snippet was aired as part of the brand's Super Bowl commercial, and Grannis received a recording contract as her prize, facilitated by Frito-Lay. Now in its third year, the company has revived the ad-creation contest and has received bigger, better-quality ad submissions, as people see it as a viable platform for launching their film careers. It has also added a $1 million "bonus" prize if the selected ad goes on to become number one on the USA Today annual Ad Meter survey, which it did: Dave and Joe Herbert, two brothers in their early thirties, beat Madison Avenue at its own game, winning the *USA Today* ad competition with their amateur (but clearly effective) work.

> Because of the success of consumer involvement in marketing efforts, [some brands will go] so far as to tap consumer participation for . . . product development.

Perhaps in part because of the success of consumer involvement in its marketing efforts, Doritos has even gone so far as to tap consumer participation for its product development. It launched its newest flavor in plain black-and-white packaging under the code name X-13D. Buyers were invited to describe the taste and suggest a flavor name; 100 of the people who submitted the more than 100,000 flavor names were selected to become Doritos "Flavor Masters," receiving a year's supply of chips and membership in a tasting panel for new flavors. But the real payoff for Doritos came first from the buzz surrounding what would otherwise have been a run-of-the-mill product launch *and* then from the buzz surrounding the selection of the winning name, to the tune of a combined 20,000 Google links.

Thanks to savvy consumer participation and all-around smart marketing on Doritos' part, X-13D became the most successful flavor launch of 2008 (it was later revealed to be "cheeseburger" flavor), outselling every other in-and-out flavor in Doritos sales history, with more than 7 million bags sold.

By building on the insight that its target audience loves to create its own experience with the brand, Doritos has been able to get its marketing back on track. Most notable, Doritos' household penetration increased to 49 percent in 2007 and was back above 50 percent in 2008.

It would probably be a stretch to find a traditional marketing tactic that would work as well for selling airline seats as for selling snack chips—but that's not true of marketing with meaning. When thinking about Southwest Airlines, nearly everyone thinks of its low fares and exceptional customer service; as you probably know, it grew as a company and continues to succeed as the low-cost leader primarily in short-haul, point-to-point routes between medium- and small-sized cities.

As we saw in the case of Alaska Airlines in Chapter 3, a significant key to success in the airline business is to vary pricing continually according to supply and demand, the goal being to fill every seat on every flight. For Southwest, its real competition often isn't other airlines, but car travel—having the option to drive a few hundred miles—or not traveling at all.

To counter this, Southwest got to know its target customer a little better and found a sizable group of younger people in each Southwest-served market who were willing to travel more often to visit one or more friends or family members, but who didn't have lots of disposable income. For example, a woman in Denver has parents in Albuquerque; while this is too long a drive for a long weekend, since this woman has few outside responsibilities, she can make last-minute travel plans. Southwest saw this insight as a significant market opportunity.

In February 2005, Southwest launched a downloadable tool or "desktop widget" that people could program to alert them when flights to certain cities went on sale.

The tool sits quietly in the lower right-hand corner on the system tray of a desktop until selected flights go on sale. Customers then hear the brand's signature "ding!" and the details of the sale appear on the screen. Usually customers have 6 to 12 hours to book a flight.

People appreciate being alerted when these fare specials become available; Southwest benefits not only by filling its seats, but also by being able to build more specific personal profiles of each of these customers. The company can then use customers' purchase histories to tailor future offers or announce new routes.

A whopping 2 million people downloaded the tool in the first year, generating $150 million in sales by the end of year two. Use of the tool is continuing to grow over time; in the third quarter of 2008, the tool drove *10 million visits* to Southwest's site.

It's always interesting to see how marketing tools "travel," and in the case of insights, Germany's Bruno Banani fragrance showcases how the Germans are applying what others have done to revolutionize snack chips and air travel to the art of seduction.

One of the key occasions on which men use cologne is for a night on the town. Since there are hundreds of fragrances on the market and many new product launches and ad campaigns each year, it was important to Bruno Banani to drive its brand awareness by standing out in a crowded, noisy marketplace. Rather than take a traditional generic approach to getting the word out, the brand cleverly chose Carnival, the flirtiest season of the year, to reach out to its target audience—specifically homing in on the men's room, where guys periodically retreat not just to relieve themselves, but also to take a time-out from the pressure of wooing women.

Banani utilized posters, mirror stickers, and floor ads in restrooms at popular bars and clubs—all of which pointed to a telephone hotline that guys could call to hear suggested pick-up lines and other manly advice. This incredibly effective campaign helped Bruno Banani boost the brand's "sex appeal" equity and capture the number one share of the German market, ahead of better-known global brands like Armani and BOSS.

Each of these examples shows how strong consumer insights can help your brand create marketing that adds value to people's lives, and thereby drives real sales results. Whether you need to turn around an entire brand franchise or come up with a low-cost promotion, a deep understanding of who your target audience is will help your business discover a meaningful path into its members' lives.

8

IDEATE, RANK, LIFTOFF

With management support and insights in hand, you are now prepared to approach the meaningful marketing development process. This is likely to be both an exciting and a frightening time for you and your team. The closest experience I can compare it to is first learning to drive a car—you're eager to take the leap and experience something new, but mastering this new skill set is much harder than it looks, and it involves a lot of mistakes and frustrations before you get it right. (At least this time your dad won't yell at you for hitting the neighbors' trash can.)

Much as when you try to teach someone to drive, it's impossible to simply recount the mechanics of developing and launching such a program in any meaningful way. It takes practice and experience to develop a tailored approach to executing something that's ultimately more of an art than a science. But this chapter will provide concrete guidance on the common pitfalls to avoid and potential pathways to success.

Just as you eventually got the knack of driving and passed your driver's license exam, any eager, committed student can develop the skills and processes needed to succeed in this new form of marketing. And like driving is for you today, over time, creating marketing with meaning will become second nature for you and your organization.

> It takes practice and experience to develop a tailored approach to executing something that's ultimately more of an art than a science.

Generating Meaningful Ideas

To marketers, the idea of "creative development" often has an air of mystery and intrigue about it. I remember my first interaction with the creative team of our advertising agency during my early days in brand management. We had to fly to New York City to meet "the creatives," and halfway through our scheduled visit, they made their entrance, wearing identical black T-shirts and fancy eyeglasses.

The purpose of the meeting was to brief the creative team on a new project. First, the people at the agency who were handling the account carefully walked the creatives through each line of the creative brief—a document that we had collectively argued over for weeks. The creatives asked a few benign questions (which mainly seemed positioned to show us that they were listening), then walked out of the room, apparently to begin the mystical creative process. Three or four weeks later, they delivered their television commercial ideas.

A lot of things have changed in the creative-development process since those days. Now, clients typically get to spend more time with their creative teams, and some are even invited into a brainstorming session or two. But to maximize its effectiveness, the shift to marketing with meaning can and should be an even more open and collaborative process that breaks apart the old-school rules of brand and agency exchange.

Why? Well, in a way, it could be argued that the process of developing meaningful marketing ideas is closer to product development than to the production of traditional advertising. After all, marketing with meaning is often about turning the marketing itself into a product or service, guided by clear business objectives and deep consumer insights. This process taps the same skills that marketers use to create, say, a product line extension or a new financial services offering, which should be some comfort to you as you strike out in this new direction. As a result, at the start of the creative-development process, my strong recommendation is that you use a model similar to the one you and your organization currently employ to develop new products or services. By narrowing down the directions in which your meaningful marketing can go, you will be in a better position to brief your advertising agency and give it a more focused box to think outside of.

As with traditional product development, it often makes sense to create a specific team for this stage of the development process. And yet, while this may make sense, and while it is arguably one of the most important steps in the process, it is also one of the trickiest to execute. You will have to manage the egos of those who are *not* part of the team and recruit the best people for the job—people who will have many other justifiable pulls and priorities.

The best teams for this type of work comprise a handful of people (usually five or six) who bring diverse perspectives to the table. Look for people who come from a wide range of backgrounds and are comfortable with playing multiple roles and working in specialty fields. Avoid bringing in people who report to one another or who put up walls rather than uncover solutions. A single leader should be assigned, but the group members should be treated as equals. It is important to select people who, in addition to their individual strengths, are intellectually curious, are willing to take risks, and have strong relationships throughout your organization. They should be comfortable working closely together, and they should be able to dedicate themselves to the process as close as possible to 100 percent over a concentrated period of time.

For initiatives that cut across a large corporation or many brands (like ConAgra's Start Making Choices program, described in Chapter 5), it is often most effective to create an entirely new, dedicated "brand team." And this is a great time to bring one or two key advertising agency players into the process—preferably a strong account planner or strategist who can balance what the business needs with what the project needs, so that the creatives can add the most value later.

Once your team has been organized and briefed on the business objective and the insight work that you have done to date, it is time to start bleeding ink onto your whiteboards, in the hope of developing meaningful marketing ideas. At this point, you and your team members

> The best new products and marketing programs do not necessarily come from eureka moments. Instead, they are the logical conclusions of deep research and lots of thinking.

should have some ideas stemming from the extensive amount of time you've spent getting to know the people who buy your products and services—and what is important in their lives. That's good, because the best new products and marketing programs do not necessarily come from eureka moments. Instead, they are the logical conclusions of deep research and lots of thinking.

Once again I feel compelled to channel master planner Jon Steel, who provides excellent guidance for the strategy and idea development process. In *The Perfect Pitch*, Steel shares an approach that has helped him and his teams develop killer ideas for brands like Nintendo, Porsche, and the NBA under the gun of the new business pitching process. If he can nail big ideas in the two-week pitch time frame with little or no available research, surely your team can do the same with years of inside knowledge.

Steel's core belief is that creative ideas come from connecting the dots among and between the business, the brand, and consumer insights, and he shares excellent guidance from another master, Kenichi Ohmae, who writes in *The Mind of the Strategist*:

> The best possible solutions come only from a combination of rational analysis based on the nature of things, and imaginative reintegration of all the different items into a new pattern, using non-linear brain power.

Both Steel and Ohmae recommend building in time for daydreaming and distractions, which I have found to be useful as well.

Here is our four-step process for meaningful idea generation, which should get you and your team thinking in the right direction:

1. *Graze.* This first step involves the purposeful dumping of data on the heads of your team members. Instead of jumping straight into generating ideas, take a step back and mentally bathe in every piece of information you have so far that has gotten you to this point. This is a good step for making sure that every player on the team—some of whom will be new to the group—is equally knowledgeable by the time ideation begins. Steel recommends that team members write key questions, observations, and early ideas on Post-it notes and stick them in a prominent team space for pondering.

2. *Search for Meaning.* Next, you should start looking for connections within your research, questions, and observations. The Post-its begin to take on a life of their own, morphing into ideas and insights that can be organized into commonalities. There is still no need to rush to an idea here, so be patient, and simply let the disparate pieces of information you have in front of you marinate.

   You may choose to conduct a team brainstorming session at this stage. I advocate "Full-Contact Brainstorming," a method created by Todd Copilevitz, director of digital strategy at JWT/RMG Connect.[1] Team members should be given the homework assignment of bringing ideas to the table and should be prepared to defend them. The team leader should be positioned at the board, directing the discussion and recording the best thoughts as they bubble up. Bad ideas do not earn a place on the whiteboard, and the best few should be further blown out as a group. Be prepared: it may take more than a one-hour meeting over pizza to get you where you need to go.

3. *Drop It.* That's right—leave your Post-its on the board, get out of the office, and do something completely

different. Go to a movie. Walk the mall. Believe it or not, when your conscious mind is distracted, 95 percent of your unconscious is still at work trying to solve the problem. This is the same process that, seemingly out of the blue, allows you to remember a name you couldn't recall hours earlier. Steel recommends that the entire team get out of the office together, ensuring that everyone gets a mental break and providing a greater opportunity for team bonding.

4. *Adapt and Distill.* One or two people from the team start sorting through ideas, questions, and comments and begin to focus in on what seems to have the most potential for success. Steel recommends "editing mercilessly, throwing away the irrelevant, and crafting whatever you believe to be useful." Begin to write up your ideas in concept form, and share them with colleagues whose opinions you respect but who have some distance from the project. Whittle away at your list until you are convinced that you are ready for research.

In case you're stuck in the idea generation phase, simply go back to what you know best by finding ways to "activate" your current advertising campaign or product benefits in such a way that the marketing itself becomes of value to your target market. For example, for decades, De Beers has brought us television commercials and print ads that tell us, "A Diamond Is Forever." These ads are meant to trigger our emotions—to get us to think about our special someone and head to the jewelry store for that memorable gift, anticipating the magic moment that will follow. TV commercials re-create so-called memorable moments of someone proposing or giving a twenty-fifth-anniversary ring, but these false "moments" shown during the Sunday football game are no more personal, memorable, or meaningful than the fake photos that come in frames you buy at the store.

In December 2008, in a move toward meaning, De Beers did something more: it actually helped create these moments for real people. The company launched the "When Forever Began" campaign, in which it erected a giant wreath of mistletoe in New York City's Madison Square Park. A group of several cameras arranged around the stage created 360-degree photos of couples kissing, which were available online for downloading and sharing with family and friends. De Beers "activated" its tagline by creating a special moment that people will remember forever.

Another example comes from Westin hotels and resorts. For years, business travelers have enjoyed one particular aspect of Westin that differentiates it from the rest of the pack—you guessed it: the Heavenly Bed. For those who have not experienced its wonders, the Heavenly Bed, introduced in 1999, has a custom designed pillow-top mattress set, a down blanket, five plush pillows, and three 200-count sheets. It is a brilliant innovation that hits on one of the most important must-haves for business travelers. After a long day on the road, we just want to crash, and before a big meeting in the morning, every spare minute of shut-eye can help us be our best.

Up until 2007, Westin funded a major TV advertising campaign that presented the Heavenly Bed along with other nonmemorable copy lines about how great it is to stay at Westin hotels and resorts. But the results from this campaign were unspectacular, as it didn't connect with the hotel's target audience. So Westin shifted to what it now calls "ambient advertising," in which it brings a sample of what is best about Westin to higher-end business travelers when and where it can add the most value to their lives. One example is a partnership with United Airlines, in which Westin has placed its Heavenly blankets and pillows in business-class seats and in the airline's red carpet lounges. Sue Brush, senior vice president of marketing at Westin, loves this marketing because "it's high-impact and it's not really done that much in our industry." And her customers love the moment of extra comfort that Westin provides in an otherwise stressful travel process.[2]

Finally, some brands have succeeded in developing meaningful marketing programs by going "back to the future"—tapping their histories and blowing out what made them special and differentiated them from the competition in the first place. One excellent example is the Land Rover Experience driving schools, which teach people how to handle their sport utility vehicles in the challenging natural elements that they were designed for, while providing a powerful brand- and loyalty-building platform.

According to Bob Burns, the 3-D experience manager for the Land Rover Experience program, when the company's Range Rover brand was first introduced in the United States in 1987, the brand did not have a large launch marketing budget, yet it needed some way to introduce people to a new brand in the new luxury SUV market. So the company went back to its roots. The first Land Rovers were sold mainly as fleet vehicles for the British military; as part of its early sales strategy, the company conducted training classes for its military buyers. The soldiers learned how to drive the vehicles properly over challenging terrain around the world. This focus on training became part of the brand's DNA.

Fast-forward to 1987, when the company used a similar approach in selling the brand to high-income drivers in North America. Land Rover dealerships added small obstacle courses to their parking lots, and two-week adventure trips were organized for owners. These unique experiences that tested the limits of the vehicles helped the brand stand out in a competitive market and helped buyers get more out of their purchases. In turn, these very satisfied customers generated positive word of mouth and repeat sales.

In 1996, Land Rover opened its first stand-alone driving school for owners of any type of SUV. Participants pay anywhere from $225 for a one-hour introductory lesson to $850 for an advanced full-day experience. They learn how to navigate steep ascents, descents, side-tilts, creek crawls, and boulders. Driving school students come away with real skills, greater confidence, and life experiences that they will never forget.

For Land Rover, this represents a test drive that people actually pay for. Trainers focus on key skills that can be applied to any vehicle, but they also point out some of the unique features that Land Rovers possess; for example, unlike those of most SUVs, its front and rear differentials are offset from the center so that foot-high obstacles can pass straight under the vehicle.

Bob Burns says that the courses uniquely introduce prospective buyers to the brand in a meaningful way, while reaffirming buyers'

> A traditional product/service development process will result in a handful of written concepts: . . . simple, straightforward descriptions of the program you wish to create [that] communicate the end benefit.

choice of a Land Rover vehicle. According to Burns, "The better education we provide, the more people get out of our SUVs."

Like many examples in this book, the Land Rover Experience program has continued to adjust and expand over time, growing to 30 driving schools around the world. The Land Rover team now operates corporate team-building events and has started a series of vacation excursions in places like Moab, Utah, and Muscat, Oman. Roughly 5,000 people participate in the classes each year, and more than 100,000 people have experienced Land Rover in this unique way since the program's inception.

Other SUV brands, like Jeep and Hummer, have tried to follow Land Rover's lead, but none of them has approached its success. By sticking with its historical differentiation and success model, Land Rover has carved out a valuable niche with a fraction of the marketing spending of these other brands.

Developing Testable Concept Statements

If you choose to follow a traditional product/service development process for your meaningful marketing, the output of your ideation sessions will be a handful of written concepts that represent the program and its benefits to consumers. These provide a set of simple, straightforward descriptions of the program you wish to create; they communicate the end benefit of the marketing to consumers and the reasons to believe that this benefit will be delivered as promised.

To better illuminate this format for writing concepts, I will use a fictional example of a real company that could use a little meaningful marketing: Visa. I have no inside perspective on Visa, but I can surmise that a key business objective for the brand is to maximize its share of cardholder purchases. I can also guess that Visa has an insight that people will use their Visa cards more often if they see the card as a value-added part of the purchasing process. Furthermore, Visa's current advertising suggests that the brand wishes to connect with its cardholders on an emotional level by enabling life experiences; taglines on the Visa Web site, for example, include "Power to do the things you want," "Enjoy life's opportunities," and "Life Takes Visa." The Visa Signature rewards card targets higher-income individuals with an even more experience-focused marketing message and provides access to special events and a concierge service.

Visa has made some of the greatest television ads in history, but it is ripe for some added-value marketing services to help it to deliver on its promising taglines. Figure 8.1 shows two potential concepts I

Concept Title	"Travel Smart"	"The Hot List"
Benefit:	The new online Visa Travel Smart tool makes suggestions on the best places to get what you need when you are on the road.	Visa presents The Hot List—an iPhone application that shows you the most popular restaurants, clubs, and stores, so you can be where the action is at all times.
Reason to Believe:	That's because every time you use your Visa card, we compile a profile of your favorite places and activities and compare it to those of other members and what's available in the cities you visit.	Visa continually mines data from millions of transactions around the world every day, allowing us to see and even predict popularity patterns. We see where the action is before the speed of word of mouth.
	For example, if your Visa purchase history includes several sushi restaurants, when your flight lands, we will recommend a Japanese restaurant within walking distance of your hotel.	For example, if you are out on the town and looking for a cool club, pull up The Hot List application and it will show you the most popular places near your location, and the times that they are hottest.

Figure 8.1 **Two potential marketing with meaning concepts for Visa Signature to explore.**

created to show meaningful marketing concepts that the Visa Signature brand could explore further with research subjects.

These are just two of dozens of potential concepts for services that Visa Signature could provide. Note that these two concepts are testably different (meaning that they are unique and can be compared in preference questions), appeal to cardholders on a different basis, and provide just enough information to allow people to understand what the service offers. Like any good new product concept, they are short and simple; if you pack too many benefits and reasons to believe in a concept, it becomes difficult to execute the resulting bloated list of features convincingly.

To Research or Not to Research

A key next step is to get feedback from your target consumers to ensure that you are on the right track, prioritize the best idea, and uncover issues that need to be addressed in the final execution. I recommend qualitative research at first, through one-on-one interviews that provide useful feedback while avoiding the groupthink tendency of focus groups. Make refinements to your written concepts, and follow up the interviews with quantitative research to test for broad-based interest in the marketing and consumers' likelihood to choose to interact with it. Quantitative research can help you narrow your choices among multiple concepts and set expectations for market results. Just realize that you might have to start over, using your new research to help refine your thinking, before you eventually get to the right result.

At the end of the day, you are going to have to make a judgment and give the green light to one direction. The ultimate recommendation should be one that is in alignment with your team's collective judgment. Trust that the plethora of research that you've mined and the depths of understanding that you've plumbed are working overtime. That 95 percent of your unconscious is powering your decision making now, and it has proven to be a very reliable compass.

But I warn you that this can be tricky; as David Ogilvy said years ago, "I notice increasing reluctance on the part of marketing executives to use judgment; they are coming to rely too much on research, and they use it as a drunkard uses a lamp post for support, rather than for illumination." Here, again, management and others in your organization with special interests may defend the status quo and question your new approach; at times, these people may delay your work by asking for even more research and data. But with a good rationale and support along the way, you can break the bonds of inertia.

> I notice increasing reluctance on the part of marketing executives to use judgment; they are coming to rely too much on research, and they use it as a drunkard uses a lamp post for support, rather than for illumination.
> —DAVID OGILVY

Even if you follow this guidance, success is far from guaranteed. But then, no marketing model that we have followed up to this point in history has ever guaranteed success. My best advice is that you do *something* to move your brand in a meaningful direction, and watch what happens. Get into the market and start learning by doing. You will make mistakes the first time, and then you'll learn to avoid them. You will happen upon successes and come to understand how to recognize them and leverage them further in the years ahead. I cannot guarantee that you will reach the mountaintop of marketing fame and fortune overnight, but by committing to the first step and starting the journey, you will be much closer to it than those who are stuck in the valley of despair.

Execute with Excellence

There are an infinite number of concepts that you and your team could arrive at, and the farther down the road you go toward marketing in a way that is meaningful for your brand and your consumer, the less specific guidance you'll need, as you'll master what's meaningful for your particular brand, product or service, and audience. There are several specific considerations, suggestions, and things to watch out for, however, that will be useful for bringing your meaningful marketing program to life.

Arming Your Agencies for Success

Unfortunately, one of the major barriers to meaning can be an advertising agency that is still focused on perfecting the 30-second ad. Much as you may want to, you cannot just walk into your agency's office and say that you expect meaningful marketing from here on out. While I believe that any advertising agency *can* shift to this type of marketing model, it won't happen if the agency merely follows the creative process of the television or print ad.

However, this is not necessarily the time to start the competitive pitch process in search of a new agency partner. If your relationship with your agency is strong, the journey to marketing with meaning should be something that you commit to together—if for no other reason than that the agency has a great deal of knowledge about your business and your consumer (often more than the brand marketers on the team, who can change often). Work with your agency to create a new process that fits with the marketing with meaning model, providing clear direction and feedback along the way. A great strategic thinker from your agency should be included on the core team, and your agency's creative team should take over after the concept-testing stage to bring the ideas to life. If the agency fails to meet your needs right off the bat, give it a chance to learn and improve for the next round.

While your agency partners may need a little extra guidance, be wary of providing too much prescription during the creative phase. Clients can sometimes be too dictatorial about the direction of the work, with the result that they may miss out on more original and surprising programs. One of my favorite stories comes from Ryan Turner, social media lead at digital agency ZAAZ. A little over a year ago, his client Microsoft asked for his help in launching the Office 2008 software line for Macintosh computers. The firm came to ZAAZ specifically seeking a user-generated video campaign. While this might have been a success, Ryan's team asked for the chance to step back and think more about the strategy before jumping right into a specific execution.

Ryan and his team focused on the business objective of helping Mac users to see the value of Microsoft's Office productivity software;

they spent time narrowing down the insight (and challenge) that Mac users are creative and individualistic, and they don't think of Microsoft as a brand that stands for what they believe in. The ZAAZ creative team

> **Be wary of providing too much prescription during the creative phase.**

decided to do something that would confront these doubters head on and show hard-core Mac users that Microsoft Office *was* capable of something special. It created a marketing program called Art of Office, an online, open-source museum of sorts where creative people are invited to upload work that they have created using Office for Mac. The site was seeded with some commissioned work, but it has become self-sufficient, with people uploading new original artwork each day.

Thanks to the creative team at ZAAZ, and its client Microsoft's willingness to let the creative process flourish, the Art of Office campaign helped recast the brand in Mac users' minds and drove strong launch results for Office for Mac 2008.

Teaming Up for Mutual Meaning

As you have probably noticed, there are many examples in this book of two (or more) brands teaming up to create meaningful marketing for their shared customers. Partnerships can help brands penetrate a new market or make it easier to get into a new area of, say, technology development or service offerings—leading to a greater impact, less investment, and faster time to market.

One of the best illustrations of this is the partnership of the Apple iPod and Nike shoes to develop the Nike+ product described earlier. This is an obvious example of two brands, each with unique strengths, that add value to the customers of both—many of whom they hold in common.

In this case, each partner brought unique value to the relationship. Apple brought Nike the iPod software and hardware, an established base that is actively used by tens of millions of people every day; Nike brought Apple another product benefit for the iPod system, along with millions of dollars in marketing support. Both brands share a similar target consumer—active people with higher incomes—and both brands share some elements of their brand equities—they are leading, aspirational brands with a history of rebellion.

Another great example is one I came across while staying at my favorite W Hotel in New York City. In my room was a flyer offering a free ride in an Acura MDX:

> Who needs a ride? Get where you're going with Acura and W.
>
> Wherever you're off to, Acura and W have teamed up to deliver you to your destination in style with the complimentary Acura Experience, an exclusive Whatever/Whenever® service. Whether it's shopping on 5th Avenue, a ride down Rodeo Drive or a swift lift to Bourbon Street, get ready for the perfect ride in an Acura MDX. Just visit the Acura Experience Desk in the Living Room, reserve your complimentary ride with a personal driver and let Acura take you where you want to go.

This is a clear example of a win-win-win for all three parties: W Hotels offers yet another service under its umbrella brand of "Whatever/Whenever," a great way to differentiate its hotels from its countless competitors around the world at zero incremental cost. Acura gets a chance to connect with W Hotel customers, who are probably just the young, higher-income crowd that is in the sweet spot for its vehicles, and who can be difficult to reach with traditional interruptive ads. Finally there's the benefit to the customer. He gets a free ride in a cozy car with a considerate driver who knows his way around town. The customer also feels appreciated, and a little bit like a big shot or movie star. This is a meaningful experience for the customer, connecting him more closely to both the W Hotel and Acura brands.

There are other successful examples of diverse brands hooking up to build mutually valuable experiences: Honda and Mattel joined forces to create a special edition of Hot Wheels collectible cars, Fox and 7-Eleven partnered to create a dozen branded Kwik-E-Marts to support last year's *The Simpsons Movie*, and Victoria's Secret staged a fashion show in the aisle of Virgin Airways last year.

These experiential tie-ins seem to work best when the brands share both a common target customer and brand equity elements—*The Simpsons* and 7-Eleven both target 18- to 34-year-old men, for example. But they also require corporate organizations that are willing to give up some control

> **Think about other relevant brands in your customer's life and consider the synergies that a partnership might create.**

and ownership. Each of the partners has to bend the normal rules and live with mutual alignment rather than sole decision making.

This is a great exercise to conduct for your own brand: think about other relevant brands in your customer's life and consider the synergies that a partnership might create, then pick up your Black-Berry and reach out. Chances are there will be another marketer out there who is similarly looking for ideas for something new and meaningful.

Meaningful Content—To Create or License?

A great many of the examples shared thus far have been brands that developed original content of some kind, be it informative articles, interactive games, or pop-up retail experiences. One of the biggest questions that marketers who are looking to create meaning have is whether they should be in the content creation business—despite the fact that all marketing contains "content" in one form or another. The only difference is making it more about something that your customer actually wants to receive.

Marketers worry that their brands and the agencies they work with cannot create video that rivals what Hollywood producers plan out over lunch, nor are they confident that they can develop iPhone applications that can match what Google employees create in the 20 percent of their time dedicated to free thinking. While your fears may be real and well founded, the only way to get past them is to per-form cost-benefit analyses and make a reason-based decision as to whether to lease or buy your way into a meaningful marketing vehicle.

There are several arguments to support brand development of original, owned content. First, original content that your brand develops on its own can serve as a powerful asset that will continue to drive results for years. The effect of simply borrowing articles or videos from another brand or media firm is almost always temporary and can come at a price, which can then be bid up by your competitors. Special K's first efforts focused on weight loss were hosted almost entirely on Yahoo!'s platform, which tied the brand to an ongoing relationship with Yahoo!-developed content. YouTube drew brands in early with low-cost video hosting and branded home pages, but as this media channel has grown in popularity (and needs to show profits), it has raised its prices for this service into the hundreds of thousands of dollars. Brand-owned content also maximizes creative control and ensures that the brand itself (not YouTube or Yahoo!) gets all the credit in the consumer's mind.

One of the great success stories of brand-owned content is Baby Center.com. Following the dot-bomb meltdown in 2001, Johnson & Johnson purchased the three-year-old online media platform for $10 million—a number well south of what a single big brand spends on TV commercials for a quarter of the year. As Christian Koffmann, worldwide chairman of consumer and personal care, said at the time, "Johnson & Johnson was attracted to the superior content and personalized relationship that BabyCenter, as the leading online parenting brand, has created with millions of parents from conception through childhood."

Today, BabyCenter provides J&J with a free, proprietary relationship-marketing platform to support its brands, many of which were used to paying millions of dollars every year for the chance to connect with hard-to-reach new moms. It expanded from 11 to 18 countries in 2008, and it enjoys visits from more than 1 million visitors each day. The company is able to glean insights from members' activities that give it a distinct advantage in this extremely competitive market. And thanks to its 78 percent market share among parenting sites in the United States, BabyCenter even makes a bonus profit by selling advertising services to competitors and noncompetitors alike.[3]

Of course, there are corresponding benefits to licensing or borrowing content from external experts and copyright holders. For example, media companies from Cooking Light to ESPN can bring high-quality content, trusted name recognition, and access to their readers and viewers. For a price, they can go as far as building and hosting your Web site and can guarantee a certain amount of traffic to it.

> The brand itself must play some kind of lead role in the action if sales growth is to result.

For example, the blogger network Federated Media worked with its writers to help compile the JCPenney Fall Shopping Guide for the holiday season. Suggestions were posted by popular bloggers like dooce, The Mommy Blog, and Confessions of a Pioneer Woman. This helped JCPenney achieve strong search results in short order, with the site rising to number two on a Google search for "fall shopping guide" (among 4 million results).[4]

Some brands are getting the best of both worlds by finding and organizing content at no cost, and hosting it on their own footprint. Purina pet foods, for example, saw a growing, insatiable interest in cute photos of pets online. So it created Pet Charts, a site that compiles the "best of" cute dog and cat pictures found on the Internet. Purina claims that it takes a trained person only 30 minutes a day to find and update the site's content. In return for this modest investment, Purina is able to connect its brand with thousands of passionate pet owners each month.

Make Sure the Brand Is Part of the Entertainment

Whether they're creating new content or licensing it from others, many brands are tempted to head into the realm of entertainment for a dose of meaningful connections with their consumers. A big thing to watch out for here is that the brand itself must play some kind of lead role in the action if sales growth is to result.

Unfortunately, some content creators and new marketing gurus claim that it is nearly impossible for brands to be a part of the show. They claim that if brands' involvement in the action is too obvious, people will notice, be turned off by the marketing "agenda," and turn their attention away. But brands like BMW have proven the naysayers wrong, as seen in the viral campaign for the "launch" of BMW's 1-Series car in the United States. The centerpiece of the campaign is a mockumentary that the brand created about a fictional small town in Germany that built a massive ramp to catapult a car across the Atlantic and into America. The town created an event around the launch, called Rampenfest, in hopes of attracting tourists. Naturally it was released on YouTube and caused much debate about whether or not it was supported by BMW's marketing department.

Early on, the company refused to acknowledge its role in the work, which further built interest and speculation, but eventually BMW owned up to the campaign and was widely praised for creating an entertaining effort that put its brand at the center. According to Patrick McKenna, manager of marketing communications for BMW, the goal was to reach a slightly younger demographic with its new smaller-budget car. The entertaining campaign "cost a fraction of a typical 30-second spot," and McKenna figured that the "worst-case scenario is that few people might watch it and it might quietly disappear."[5] Instead, the campaign got wide media attention and thousands of views, and helped the 1-Series get off to a strong start.

Don't Settle for Short and Small

Marketing with meaning means that you have to do more than buy into a short-term effort that is aimed more at generating media attention than at truly touching a significant number of people's lives. Drew Neisser at Renegade names a couple of the worst offenders, one being the handful of "Warming Taxis" sponsored by Tylenol that offered free rides to Manhattanites during a single week in early November (when it's not even that cold). Another culprit is Kraft's Stove Top Stuffing brand, which installed only 10 heated bus shelters in Chicago, while the other 49 city bus shelters the brand advertised on left riders out in the cold. Neisser calls this a "thin commitment . . . an insincere stunt that Kraft hopes will inspire lots of PR."

Compare these stunts to Neisser's agency's ongoing program of branded cab rides by HSBC, which has been running for six years straight, or the CVS Samaritan Van, a service that provides roadside assistance in nine major metropolitan areas. The CVS program began in Rhode Island during the "Blizzard of '78" with one help van, and it is still going strong 30 years and a million assisted drivers later.

Another common mistake is to "launch and leave" your meaningful marketing program. Far too often, marketers move on to the next project the day after the current one goes live. The result is that the marketing program gets neglected at exactly the time when it may need the most attention. Piers Fawkes, a top digital marketing strategist, suggests that customers can actually sniff out a marketer's lack of commitment: "One of the problems . . . is that brands can see campaigns as a very short-term project. If you create something that you don't care about, consumers sense it."

Launch, Learn, and Adjust

When your program finally hits the market after months of hard work, take a few minutes to pop the champagne—then get right back to the hard work of making sure that the program performs to the best extent that it can. Instead of launching and leaving, smart marketers make the extra investment to launch, learn, and adjust.

Make sure you are following the results data, tweaking the program, and testing improvements. Build an extra month or two into your project timeline, and save some budget dollars for these changes. Despite all of the research and modeling effort before launch, you never know what will happen until actual consumers begin to interact with your campaign and make it their own.

In our Healthy Choice "Working Lunch" campaign, for example, we actually broke up the program into two "seasons," in November 2008 and January 2009. The main reason was that we knew that the holidays would mean low viewership for our program, since a lot of people take vacations during this time, but we used the December break to our advantage by looking at, learning from, and adapting everything, from our media buy to our final casting. Our second season in January experienced improved results because of our changes.

Although, in Chapter 6, I called the OfficeMax "Elf Yourself" program a campaign that needed a more direct link to sales, it does serve as a strong example of an alternative way to let the market decide which is the most buzz-worthy. Bob Thacker, OfficeMax senior vice president of marketing and advertising, originally commissioned 20 viral games at roughly $20,000 each for the 2006 holidays. Elf

> Make sure you are following the results data, tweaking the program, and testing improvements. Build an extra month or two into your project timeline, and save some budget dollars for these changes.

Yourself happened to be the one that took off and led to 250 million selves elfed after three years. This story suggests that the marketplace might be a better way to sort out the winners and losers than in a focus group session or corporate boardroom.

Steve Sullivan, senior vice president of communications for Liberty Mutual, tells a similarly interesting story. A relatively small player in the very competitive auto insurance market, Liberty Mutual was looking for a new way to grow sales. It lacked the huge marketing budgets of brands like GEICO and State Farm, so it sought a differentiated angle of approach.

The brand and its new agency, Hill Holliday, were smart enough to start the process by looking within. They harked back to the company's mission statement, which ended with the line "Helping people live safer, more secure lives." They then interviewed employees to understand what they felt was special about Liberty Mutual. This research led to a strong overall belief that "at the end of the day, we do the right thing."

Through this in-house research, Liberty Mutual arrived at a connection between its employees and the customers it most coveted: a shared belief in the importance of personal responsibility. Luckily, the team was smart enough to realize that another 30-second ad would not be enough. The challenging questions, according to Sullivan, were "How do you really make something like that tangible?" and "How do you connect with people in a way that's not just another claim from a big insurance company that people are going to disbelieve?"

The marketing team's solution was to use television and print ads to build awareness of the importance of personal responsibility, then drive them to engage and discuss the issues with others. The hub of this deeper engagement has been a Web site called the Responsibility Project that includes video stories of personal choices involving responsibility. And Liberty Mutual poses engaging debate questions on popular news sites—for example, asking if government should be responsible for regulating trans fats in restaurants.

New opportunities for adjustment came early on in this campaign—within months of launch, the company received more than 3,000 requests thanking it for promoting this message and asking for copies of the commercials that they could share in schools and churches. One man who didn't even own a car sent in a $20 donation to Liberty Mutual's "cause." Sullivan says people "started a dialogue that they obviously wanted to have. I say 'obviously' because they keep contacting us."

So Liberty Mutual started making its videos more widely available on its Web site and other locations. It provided other educational pieces that people could download from its site for free. And it partnered with NBC to develop two made-for-TV movies that promote the theme of personal responsibility.

And at the end of the day, this campaign seems to be a significant business builder. Liberty Mutual's premium revenue in auto insurance was up 17.4 percent, to $3.6 billion, in the six months after the campaign launch, in part because of "strong customer retention and new business growth." The added benefit is that by bonding with people who believe in personal responsibility, Liberty Mutual is keeping and attracting the most profitable customers—the ones who take personal responsibility for not getting into auto accidents in the first place! (Sure enough, the six-month numbers show that auto liability losses are down.)

There is a strong long-term benefit to be seen in marketing with meaning and in this specific example. While GEICO might be long remembered for its cute cavemen and dapper gecko, Liberty Mutual has a chance of becoming deeply linked in our minds as a company that stands for something that is uniquely important to our lives and to society overall.

Prepare for Dramatic Success

One of the greatest tragedies in developing meaningful marketing comes when companies fail to use scenario planning to anticipate tremendously positive results. Such situations can turn your wildest

> One of the greatest tragedies in developing meaningful marketing comes when companies fail to use scenario planning to anticipate tremendously positive results.

success into a sleepless nightmare. I have seen this most often around digitally focused programs that fail to anticipate a surge of traffic.

Suppose, for example, your online store goes down on the biggest shopping day of the year. In online retail, the first Monday after Thanksgiving is known as "Cyber Monday"—a day when people get back to the office after a few days off and take some free time to shop online. On this day in 2008, both the Old Navy and Gap sites were temporarily down for maintenance. Whether it was for a few minutes or for hours, this maintenance should have been planned earlier or conducted during the late night shift.

But the grand prize for missed opportunities should probably go to Dr Pepper. Back in March 2008, an individual on the Dr Pepper brand team released a blog that promised to give a free Dr Pepper to everyone in the country if the long-delayed new Guns N' Roses album, *Chinese Democracy*, was released before the end of the year. It did not seem to be an official Dr Pepper marketing effort, but the buzz built, and people started anticipating a big payout by the brand. Sure enough, in October, the band announced that the album would hit the stores in November, and the blogosphere wondered whether Dr Pepper would make good on its promise. Two weeks after the initial challenge announcement the brand had received 300 million PR impressions.[6]

Dr Pepper surely needed the buzz; the brand continues to fade from the soda scene, both because of the continued strength of the Pepsi and Coke franchises and because of the rise of new upstarts such as Red Bull and Monster. Dr Pepper is now using long-retired basketball legend Dr. J in its TV advertising, which isn't helping much, given that most of its target audience never saw him play. So in August 2008, when Guns N' Roses' lead singer, Axl Rose, officially announced that the album would drop in November, Dr Pepper scored more news and promised to uphold the deal. All it had to do was fulfill its promise and get free soda coupons into consumers' thankful hands.

But the brand completely mishandled the payoff. It announced with short notice that people would have to register for their free soda coupon within one 24-hour window. And, when people dutifully visited the brand's Web site, they found the server down continually. The brand responded weakly by extending the promotion into the next day for a few hours, but the server still failed often. Those who did manage to successfully register had to wait four to six weeks for the coupon to arrive.

So here, into the laps of the marketing team, dropped the culmination of a very successful, low-cost buzz campaign—a campaign that succeeded in attracting the young, connected generation that all soda brands covet. (There were more than 100,000 Google results for "Chinese democracy dr pepper," and 7 of the top 10 Google search trends were related to the supposed payoff.) The coupon sign-up process, if it had been conducted correctly, would have given Dr Pepper a great chance to harvest the e-mail addresses of new brand fans. The brand team should have been high-fiving, but instead, it seemed to be in hiding.

Naturally, the same blogosphere that promoted the brand began to damn it for its poor execution on its promise. As word-of-mouth agency leader Ted Wright said, "Nobody is really mad about an 89-cent [soda]. They just wanted to be part of the fun, and they took all the fun out of it." Even Axl Rose—who supported the free sample buzz—went on the offensive, demanding that Dr Pepper reopen the free offer and print a full-page apology in major newspapers. Alas, his demands went unheeded.

Institutionalize the Lessons

As your new meaningful marketing program is taking hold and (hopefully) proving successful in the marketplace, it is important that you step back and take stock of what you as an organization have accomplished. Going back to the lessons learned in Chapter 6, it is essential that you ensure that your changes are taking hold and that the broader team has institutionalized lessons large and small. This will keep your organization's eye on the process of change, and make it easier to take the same steps for the next program you launch.

One example of an organization that learned and broadly shared the internal lessons of its move into meaningful marketing is the Levi's brand. Speaking at the Forrester Marketing Forum in April 2008, Patrice Varni, vice president of Levi.com, shared her team's experience in launching a user-submitted blue jeans design contest as part of a tie-in to an episode of the hit show *Project Runway*.

Varni described how she inherited the project after it was already in the works. A different group at Levi's had negotiated the show placement, but had no other tie-in for the brand. Patrice and her digital agency, Razorfish, scrambled to build an added-value tie-in. They developed the contest idea, and they created a detailed map of all of the touchpoints of the program, making sure that each of them had something to do with selling the featured jeans.

As the promotion was launched, the Levi's team learned that the word of mouth from blogs and social networks was having more impact on driving awareness than the show itself, as 38 percent had become aware of the promotion through digital social media, while only 30 percent had become aware of it from the television program (which had a weekly viewing audience of 3 million). This revelation helped manage the brand's expectations for future work and put a clear priority on social media.

After the brand chose a winner, there were negative comments from the losers (and the fans of these losing designs) on the Levi's site, but Varni's team decided to let the conversation proceed untouched. Soon, other brand supporters in the community stepped in on behalf of Levi's and beat back the sour grapes.

During the five weeks of the promotion, Levi's saw its sales increase significantly and shift to a younger audience. However, while the campaign exceeded expectations, trends returned to normal after the promotion ended. Now the brand is trying to figure out how to keep the sales lift and youth shift after the original promotion period.

Varni said that the project was a turning point for the entire marketing organization. Now Levi's digital and traditional marketing teams work together, and they expect more meaningful marketing with even better results.[7]

This case study, among many others, shows a common element in meaningful marketing activities—they count on brand managers and agency partners to continually learn from and improve upon their efforts. Since this type of work is new for nearly everyone involved, you can expect to be in heavy learning mode at all times. But to best judge your success and learn from your mistakes, you must ensure that you are properly *measuring* your work across multiple variables.

9

MEASURE, ADJUST, AND KEEP GROWING

If this book has succeeded at anything by this point, it is, I hope, illustrating how many of the marketing processes and models that we have relied on for years have become (and are increasingly becoming) obsolete. Thus, as the process of creating and distributing traditional marketing becomes defunct, the methods we use to measure it are also desperately in need of an upgrade.

Peter Daboll, a marketing measurement veteran who spent much of his career at Information Resources, Inc., and is now CEO of Bunchball, a company that enables brands to measure and drive consumers' most valuable behaviors, perhaps sums it up best: "I have studied consumer behavior for 25 years. . . . One thing is undeniable: In almost any set of metrics or test results, the impact and influence of the current advertising approaches are diminishing." Clearly, a move to marketing with meaning demands a new set of metrics, to measure both the impact that this new approach is having on your business and the impact it's having on consumers' lives. Creating measurement plans for both of these objectives and turning your initial efforts into a long-term business-building asset are essential for achieving success.

> *If baseball were measured like advertising, you would only count the pitches.*
>
> —PETER DABOLL, A MARKETING MEASUREMENT VETERAN

Why bother to formulate measurement plans? They help your team prove, both to management and to the rest of your organization, that this approach has had positive results. Great results can help to convince the doubters and ensure that this new approach is more than just a one-time test. Measurement helps you learn specifically what went well, what did not go well, and why. As you begin a new journey of meaningful marketing, these early data are critical to helping your team understand how to connect higher-level equities to higher-level needs. And these early results become the base for comparison to future work.

Unfortunately, many marketers and their agencies fail to follow through with a robust measurement program. Sometimes it's not baked into the project costs up front, and asking for money after the launch takes guts of steel. Other times, the team simply cannot agree on an appropriate way to track and measure success, which is a great shame, but nonetheless a reality. Firm numbers such as GRPs and CPMs are difficult to replace with the number of site visits, YouTube views, and Facebook friends. However, despite the discomfort of mining new territory, the data are out there. In fact, it should come as no surprise to learn that marketing with meaning often generates more useful data than the traditionally culled numbers have historically provided.

There are three key areas by which to measure marketing with meaning, each of which provides evidence of whether or not you are achieving your objectives (see Figure 9.1). Engagement is the measure of consumer involvement with your marketing. This is the single measure that is most likely to replace reach, frequency, and

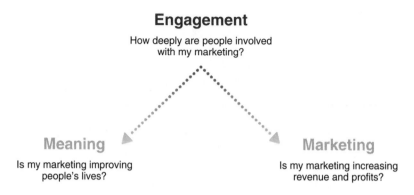

Figure 9.1 **Engagement is the measure of consumer involvement.**

impressions. It is also a measurement that you can use to compare all media equally.

Engagement is your foot in the door of the consumer's mind. Once you capture conscious, positive attention, *meaning* measurements are used to determine whether or not your new marketing is, in and of itself, improving people's lives and helping them achieve their higher goals. Finally, and most important, *marketing* measurements are used to ensure that this kinder and gentler new marketing model is actually driving hard-core business results.

Measuring Engagement

Engagement is the linchpin for defining successful meaningful marketing—and I am certainly not alone in thinking so. Over the past few years, a near consensus has formed around the importance of engagement, to the point that it is fast replacing traditional advertising measurements such as reach, frequency, and awareness—which are dull instruments that show only exposure to an advertisement, rather than a genuine willingness to connect on the consumer's part. The hypothesis that brands around the world are proving each day is that a consumer's conscious, positive experience with marketing is significantly more valuable than an unconscious, interruptive advertising impression.

While there is no consensus among new media gurus on the definition of "engagement," three sources (see Figure 9.2) point to a common theme.

Figure 9.2 **Definition of engagement.**

In a model in which we aim to add value through our marketing, we must first measure whether or not people find this marketing worthy of being allowed into their lives. When people are attracted to your brand messages and direct their attention specifically to them, you have achieved engagement. To make the matter a little more complicated, but intellectually rigorous, the *degree* of consumer engagement can be measured in different ways, depending on the type of marketing and the media through which it is presented, such as:

- Read text (consciously)

- Hear audio (consciously)

- Watch video/motion and sound (consciously)

- Play games

- Forward/share

- Vote

- Comment

- Create text/graphics/audio/video

- Participate in a community

Every item on this list requires the consumer to *choose* to pay attention to your marketing—some more than others. For example, writing a comment shows a deeper engagement than simply reading text. In our agency's meaningful marketing, we have found repeatedly that the more consumers personally engage, the more product they buy (and the greater the loyalty that forms). One of our sister agencies, ZAAZ, in Seattle, has created an Engagement Index that measures the correlation between the degree of engagement in an activity and the likelihood of purchase. For example, it can estimate the sales that result from a consumer who spends time reading an e-mail article, and compare that to time spent on another activity, say, watching an online video. These measurements can help provide an estimated return from creating these kinds of content and can help prioritize where the next dollar would best be spent or how traffic is directed.

While admittedly imperfect, engagement is the closest thing we have to the next holy grail of marketing measurement, and it lives up to the hype it has received. First, engagement fits with the common-sense approach that marketing with meaning is based on. It suggests that if people get more personally involved in your marketing, they are more likely to develop a favorable impression of your brand and learn something important about your product or service, which, in turn motivates them to buy from you.

Engagement also highlights the importance of consumer choice. Anyone can easily buy the right to spam consumers' eyeballs, but if consumers are not interested in what you're offering (or are too jaded to care), you really have no chance of influencing their behavior.

Second, engagement is extremely measurable. Nearly every digital device that is currently available allows for reporting on some type of engagement. Web sites track the number of visitors, the duration of the visit, and the number of pages visited. Rich media banner ads can now expand to allow consumers to watch a video, play a game, enter a contest, chat, or request a sample, all without leaving the site they are on—and all of this interaction is trackable.

A company called NuConomy offers a service that shows marketers a dashboard of engagement metrics, allowing brands to customize the weight of each measure. If, for example, you find that site visitors who leave a product rating are more engaged (and thus more valuable) than those who send to a friend, you can adjust the formula accordingly. The software can also calculate correlations between activities. For example, it may show that visitors who upload content are more likely to click on promotional messages or buy products, which can help you prioritize which features to create or highlight.

> Engagement is marketing's new key metric.
> —FORRESTER RESEARCH

Third, engagement is versatile enough to work across all forms of media. One of the barriers to advertising in new media has been the lack of good, comparable data. But with engagement, this barrier disappears. For example, banners and search ads can be placed on any type of Web site, mobile Web page, social networking site, or RSS reader—and all allow for comparable click tracking. Widgets and Facebook application developers can instantly read how many people are using their code and what the resulting consumer actions are. Apple can read iPod data to see which podcasts are most popular. Anyone can see exactly how many YouTube views your viral video has earned. TiVo and Nielsen are now even reporting which TV commercials are skipped most and least often, and which ones consumers actually choose to watch again. Net, even "old media" can be studied through the lens of engagement.

Finally, changes in consumer media habits suggest that engagement will become even more important going forward. We are spending more of our media time in "lean-forward" mode (i.e., online). According to a Forrester Research report that called engagement marketing's new key metric, "Passive consumption of media is waning. Individuals dismiss or ignore marketing messages in lieu of information available from an ever-increasing number of resources, such as product review sites, message boards, and online video."[1] And even the "lean-back" world of television is adding active participation through live voting via mobile phone and e-mail responses during talk shows.

The biggest downside to measuring engagement is that it requires thought and processing, rather than just counting eyeballs. Engagement is multidimensional, which can translate into different results for meaning and marketing measurements. You and your

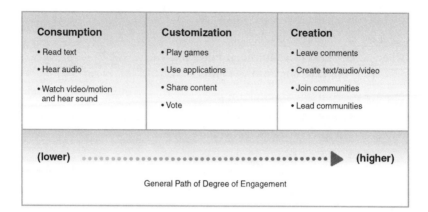

Figure 9.3 **The range of engagement.**

agency team must work to define the right engagement measures up front for the specific program you develop.

But there are simple places to start from, and common sense is often your best guide. Our company generally groups and measures engagement using three categories (see Figure 9.3), moving from lower to higher engagement (and usually lower to higher sales impact).

The range of engagement and measurement that can be derived from a single program can be seen in the example of a program our agency conducted for Folgers. Working within an integrated team of several agencies, we developed a campaign in support of Folgers Gourmet Selections, a new brand extension into higher-quality flavored coffee. Our key insight was that the target consumer for home-brewed gourmet coffee was someone who was willing to pay a little more to add a more enriching experience to her daily routine.

We jointly developed a campaign that highlighted the morning habits of approachable celebrities and suggested that Folgers Gourmet Selections could help people make every day special. A television campaign featured celebrities Lisa Ling and Chandra Wilson, giving morning viewers a peek into how they get ready for the day— and how they make their routines a little more special with their favorite flavor of Folgers Gourmet Selections. A callout at the end of the ad directed viewers to www.wakeupspecial.com, where visitors could request a sample and show others how they make their mornings special. Our agency's specific role was to deliver this meaningful online experience.

At www.wakeupspecial.com, people could upload a few personal photos, type a short description of their waking-up routine, add music, and then pick the Folgers flavor that most appealed to them. The result was a personalized slide show that people could download, post, or share with friends. We sent these people a sample of their favorite flavor, and all entries were posted live, where votes could be cast for the favorites. We gave visitors the code to publish their slide shows on their own Web sites, blogs, or social network pages. Meanwhile, a rich media banner campaign ran on key online networks during the mornings. Consumers who rolled over the ad units could watch the Chandra Wilson commercial, request a sample, and type in what makes their morning special while reading the simultaneous comments of others—all within the banner ad itself.

This program permitted several engagement measurements, including:

- Site visits that coincided with the television media schedule (the URL was given at the end)

- Number of site visits and time on site

- Number and type of samples requested

- Time spent watching others' slide shows, and number of votes cast

- Number of slide shows created

- Number of "Send to a Friend" e-mails sent and posts on blogs or MySpace pages

- Percentage of people who interacted with our banner ad

We were able to compare these data to those for other programs within and outside of the company. In tracking actual results, we found:

- About 10 percent of consumers interacted with our banner ad

> Don't forget that this new model of marketing rests on the hypothesis that, by creating meaning through your marketing, you will win both immediate business results and long-term loyalty.

- Roughly a million visitors came to the site

- On average, people spent five minutes creating their slide shows

- There were hundreds of thousands of impressions from blog posts

- There were 1.5 million sample requests from the site and banners in the first nine weeks

These results helped us confirm that the program was helping to drive the success of the Gourmet Selections initiative and, in turn, served as a base for setting future goals and objectives. Best of all, the product launch itself was a big success.

While it's important, engagement is merely the leading indicator of success within a meaningful marketing program, and it's just the beginning of your brand dialogue with consumers. Once you have established that people are voluntarily paying attention, you've got to get down to measuring the nitty-gritty—improving their lives and selling some product.

Measuring Meaning

It's tempting to consider measuring only engagement; it's also natural to want to skip ahead and check the business results of the marketing plan you launched. But don't forget that this new model of marketing rests on the hypothesis that, by creating meaning through your marketing, you will win both immediate business results *and* long-term loyalty. All three legs of the measurement stool—engagement, meaning, and marketing—work together to present a clear picture of what's working, what's not working, and why.

The good news is that, once again, your gut instinct and common sense about what makes people tick can translate into real, quantitative success metrics. The bad news? As with engagement, you're going to need to do some additional thinking, up front, about the right measures to use. In our experience, there are really three general ways to measure to evaluate meaning.

Are We Having a Positive Impact on Consumers' Lives?

You need to know how participants feel after they engage with your marketing. Here, measurement should encompass both the breadth (number) of consumers touched and the depth to which they are affected. For breadth, you can track the number of participants through site visits, registrations, and the number of times a tool is used. For depth, you can use surveys to judge the impact of consumers' experiences. A good survey will start at the bottom of the Hierarchy of Meaningful Marketing and move up—first asking questions about relevance and interest, and then moving into higher fields such as whether or not the program led to a significant life experience or change.

In working with one of our health-care clients, for example, we asked program participants to complete a pre/post survey to see how they felt before and after their experience, and we found that they felt better about the decisions they were making regarding their health and more confident about which steps to take going forward. For another client, we created an online game; in addition to measuring the number of participants and the time spent playing, we asked them how much fun they had had and whether they would play it again.

Is the Brand a Part of the Positive Impact?

You can spend a lot of money helping your consumers reach personal nirvana, but if your brand is not directly benefiting from your marketing, you can't pay the bills. Therefore, it is important that you measure the extent to which people are giving your brand credit for the meaningful content that you have created. A positive number here will add confidence that they will repay you with sales and loyalty.

Marketers sometimes feel that consumers will not trust or engage with marketing that overtly introduces a brand into the equation. And while it may, in fact, be more difficult to get consumers to get past what they perceive as a blatant product pitch, it is sometimes the only way to actually drive sales. One client (who shall remain unnamed) spent millions on a viral video and went along with its lead agency's demand that there be almost no branding of the effort. The work was incredibly brilliant and got some decent buzz, but the brand itself got no credit; its sales actually declined during the effort.

You might be surprised to learn that consumers are sometimes more than willing to get involved with brands directly—and will reward those brands for the benefits that they receive for doing so. For example, we received hundreds of consumer-generated original songs and videos for a "Jingles for Pringles" campaign that was cross-promoted on *American Idol*. Like it or not, brands are with us virtually from birth (the first outdoor sign my daughter recognized was "McDonald's"); they are part of our lives, and people are willing to interact with them directly as long as they feel the brands are adding value.

So make sure that your measurement program includes a survey of loyalty, equity metrics, and the degree to which people have feelings of reciprocity toward your brand.

Do People Recommend You to Others?

One of the most important drivers of a successful meaningful marketing program is getting your target consumers to spread the word for you. After all, with mass media playing less of a role, and people increasingly relying on word of mouth and social networks to screen for what is important, a good measurement of both the meaningfulness of your program and its potential to spread positive buzz is a must.

A favorite tool that is increasingly being employed across a wide variety of businesses is the Net Promoter Score (NPS), which was created by Fred Reichheld and is the focus of his book *The Ultimate Question: Driving Good Profits and True Growth*. The (ultimate) question is, simply, "How likely is it that you would recommend this (product/service/brand/marketing) to a friend or colleague?" This tool is used by such organizations as GE, Intuit, American Express, and our own agency. Any product or service can use customer surveys to ask the question; respondents are asked to provide a score from 0 to 10, with

10 being highest. Respondents can then be separated into three groups based on their scores: Promoters (9–10 rating), Passives (7–8 rating), and Detractors (0–6 rating). The Net Promoter Score is the number of Promoters minus the number of Detractors. Anything in the high double digits is a great score, and anything below 0 percent is a sign of great concern. Reichheld's research shows that a high NPS score is correlated with sustainable growth across many industries.

The beauty of the NPS is that it can be compared across a wide variety of consumer engagement points, from e-mail subscriptions to customer service exchanges. You can track the score in broad strokes over the long term, or you can use it to drill down on an individual, customer-by-customer basis. And it can measure the effectiveness of specific marketing tactics as well as consumers' perceptions of the overall brand.

The answers to these questions about engagement and the impact on people's lives lead to the final piece of the measurement puzzle: judging the impact on the business.

Measuring Business Results

This last leg of the measurement process brings you back, full circle, to the business objectives outlined in Chapter 6, in order to evaluate whether you achieved what you'd hoped to achieve with your program. Recall the eight key business drivers:

- Awareness

- Consideration

- Trial

- Loyalty

- Advocacy

- Equity

- Trust

- Identification

You probably already have a preferred model for measuring these drivers that you are using to measure the performance of the traditional marketing you are doing today. Little is different in the marketing with meaning model; awareness, consideration, trial, equity, and trust can all be measured through either national research or pre/post surveys of people who engage with your marketing.

Nearly any measurement system you are using today will fit with a meaningful marketing program. Marketing mix modeling, which attempts to look back in time and measure the ROI for each dollar invested in each marketing tactic, can also encompass many of the outputs of a meaningful program. And if your business sells direct via phone or the Web, you already know that you can code your marketing efforts to show how specific marketing tactics are driving leads or growing sales.

In some ways, though, marketing with meaning can lead to even deeper, more accurate data and useful information. Since there is often a direct engagement with individual consumers, brands have a chance to track marketing interactions all the way through to final sales. For example, if people like your program, they will provide their name and address in order to enter a promotion, receive a sample, or request more information. The resulting household-level database can be matched with the panel data from a company such as ACNielsen, and this can help your brand uncover even more accurate data on the purchase behavior change of consumers in your program.

Despite all the positives and consistencies in measurement, however, the biggest shock to most marketing organizations is the smaller scale of engagement as compared to mass-marketing metrics like reach. Instead of hitting many millions of eyeballs, meaningful marketing programs often have total engagement numbers in the tens or hundreds of thousands. Nike+, arguably one of the best examples of a long-term meaningful marketing program, offers one example of the difference. While a television commercial on the Super Bowl might hit 100 million people, there are only a little over 1.2 million global members in the Nike+ program, and only just over 250,000 members have logged at least 100 miles. A mass marketer will no doubt ask: how can this add up to building the business?

Remember, marketing with meaning is based on the hypothesis that higher-quality engagements with a small group of people will generate more short-term sales and long-term loyalty than an interruptive message that hits (but does not necessarily get noticed by) 10 to 100 times as many people. For Nike, the ROI might mean getting a majority of its Nike+ members to spend $100 on shoes and apparel each year. For Healthy Choice, it probably means selling just one extra meal per month.

One example of the power of Nike's small but highly engaged audience comes from its Human Race 10K event in 2008. The brand tapped its Nike+ network and used only $450,000 in media to promote the race. There were 25 race events in major cities, and Nike+ users could participate on their own at home. All 10K times were uploaded to a single Web site. A total of 780,000 people in 142 countries participated in the real and virtual race on a single day, suggesting that a large percentage of a small but powerful group can come together for a meaningful event.

> *[The Human Race] was a customer experience we couldn't get anywhere else. Our revenue climbed as running became our fastest-growing category. And, more importantly, it showed us how we could combine consumers' physical and digital experiences to create powerful new connections with our consumer.[2]*
> —JOAQUIN HIDALGO, NIKE BRAND CHIEF MARKETING OFFICER

The results of Nike's move to deeper relationships with fewer people are incredibly powerful. According to market tracking service SportsOneSource, the company's global running-shoe sales were up from $8 billion in May 2006 to $9.7 billion in May 2008—a 21 percent increase. Market share also increased from 48 percent to 61 percent in that time.

The scale of the sales results gleaned from a meaningful marketing campaign might be the single biggest issue for your organization to overcome. I'll admit, it takes a bit of a leap of faith to believe that personal engagement with a few hundred thousand people can move the needle as much as or more than a 30-second spot that's seen by millions. But our experience—and that of all the companies profiled in this book—proves that this is an ROI model that you can build and a hypothesis that you can trust. Not only have we never seen a major meaningful marketing effort fail to pay off, but with the rising costs and falling results of traditional mass media, you may have no other choice.

Leveraging Meaningful Marketing into Long-Term Success

If everything goes according to plan, your new meaningful marketing program will have resulted in strong engagement scores, very satisfied consumers, and an obvious bump to your bottom line. At this point, your default habit would probably be to start from scratch on the next program, to be launched in the months ahead. But not so fast—if you skip this next step, you might be missing out on one of the biggest benefits of marketing with meaning. Meaningful marketing can help you score similar long-term returns if you make a commitment to stick with it and continually add new life and fresh elements to your program.

Keeping a program alive can benefit your brand in several ways. First, if the program has worked in the past, there is less risk in expanding it further than in starting from scratch with something completely new. Second, existing programs indicate that there is a base of consumer interest—and if consumers have signed up for your mailing list or installed your widget, you have a built-in audience to take the program further. People who have had a positive experience in the past will want to know what you are going to do next. Third, existing programs enable you to recycle some of the assets you have already created, which allows you to spend less or put new money into novel tactics that will add incremental returns.

Charmin is one brand that is building on one year's success as a platform to go even further. Not only did the marketing team bring the branded restrooms back to Times Square for the third consecutive holiday season, but its third year was bigger and better than ever. Improvements included a family photo area for pictures with Santa's sleigh and a life-size Charmin bear. Charmin also enlisted a fellow P&G brand, Duracell, to sponsor the Duracell Power Lodge, where guests could recharge their cell phones and cameras. This partnership with another brand shows how proven programs can effectively recruit others to help defray the costs and add further value to consumers' experiences.

NIKEiD, the design-your-own-shoe program mentioned in Chapter 4, is another great example of a meaningful program that continues to attract new and repeat users by evolving. After launching the program in 1999, Nike soon realized that it had legs beyond being a short-term novelty. NIKEiD is investing in the program by tapping into the hottest technology tools to make the experience more rewarding. The latest chapter arrived in June 2008, when Nike launched PHOTOiD, a mobile phone–based tool that analyzes any photo, matches the two most dominant colors to the NIKEiD shoe design palette, and applies the colors to a chosen customized shoe design. The general idea is that kids walking down the street can turn an image from graffiti art or a customized car into a personal shoe statement in seconds. That's pretty cool—and buzz-worthy.

Brands can also evolve long-running programs to reach new levels in the Hierarchy of Meaningful Marketing. Kraftfoods.com provides an excellent example of this, having started with a magazine that focused on recipes and evolving to include not just ideas for what to cook but lessons on actually how to cook. Kraft's online Cooking School includes how-to videos, step-by-step instructions, information on cooking techniques, tips for creating authentic ethnic cuisine, and message boards where visitors can help one another pick up the skills needed to make a great meal. Not only does this lead to deeper engagement and loyalty than a simple recipe, but it helps Kraft meaningfully address the business issue of a decline in homemade meals.

Brands are increasingly building long-term thinking into their meaningful marketing efforts from day one. Mountain Dew's branded online game "Dewmocracy" was an engaging way for fans of the brand to get involved in choosing its next flavor. According to Frank Cooper, vice president of marketing for Mountain Dew, "the idea was based around the fact that we know consumers want to get more involved in creating their own content as well as developing their own

A final benefit of a long-term commitment to a single meaningful marketing platform is that it can become a tool that invites participation and investment from other brands.

products." In Dewmocracy, players helped an on-screen hero in his quest for an elixir that "will change everything."

After only a few weeks, the game shows signs of success; the first phase attracted more than 700,000 unique visitors and 200,000 total players, who spent an average of 28 minutes per session playing the game. It is a great fit for Mountain Dew's young, male target that loves to stay up gaming all night (and needs the caffeine to do so). The business responded as well; according to John Sicher, editor and publisher of *Beverage Digest*, Mountain Dew "significantly outperformed" its competition in 2008 and grew share in a tight market.[3]

But this is no mere one-and-done promotion. The game was designed to be a deep, massively multiplayer game to which players can add levels and quests over time. It clearly has to boost short-term results, but Cooper is thinking long-term: "If we get a significant reaction, we think there's an opportunity to expand this game into a broader online property. We're seeking feedback from the consumer about what parts of the game they enjoy; is the story line resonating? And if it is, we do have plans to expand it."[4]

A final benefit of a long-term commitment to a single meaningful marketing platform is that it can become a tool that invites participation and investment from other brands. In a world where consumer attention is critically important, yet spread thinly across many media, brands that manage to hook and hold consumers often find themselves flooded with offers from fellow marketers. Charmin's link with Duracell provides a good example, as do J&J's BabyCenter platform and Coke Rewards. With more than 7 million members visiting its site weekly, Coca-Cola suddenly has its own media channel that rivals major magazines and television networks in terms of size and engagement. The company uses this audience to attract favorable offers and discounts from brands like Xbox and Southwest Airlines, which, in turn, make the program more valuable to Coke Rewards members, while reducing the cost of redeeming loyalty points.

Putting It All Together: Diabetes Control for Life

Nearly every successful advertising agency can plot its evolution and growth against a handful of marquee clients and projects. These few, precious relationships drive mutual success for both the client and the agency, and ultimately become the stuff of countless case studies. For example, Grey Advertising won its first major client, Procter & Gamble, in 1956. Ogilvy points to its winning of Maxwell House and Kraft in 1959. TBWA\Chiat\Day rose with Apple in the 1980s. And Crispin Porter + Bogusky hit the big time with the MINI launch in 2001.

For Bridge Worldwide, our relationship with Abbott Nutrition has been one of those defining partnerships. I share this tale of a program that helped to define us as an agency, define Abbott Nutrition as a marketing leader, and define the path to marketing with meaning here because it serves as an excellent summary of virtually all the lessons from the previous chapters, and it specifically highlights a world-class example of measuring success in meaning and in business.

Formerly known as Ross Products, Abbott Nutrition develops and markets a wide range of science-based nutritional products that improve health and wellness for people of all ages. Located in Columbus, Ohio, it is a division within Abbott, one of the largest and most diversified health-care companies in the world. Abbott Nutrition manufactures and markets several institutional and consumer brands of nutrition products, including Similac, Ensure, EAS, and Pedialyte.

In 2004, Abbott Nutrition selected Bridge Worldwide for an assignment to serve as the interactive and relationship-marketing agency for its adult nutrition brands mainly because of our shared belief in the importance of relationship marketing. For Abbott, relationship marketing has been the dominant philosophy of all its brands, based on its rise with a decades-old Similac program that puts formula samples directly into the hands of new mothers in hospitals throughout the nation. At Bridge Worldwide, we saw the traditional marketing model breaking down, and while digital dollars were coming our way, we believed that long-term success lay in using digital media to build deep, direct relationships with individual consumers. From our first meeting, the Abbott/Bridge connection was a perfect fit.

> Change was needed, and our relationship-marketing program was the focus. This drove us toward objectives involving educating new consumers . . . and converting light-consuming members into high-consumption households.

One of our first assignments was to help the Glucerna brand crack the code on its marketing strategy. Glucerna is a brand that was launched to meet the nutritional needs of people with diabetes, and its product line includes meal replacement and snack shakes, snack bars, and cereal. Glucerna's key benefits? It is designed to meet the health needs of people with diabetes, taste great, and not increase their blood sugar.

As we began working together, we found that the Glucerna brand had a decent awareness within the diabetes community, but that people struggled with how, when, and why to use the product to manage their disease. Marketing efforts had focused on print ads in diabetes-related magazines and on frequently mailed product coupons sent to people who had opted in to ongoing communication.

In recent years, however, the brand's sales had been falling behind expectations and its competitors were catching up to Glucerna, despite its position as the market leader and the rising number of new diabetes diagnoses (especially resulting from an epidemic of obesity). An increase in targeted print ads was not working; in fact, consumers were becoming less responsive, and awareness and sales were decreasing.

Change was needed, and our relationship-marketing program was the focus. Early on, a team from Abbott and Bridge Worldwide worked together to establish objectives for the project. We focused on the problems and opportunities that we believed a relationship-marketing program could specifically address; this drove us toward objectives involving educating new consumers on how to incorporate the product into their lifestyle and converting light-consuming members into high-consumption households. We believed that ongoing communication would have a good chance of achieving these objectives. We also knew that management was always looking to drive efficiency and that the brand's historical results were worsening; this led us to focus on finding ways to improve efficiency in the budget that was already being spent on relationship marketing. Jason Ruebel, the director of the Abbott business at Bridge, summarizes the strategic planning process: "As we looked at the current print program, brand challenges, and clinical data available, we realized that there was an opportunity to not only increase consumption and retention by adding value to consumers' lives, but by creating a differentiable asset in the category."

From the beginning, we set up the objective as being to create a program that would become a valuable asset to the brand and would be recognized by the diabetes community for its importance. I clearly remember pounding my fist in an Abbott conference room a few years ago, promising the Glucerna marketing director, Brian Woo, that "we will create a program so large and successful that media companies will be calling *us* to see how they can be a part of it."

Finally, as a single client/agency team, we signed ourselves up for clear, numeric measurement goals at the start of our work, which looked a lot like Figure 9.4.

Objectives	Goals/Measurements
Convert consumers from trial to high consumption.	• Significant increase in overall product consumption
Significantly improve efficiency of marketing spending.	• A 50 percent increase in consumption among program members
Build viable platform for future product and marketing initiatives.	• Significant increase in ROI of marketing spending
	• Greater than $1 return on every $1 spent
	• Significant awareness of program among diabetes community and thought leaders
	• Membership of more than 100,000 consumers

Figure 9.4 **Bridge Worldwide's objectives and measurement goals for the Glucerna brand.**

With our objectives and goals in hand, we proceeded to derive a deeper understanding of our consumer. As the new agency on the brand, it was easier for us to start with a blank slate. We dove into hundreds of pages of historical consumer research with no preexisting beliefs or ties to past decisions. It also helped that our entire client/agency team was able to make the mental shift to "try something new" around relationship marketing.

We homed in on the experiences of people who had been newly diagnosed with diabetes (the market entry point, discussed in Chapter 7), and we asked ourselves the question "What does a person with diabetes need in life?" As you can imagine, this diagnosis is a significant wake-up call. Often people go to the doctor with symptoms such as light-headedness or frequent urination, and come out with the knowledge that they have a lifelong disease.

In the days and weeks following diagnosis, diabetics learn that they must test their blood glucose levels often, and that they must use a combination of meal management and medication to ensure that their disease does not progress to more complicated stages, or even death. They are advised to exercise and limit their calories to lose weight, but at the same time, they're told that exercise and diet can cause blood glucose to spike or bottom out.

We learned that, as the months go by, people with diabetes soon break down into one of several segments across a continuum of disease management. At one end, about 20 percent of diabetics are type A personalities who test their glucose levels three times a day and know exactly what changes in their diet, exercise, and mood will do to their bodies. On the other end of the continuum, about 20 percent of diabetics either are in denial or have resigned themselves to gradual decline. They have no interest in monitoring their disease and are not asking for help. We decided that there was little chance of creating meaningful marketing for these two groups, so we instead chose to focus on a group we called Confident Controllers. Confident Controllers are somewhere in the middle of the management continuum. They do some testing and monitoring, but they are not consistent enough. They fear that their disease will advance, and they know that they should do more. They are actively looking for tips, advice, and other help, and they appreciate the assistance they receive.

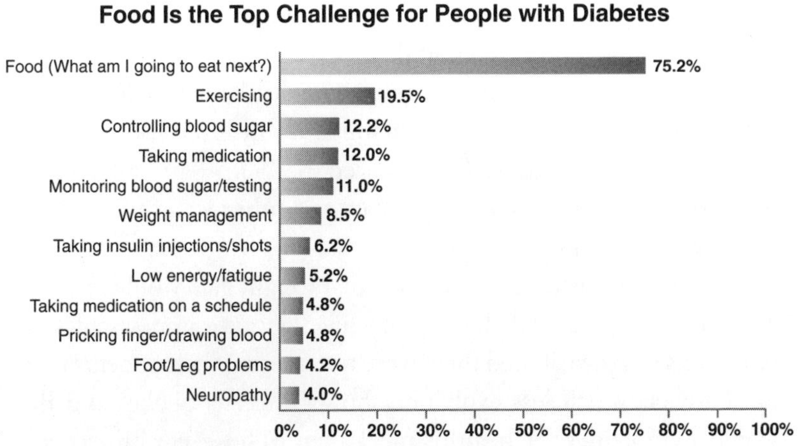

Food Is the Top Challenge for People with Diabetes

Figure 9.5 **Challenges for people with diabetes.**
Note: This chart is based on responses to the question:
"What do you feel are the most difficult challenges in living with your diabetes?"
Source: Diabetic Unmet Needs Study, August 2000, by Abbott Nutrition.

Specifically, we saw their unmet need for help in meal planning. As seen in Figure 9.5, this was by far the number one concern—and the need that had actually driven Abbott Nutrition to launch Glucerna in the first place.

While choosing food is important, Confident Controllers' needs go far beyond their daily menus. Altogether, the challenges of a diabetic involve a long tail of issues and concerns, ranging from building an exercise habit, to finding alternative places to test blood sugar, to watching for signs of diabetes in your children. Getting a handle on food choices is a start, but we saw an opportunity to help people with diabetes control a wide range of issues around their disease.

It is important to note here that age, income, and household size had nothing to do with our decision—rather, a blank-slate look at attitudes, perception, and meaning drove our direction. Demographics are just another by-product of the reach-based model we have grown up with. It is habits, attitudes, and psychographics alone that will power the engagement-based marketing of the future.

We next considered how brands and marketing fit into the lives of people with diabetes. We dove into competitive assessments, and we looked at related categories such as insulin drugs and glucose monitors. We also asked people what they thought of our product and our advertising. Loud, clear, and consistently, we heard that while people understood that Glucerna was "the drink for people with diabetes," they had very little understanding of why it was special or how it could fit into their lives. They figured that Slim-Fast had the same benefits, when, in actuality, Slim-Fast and other weight loss shakes can significantly spike blood glucose.

Physicians warned their patients that weight gain would probably worsen the progress of diabetes. But while they gave away samples, the physicians who distributed them were not offering their patients much meal advice, much less explaining how Glucerna Shakes and Bars would complement a healthy meal plan. Those consumers who received our high-value coupons were trained to wait until the next ones arrived before they headed to the store. It sure didn't feel good to hear this, but it did give us the insights we needed to affect our strategy development.

Diabetics told us that they sometimes spent time on brand Web sites in their frequent pursuit of knowledge about disease management. In fact, diabetes is in the top five of all health topics researched online. But they felt that many of the Web sites out there were either incomplete or too commercial. We began to see an opportunity.

With our research complete, we began to move into the process of strategy development. As with any strategy project, we took the time to go back to our Glucerna brand equity, which follows a typical progression from base attributes and benefits to higher-level brand values and character. The Glucerna equity positioned the brand around great-tasting control—something enjoyable that patients could count on to help them improve their A1C levels. As we looked at the program, we realized that there was a higher-order benefit that we called "Enlightened Diabetes Management." While we did not specifically use Maslow's hierarchy of needs, by this point we had internalized the range of needs for our Confident Controller. If it was put into a Maslow framework, it might look something like Figure 9.6.

By putting these frameworks side by side, you can see a powerful connection. The Glucerna brand aimed to bring its consumers control, while the Confident Controller longed for a higher-level mastery of her disease—a full life with no limitations. The Glucerna

Figure 9.6 **Bridge Worldwide's "Enlightened Diabetes Management," if put into a Maslow framework.**

brand character, a "Positive, Practical Teacher," fit well with consumers' desire to connect with friends, family, and a community that would help them control their disease. All we needed was a spark of strategy and creativity to charge our program-development process.

And, as many marketers know, luck sometimes shines down upon you. (Louis Pasteur believed that "chance favors the prepared mind.") As we were reviewing research and developing strategies, we became aware that Abbott Nutrition had been running a clinical study of a 24-week diet and exercise program with hundreds of people, in hopes that it would provide data that could be used in Glucerna marketing.

The results for program participants were very positive. A majority of them experienced improved glucose levels, were more physically active, made better food choices, maintained or lost weight, and improved their A1C levels (a key measure of long-term glucose control). By helping people make better decisions about their meals, the study actually helped diabetics understand how Glucerna could help them manage their calorie intake and blood glucose levels. So, in addition to improving people's health, we could sell more cases of product.

The power of this study rose to our collective consciousness and gave us the lead on a powerful angle for our relationship-marketing program.

Putting it all together, we chose to create a comprehensive, customizable program that would help diabetics learn about and better manage their disease. We would specifically feature the free, clinically proven 24-week meal and fitness program as the killer app. This proven, innovative program would draw broad interest and differentiate our campaign from those of leading diabetes media players such as WebMD and dLife.

We chose to create a new brand—Diabetes Control for Life—in order to communicate the foremost purpose of the program, and to ensure that consumers did not confuse our intentions with just another Glucerna marketing program. At the same time, we clearly identified Glucerna as the source of the program, featured brand messages in meaningful ways (recipes, suggestions, and solutions), and built the brand into the meal planner as an alternative. We moved the entire program online at www.diabetescontrolforlife.com in order to reduce expenses and allow for a deeper experience.

In a matter of months, we took rounds of work through consumer research to continually hone the idea and move closer to market. We tested early concepts, asked consumers to prioritize features and functions, and got their feedback on site design and usability. In addition to the 24-week meal and fitness program, we added other content that would help fulfill the mission of the site. A monthly newsletter included original articles about diabetes and its management. We added helpful tools such as a recipe finder, calorie burn calculator, portion control quiz, diabetes glossary, and vitamins guide.

When Diabetes Control for Life went live, it felt like the end of a long ride, but it was really only the beginning. We had a new business on our hands, and we immediately set out to learn more and improve it.

Data came in immediately as consumers found the program through messages on our product packaging, e-mails to our existing database, and a significant online media buy. Engagement results were immediately in the league of some of the best relationship-marketing programs we had ever seen. On e-mail, for example, we saw 39 percent open rates on weekly communications and 46 percent click-through to the site. This gave us confidence that the program was indeed highly valuable to our target consumer. We also began to monitor the content that site visitors found appealing, and we closely watched how consumers joined and stuck with the 24-week plan.

Over time, we used consumer surveys to measure how meaningful the program was to consumers' lives. First, we received confirmation that the results of the online program matched those of the clinical study that Abbott Nutrition had commissioned. In fact, 75 percent of people checked their blood glucose more consistently, there was a 5 percent average weight loss, and 65 percent said that they felt better all around. Meanwhile, our membership rose above the 100,000 mark.

Finally, and most important, we were able to judge the program's impact on the Glucerna business. We had hoped to increase consumption by 50 percent among members—but we saw a 400 percent increase instead. We had hoped to return more than $1 in profit for every $1 spent on the program—but instead we saw $3. We had hoped to build a leading program with 100,000 members—but we attracted 250,000.

In the two years since this program was originally launched, our united client/agency team has continued to build on its success and momentum. Like a true media property, we have redesigned and upgraded the program annually to take advantage of the latest developments in technology and aesthetics. We have added features, such as an instant message service that allows people to chat with a nutritionist at no charge and a Google Maps mash-up that allows members to plot out a walking course and calculate the mileage.

Hospitals are now sending their newly diagnosed patients to Diabetes Control for Life. Large retail chains have asked for a version of the program that they can offer their shoppers. Other noncompetitive manufacturers of products for diabetics have called to see how they can participate in the program. And even the diabetes media have called, asking to team up on the site.

Based on our success and that of others, I have every confidence that you will find marketing with meaning to be revolutionary in concept, and simple and straightforward in terms of process, ideation, and measurement. The most difficult challenge you will face is changing the mental habits that you, your partners, and your organization have followed for so long; but once you can get beyond these and open your mind to charting a new course, your business and personal successes will snowball.

THE FUTURE OF MARKETING WITH MEANING

We human beings have always had a fascination with predictions; from the songs of the Greek oracles to the forward-looking Mayan calendar, and from the mysterious quatrains of Nostradamus to the annual *BusinessWeek* "What's Next" issue, we are compelled to try to understand what is coming next in order to gain an edge on the future. The marketing world is certainly no different; we, too, look out toward the horizon to try to foresee where we should be putting our time and dollars in order to maximize our return on investment.

Over the past few years, we've heard all about how the rise of Web 2.0 will change everything (the implications of which most of us still do not understand). Others have claimed that marketing is on the cusp of "the Age of Transparency" or "Conversation" or "Openness." Some even go so far as to suggest that we are on the brink of reaching "the singularity"—a transcendent time when artificial intelligence will improve at an accelerating, exponential rate, soon exceeding the brainpower of human beings. At that point, either we will download

> I believe that marketing with meaning will become a mainstay that you . . . can implement to bring about real change in your brand.

our minds onto computer chips and live forever, or Skynet will gain control of the military, nuke humanity, and send Arnold Schwarzenegger back through time.

The easiest marketing prediction to make—and probably the most accurate—is that most, if not all, of these predictions will fall flat. Certainly there are kernels of truth in all of these concepts. The brands that succeed in the future will probably tend to be more accessible, more open, and more human. But none of these concepts provides a new marketing model that those of us in the trenches can turn into a success model *today*.

Based on my experience, and that of the other brands profiled in this book, I believe that marketing with meaning will become a mainstay that you, dear reader, can implement to bring about real change in your brand. But that old adage "the only constant is change" (which, perhaps appropriately, is attributed to Isaac Asimov) happens to be true, and so my hope is that, in addition to revolutionizing your short-term sales results and long-term customer loyalty, marketing with meaning can also serve as a useful lens through which you can evaluate which new trends and tools are actually worthy of your attention.

The following, in no particular order, are some of the changes that I believe we are likely to experience in the next three to five years, a time period that's long enough to allow for successful habit change to occur, but doesn't require venturing too far out into the murky unknown.

The Bar Will Rise for Everyone

No doubt you've noticed that your customers are becoming more demanding. Perhaps you've even caught yourself coming down harder than you used to on the businesses you patronize. The fact is, what passed for good service yesterday may not cut it tomorrow, and meaningful marketers may be the only ones who are prepared to rise to the occasion.

Multiple data sources suggest that people are becoming tougher customers across the board. A poll conducted by Harris Interactive in 2007 found that 80 percent of more than 2,000 adults polled had vowed never to buy from a particular company after a negative experience. This was way up from 68 percent in 2006—a 12 percent increase in only one year. Another global study by Accenture in 2007 found that 52 percent of more than 3,500 people surveyed said that their expectations for service had increased over the past five years. And one-third said that their expectations had risen in the past year alone.

I believe that improved service in some industries is increasing customer expectations for all businesses. Apple Stores set the bar that every other retailer, regardless of what it sells, is now compared to; and if Twitter can send mobile updates on what your friends are doing, the airlines had certainly better send alerts when flight details change. Brands are no longer competing with just the other brands in their category—instead, they are competing with every other brand or service that their target audience comes into contact with. Whether it's an airline, a retailer, or a software company, we expect any company that wants to earn our business to treat us with respect, in a standard, high-quality manner—to take our phone calls promptly, be available at all hours, and create marketing that adds value to our lives.

This means two things for marketers. First, it suggests that interruptive marketing could die off even sooner than we think as people become more unwilling to be annoyed and more inclined toward meaningful marketing. In the fall of 2008, for example, Toyota bombarded the television networks with its "Saved by Zero" campaign. It was really just another irritating ad for an automobile brand offering zero percent financing, accompanied by a poor rendition of the song "Saved by Zero" from the 1980s alternative band the Fixx. People have absorbed thousands of ads just like it for years, yet this particular ad seemed to create a tipping point. It spawned a Facebook protest group with more than 10,000 members. And the Facebook protest group, in turn, generated media coverage in the *New York Times*, the *Wall Street Journal*, and *Time* magazine. The ad caused ire, and that ire was newsworthy because people today are demanding more from

> Marketing with meaning creates a kind of brand meritocracy, where it's literally possible for a brand to come out of nowhere with new and improved services and beat the competition.

marketers and can access social networks to make their demands more vocal.

Second, these accelerating demands mean that meaningful marketers must invest in continually improving the services they provide. We often see this in our relationship-marketing programs for brands like Similac and ConAgra Foods. Instead of looking at competitors in the market, we model our upgrades on the latest features offered by Google or WebMD. We know that we are competing with all of these properties to provide information and win return visitors, and this goes far beyond the Web. No doubt one of the reasons that Charmin upgrades its Times Square facilities each year is that the standard for brand experiences keeps rising—especially in the ultracompetitive nexus of New York City.

While this means even more hard work for we weary marketers, the good news is that marketing with meaning creates a kind of brand meritocracy, where it's literally possible for a brand to come out of nowhere with new and improved services and beat the competition. Take a look at what today's category leaders might be missing, and you'll be surprised to see how quickly you can race past them.

Leapfrog Marketing: New Media

As well as promoting buzzwords, new media prognosticators especially love to trumpet the latest and greatest technology that is sure to turn the marketing world on its head. I have lived through several rounds of this hype cycle, which always seems to follow a similar pattern: a handful of gurus fall in love with the new killer app (full disclosure: their support often arises when they join start-ups connected to the killer app) and laud it as the next great solution to the industry's ills. After a year or two, one of the business weeklies turns it into a cover story that introduces the concept to the mass-marketing audience. Then either the buzz flames out or the technology establishes itself by providing some modicum of usefulness for the right brands and initiatives. Two successful examples are blogging and e-mail; flameouts include Second Life stores and Instant Messenger ads.

Interestingly, it seems lately that the newer the media, the higher the level of consumer ire they can evoke. Take mobile marketing. Clearly, mobile phones and other devices are becoming a more integral part of our lives, and the technology will only continue to improve over the next few years. The December 2008 Pew Internet report predicts that mobile devices will be the primary tool for connection to the Internet for most people in the world by the year 2020. As a result, new media marketers have been quick to jump on the mobile bandwagon, envisioning a system for putting micro-banner ads on all those mobile pages we visit. They giggle with glee at the thought of the geo-targeting possibilities—sending an alarm to your phone when you walk by a Starbucks, say, and inviting you in for 25 cents off a Venti Latte.

But consumers want none of this, and they are downright worried about this most personal of devices falling into the wrong marketers' hands. An October 2007 ACNielsen study that culled consumer perceptions of different forms of advertising from 47 markets found that mobile marketing came in as "least trusted." Another Nielsen study, which labeled "likely mobile ad targets" as those people who are using these devices for more than talking (like surfing the Web, sending text messages, playing video games, or buying ringtones), found that the most mobile-active people are, in fact, also the most advertising-resistant:

- Only 10 percent responded to ads on their mobile phones.

- About 11 percent viewed the ads but did not respond.

- A full 79 percent did not even view the ad.

- Some 67 percent found it unacceptable to have ads on their mobile device.

The aggregate point? *These people may look like your ideal target audience, but they don't want any ads whatsoever on their phones.* Interestingly, this anti-ad attitude has kept service providers from creating a mobile platform for marketing. In a world in which service providers are battling one another in stiff competition, they cannot afford to anger their customers just to make a few extra bucks. One Verizon spokesman confirmed that "the incremental dollar value of advertising pales next to the cost of losing customers who don't like ads."

So what's a marketer to do—just give up on this promising "third screen"? Actually, you can skip the interruption entirely and go straight to marketing with meaning. In fact, a general consensus has already taken hold within the mobile-marketing industry that the only way to win in this sphere is to add value to consumers' lives by providing useful services and fun tools. According to Zaw Thet, CEO of 4INFO, a leading mobile media company, "Brands can no longer just show up and expect that their message will be heard. Consumers trade attention for value, whether it's the entertainment of a game, or savings through a loyalty program."

Several smart marketers have already entered the mobile game meaningfully. CoverGirl created a "ColorMatch" application that recommends shades based on complexion and on clothing and accessories colors. According to a brand spokesperson, "Women would not have their computer with them at the store, making the mobile phone an ideal choice." AT&T used mobile to create tools that allowed spectators at the Ironman World Championship triathlon in Hawaii to track participants' progress at checkpoints, resulting in 15,000 sign-ups and 100,000 brand impressions. Visa created a tool that suggested wine-and-cheese pairings to supermarket shoppers on behalf of its high-end product, Visa Signature.

The rise of the iPhone and its App Store could further fuel this opportunity. Kraft, for example, has already developed the "iFood Assistant," which includes more than 7,000 recipes and a smart shopping list and store locator. It is even selling the tool for $0.99, and people are eating up this example of meaningful marketing. Just one month after its launch, the iFood Assistant had become one of the top 100 most popular paid apps, and number two in the lifestyle category. According to Kraft's director of innovation, Ed Kaczmarek, the iFood app brought the brand millions of dollars in PR coverage, hit its three-year download goal in a matter of weeks, and has brought in a high percentage of Gen Y and male consumers.

> *[The iFood app] brings us closer to becoming an indispensable food resource for consumers' meal planning, preparation, and shopping needs.*
>
> —Ed Kaczmarek, Director of Innovation, Kraft

Another example is Vicks, which funded a cold- and flu-tracking application that each day sends a zip code–level update on daily weather conditions and the severity of cold and flu outbreaks. Nationwide insurance recently launched an iPhone app that helps walk people through the steps they should take if they get into a car accident.

The term *leapfrog technology* is being used increasingly to refer to the way developing nations are benefiting from the trial and error of our evolving technologies by skipping the middle steps and going straight for the best-in-class standard. In Africa, for example, villages are going from no phones to mobile phones, not bothering to put up landlines. In Brazil, consumers leaped straight from cash to debit cards, mainly skipping checking accounts and credit cards. In Pakistan, rural villages are bypassing expensive, polluting coal-fueled power plants and going straight to solar power.

Marketing with meaning can similarly facilitate a leapfrog approach for marketers. Instead of regressing to interruptive advertising when these new media options arise, we can leapfrog straight to meaningful marketing because it simply makes too much sense for consumers and companies alike.

Video games, a mature medium that keeps growing and diversifying, offer another example of the leapfrog concept. By 2008, the average American gamer had been playing for 12 years and was 35 years old. But the fact is, people of all ages and demographics are playing any number of games on any number of platforms—from teen boys fragging on *Halo* to middle-aged women playing *Bejeweled* on their laptops.

As with mobile, this increase in eyeball time has marketers salivating. According to Nielsen, gaming consoles are effectively the fifth largest "network" in terms of nightly audience. Large and small companies alike are building systems that will allow marketers to buy placement in games, just as they do on television or in newspapers. In fact, President Obama drew some attention to the possibilities when his campaign bought a virtual billboard on the Xbox 360 driving game *Burnout Paradise*. But as Millward Brown's chief global analyst, Nigel Hollis, observes, "Sticking a . . . logo by the side of a street in a racing game is nowhere near as compelling as integrating a brand into the game's content so that the player interacts with it . . . the big challenge for advertisers is to use the interactivity of gaming to engage people with their brands, not simply use it to present a virtual billboard."

There are very meaningful ways to get involved in gaming, as seen in Paramount Pictures' support for the movie *Tropic Thunder* and its tie-in with the game *Rainbow Six Vegas* by Ubisoft. The film actually sponsored a new "scavenger hunt" level for the game that players could download at no cost, the mission of which was to search for a series of nine branded clues; those who completed the mission got a chance to win prizes such as a VIP game map and other Ubisoft games.

The key here is that the *Tropic Thunder* marketing actually added value to the gamer's experience. Paramount realized that these kinds of downloads create huge word of mouth among gamers and would get them talking about its movie right before the critical opening weekend of the film.

Marketing to Millennials

The concept of leapfrogging straight into meaningful marketing also provides a powerful way to look at how brands should approach the rising generation of Millennial consumers. You probably know who they are by now, thanks to the media hype and the fact that they are beginning to join the ranks of your company. You might even have one or two of them living under your own roof—providing the perfect laboratory test subjects. The idea of grouping together 80 million people born between 1977 and 1998 into one bucket of trends can be troublesome, but there are some generalities that are relevant for meaningful marketers.

The first thing to notice about people in this generation is that they are well aware that we are eager for their business, and they aren't afraid to play hard to get. This group grew up under a microscope of advertising attention that was rivaled only by the attention heaped upon them by their helicopter parents. As a result, they are street smart and wise to the fact that companies are mainly motivated by the desire to pry a dollar bill out of their hands.

Nor can you fool these consumers into thinking that your professionally created viral video is homemade; these are the same consumers that Frito-Lay's Doritos brand found to be skilled at using technology not only to create their own entertainment, but also to contribute to their favorite brands' marketing (recall "Crash the Super Bowl"). This willingness to participate demonstrates an openness to marketing when it is done well.

> *Millennials . . . have never known a world where they didn't control the experience. [They] have always been encouraged to believe that they are right, that there are no bad questions, and that everything matters.[1]*
> —JOHN GERZEMA AND ED LEBAR, AUTHORS OF
> THE BRAND BUBBLE

Millennials are also a group-oriented generation that has the tendency to define itself by affiliation, which provides brands with the opportunity to play a pivotal role. A Facebook group of Pringles lovers, for example, surged to more than 1 million fans around the world before the Pringles marketing team even knew it existed.

As those with teens in the home no doubt know, the Millennial generation is also leapfrogging over traditional media formats. Many of them skip the television altogether, opting for the laptop, where they can watch video clips, chat with friends, and update their blogs at the same time. They are also adept at using technology, like the DVR, that their parents still don't completely understand. So it's really a nonstarter to think that you'll have any chance at all of reaching this generation with traditional advertising media.

Capri Sun provides a great example of how marketers are thinking differently to reach this generation. After a self-imposed advertising hiatus, during which it reformulated its product to reduce the sugar content, Capri Sun needed to recapture kids' attention. Starting

> Millennials are increasingly choosing to live their lives transparently, . . . [which] opens up vast opportunities for marketers.

somewhat from scratch, the brand gave the marketing team some freedom to ignore the traditional media path.

In a move that illustrates the discussion of gaming in the previous section, Capri Sun tapped gaming to connect with kids in a meaningful way. Knowing that the 8- to 12-year-old kids in its sweet spot are big video gamers (98 percent of boys and 84 percent of girls play them), the brand partnered with the Wii game *Rayman Raving Rabbids TV Party* to include added-value mini-games built around branded characters. The game was featured in 50 million packs and in a nationwide mobile tour.

The results blew away every brand promotion in history and drove a significant sales lift. According to Maria Mandel, executive director of digital innovation at Ogilvy, who created the tie-in for this Kraft brand, it was hard to sell the idea at first. But the brand took a risk, saw incredible results, and is now working on even bigger game-related promotions using this most recent experience as a guide.

Along with being the most analyzed generation in history, Millennials are sharing more about their lives than any group that's come before. Whether their parents or their future bosses like the kinds of photos and comments they find or not, Millennials are increasingly choosing to live their lives transparently—using digital tools like Facebook and Twitter to share their triumphs and tragedies with the world. This actually opens up vast opportunities for marketers, as they can use this openness to learn about what these consumers are looking for and help them find it.

Aside from leapfrogging over traditional media habits, the most significant difference between the Millennial generation and any generation that's come before it is its propensity to leapfrog culturally, skipping traditional careers and the accumulation of material goods, and moving right into a more personally meaningful mission in life. Kids who graduate from high school are increasingly taking a year off before college to travel the world or volunteer. A study by UCLA's Higher Education Research Institute found that 66 percent of freshmen said that it is "essential or very important" to help others—the highest percentage in 25 years.

This trend toward service and meaning is what excites me most about the future, both as the author of this book and as a citizen of the planet. If the Millennial generation demands that brands give value back to the world, it could unleash a powerful force for positive change, rewarding those companies that are most committed to improving their customers' lives and creating marketing with meaning.

Marketing in Developing Nations

Although most of the examples used in this book so far have focused on brand marketing in developed economies, there is no reason to assume that meaningful marketing stops at the border—nor that it is limited to wealthy countries where, say, a majority of homes have broadband connections. The reality is that this model can be applied anywhere that a company can uncover useful localized insights and find a way for brand marketing to deliver value.

As you might expect, going digital is often not the first choice for consumers in developing nations. This is unfortunate, because digital is an effective way to provide information or connect with people on a one-on-one basis. The good news in developing nations, though, is that human labor is often more affordable and can provide an even more personal experience than the Web.

Some of the most meaningful marketing I have seen has taken place in developing nations, where one-on-one interaction occurs routinely. For example, the Ariel detergent brand provided a safe place for women to do their laundry during civil unrest in Venezuela. And in Africa, P&G's feminine care brands teach girls about their periods—a topic that is deliberately ignored by most village schools.

Creating and distributing valuable content can be a powerful way to win over these consumers. For example, the Caltex chain of gas stations in South Africa launched a free comic book around a fictional soccer team named the Supa Strikers. The series of comic books helped children learn English and created a bond between the brand and parents. It was so successful that it was rolled out into an additional 21 countries, adapting to local favorite sports (including a cricket team in Pakistan).

At times, brands can act fast to take content ideas global. One of my favorite examples is a television program in China called *Shining Journey*, which was created by the Pantene brand and its agency, MediaCom. This reality television show sought contestants from throughout the country who competed in showing the improvement in their physical and inner beauty. The program attracted 40 million viewers per week, who followed the transformation of the contestants and learned the secrets of beauty transformation themselves. Sales throughout China grew 10 percent during the program.

Even though going digital is often not the first choice for meaningful marketing in developing nations, the fact is that household penetration of digital media is rising fast, and people are quick to catch up with new technology. In China, for example, where there are already more Internet users than in the United States, people are engaged in some of the latest cutting-edge digital habits; a survey from Netpop shows that user-generated content, like consumer reviews and blogs, influences 58 percent of Chinese Internet users, compared to 19 percent in the United States, and 47 percent of Chinese broadband users regularly post comments, compared to only 25 percent of people in the United States.

Marketers must also remember that "digital" does not necessarily mean just broadband and Web sites. In the Philippines, for example, more than 46 million people have cell phones (60 percent penetration), and people use cheap texting for a growing range of services. (That's one of the reasons that Pope Benedict started texting fellow Catholics in August 2008.)

Engagement-Based Media Planning

Another prediction: marketers' embrace of engagement as the single best measure of advertising success will spawn (another) model of revolution in the marketing world—this time, in the way that media are planned for and purchased around the world.

Traditionally, media agencies have almost always used "reach-based" planning. This means that their job is to identify the target

consumer as clearly as possible, then
identify the media vehicles that will
maximize the percentage of consumers who will see the advertising
message (reach). The shortsighted-
ness of this is not the planners' fault;
after all, they are simply running with
the marketing model that their brands
have dictated for decades. Very good
media planners have begun to look more deeply than eyeballs, however, and may use "receptivity" research to understand what types of
interruptive media have the best chance of breaking through
consumers' defenses.

> Marketers' embrace of engagement . . . will . . . [influence] the way that media are planned for and purchased around the world.

Going forward, however, the media-planning model will shift
away from reach-based planning and toward engagement-based planning. As described in Chapter 9, engagement depends on attracting
people who choose to pay attention to and interact directly with your
brand. An engagement-based plan identifies places where brands can
find people who are looking for value-added marketing, and it can
lead to some pretty significant shifts in thinking. Instead of buying
magazine space, for example, it might direct brands to build up an
e-mail database, create a Facebook group, or try to earn a spot as a
merchandise sponsor in Coke Rewards.

From a media agency perspective, this represents an enormous
opportunity to pull ahead of the curve and help clients make the shift.
The fact that creating engagement-based plans requires more work
and deeper intelligence than developing formula-based reach plans
means that marketers will be willing to pay a premium for talented
planners' specific skills.

Meanwhile, media producers will have to adapt in order to provide avenues that engage consumers in real, measurable ways. Magazines, for example, are losing advertisers to the Web, in part because
the latter has a chance of gaining deeper consumer connections. Look
for magazines to move more quickly to give priority to the Web and
push into new digital reading devices such Amazon's Kindle and the
Sony Reader, which permit more engaging experiences for consumers
and advertisers alike.

Overall, engagement-based planning is still in its early stages. For now, ask your media-planning and media-buying agencies to modify their approach more toward the receptivity of your core target market. And if your media agency has not heard of engagement-based planning, it is time for you to look for a new partner.

More Advertiser-Developed Content and Channels

Despite some of the challenges outlined in Chapter 8, the balance of meaningful marketing seems to be shifting toward companies that jump into the content creation business. Technology is making it cheaper for brands to both produce and distribute content, and the costs of sponsoring or advertising via traditional mass media keep escalating.

One of the places in which brand-created content is most visible is in the rise of new brands. Love 'em or hate 'em, the Crocs brand is an upstart that is forging a new content-driven marketing model. In 2008, the brand created "Cities by Foot," a hub for video city guides with suggestions on places to eat, shop, and play in places like Las Vegas, Denver, San Francisco, and New Orleans. According to Tom Flanagan, CEO of Red Robot, the agency behind the effort, "Instead of allocating additional marketing dollars on traditional media, we think it is more relevant and timely to create an online video-based platform that will consistently provide both local business and travelers with something of real value."

Even so-called failed attempts at creating content might be smarter than the cynics assume. Take Bud.TV, an online property from Budweiser that includes original content like an interview show, viral videos, and a sci-fi/drama series. Bud.TV was an attempt by the Budweiser and Bud Light brands to deploy the humor that makes the brands special without being tied down by 30-second limits, expensive media buys, and growing pressure from parents who don't like their kids to see beer ads during the ball game.

Analysts panned the company's efforts, suggesting that it failed to secure a critical mass of visitors for its $30 million investment. Expensive as it sounds, though, the program was a worthy experiment. For starters, $30 million is a drop in the bucket for two brands with a combined annual media budget of $500 million. Furthermore, the company's early mistakes afforded learning opportunities. For example, when its original programming was slow to gain a following, the brand resurrected and promoted popular commercials like "Swear Jar" and Bud Light's "Real Men of Genius." Budweiser found that Bud.TV was a way for these videos to build buzz and attract deeper interest online.

The lesson here is not to let Bud.TV's struggles or $30 million investment deter you from lunging headfirst into content development. As the costs fall and the global reach of content rises, the biggest risk is not testing and learning today so that your brand is ready for the inevitable tomorrow.

Taking Online Features into the Physical World

The ever-improving features and penetration of digital technology will obviously inspire a steady migration toward online marketing, but in the years ahead, look for these online experiences to also infiltrate our physical world. One of the main areas where online and offline will blend seamlessly is retail, where we should expect the best features of e-commerce to find their way into brick-and-mortar stores. Microsoft is already partnering with ShopRite stores in five northeastern states to create smart shopping carts, which customers activate with their loyalty cards upon entering the store. The carts provide useful information, like where to find hard-to-locate items and a running tally of the total cost of the items to be purchased. And like a top e-commerce engine, these smart carts can present offers based on shoppers' purchase history and location in the store.

But instead of smart carts, mobile devices are likely to be the killer technology that enables a broad range of services like this. For example, personalized coupons could be sent to a mobile phone or directly to a shopper card, or multidimensional UPC-like "QR codes" could be placed next to price tags in stores. A scan of the QR code could link a mobile browser to more product details, reviews, and, say, wine pairings.

The technology is already available—just unevenly distributed. Both Sephora and Intuit are experimenting with mobile reviews that

> Mobile devices are likely to be the killer technology that enables a broad range of services.

allow people to see what others think before they buy, facilitating higher closing rates and customer satisfaction. Signage in Sephora and Office Depot stores, respectively, encourages shoppers to read reviews at m.sephora.com and m.turbotax.com. "Here's a platform people are already walking into the store with and there's nothing that the in-store retailer has to do," said Sam Decker, chief marketing officer at Bazaarvoice.[2]

Mobile devices will rapidly grow more intelligent as well, providing users with an always-on, always-handy tool for whatever their needs may be. My favorite example is a free iPhone application called Shazam that can recognize a song that you hear and pull up a page with the artist's name and a link to buy it from iTunes. Imagine a tool from *Motor Trend* that allows you to take a mobile photo of any car and link to a page listing its exact make and model, along with driver reviews and other comparison information.

Earn Money by Watching Ads?

Despite my bias toward marketing with meaning, I would be remiss if I avoided mentioning some of the innovations that are going on in the interruptive marketing world. As you might imagine, the leaders of this world are not sleeping easily, and the movement of billions of advertising dollars toward new media has attracted a lot of new ideas. Perhaps the most interesting concept is the idea of directly compensating people for engaging with advertisements.

As people become increasingly more difficult to reach and give their attention more sparingly, the value of a true marketing interaction is rising rapidly. It is not a great leap to imagine a more direct "value exchange" between marketers and consumers, and several services are experimenting in this area. For example, Blyk is a mobile network in Europe that is completely funded by advertising. The more advertising you view, the more free service you receive. Blyk targets young consumers, who are the hardest to reach, yet most in need of free cell service. It has run ads for brands like Coke, L'Oréal, and

NatWest Bank. The company claims to be growing more quickly than expected—hitting more than 100,000 sign-ups in the United Kingdom in its first nine months, nearly six months ahead of its plan.

This kind of exchange can sometimes look more like a reframing of traditional advertising that simply shows people what a marketer is doing for them. For example, Dell recently sponsored free access to the subscriber-only section of the *Economist*. And in 2007, Philips bought up ad space in *Fortune* magazine and the *NBC Nightly News*, pointedly "giving it back" for more content as part of its "Sense and Simplicity" campaign. (The NBC news effort actually resulted in 8 percent higher ratings and more than 9,000 thank you e-mails.)

On the cutting edge of this trend is a company called Apex in Japan, which serves free drinks in ad-supported vending machines. The customer is exposed to a 30-second video advertisement while the drink is being prepared, and it is served in a branded disposable cup. There are already 35,000 such machines in place across the country.

It will be interesting to see if this becomes a bona fide trend, with its own *BusinessWeek* cover story and crop of me-too start-ups. Of course, I think it has potential because it's actually a form of meaningful marketing: instead of trying to steal our attention, it is marketing that does add direct value, and it is obviously an opt-in model. What's questionable is whether appealing to the base level of value—free stuff—will enable brands to make the most meaningful connections with the kinds of consumers that they want to reach.

Google Life

While pay-per-view advertising offers some potential for success in the years ahead, the real hope of the interruptive marketing industry is that someone can figure out how to tie together multiple media with individual personalization. Right now, that someone seems to be Google, and it seems to be working nonstop to deliver the solution. The "Google Life" future might well either ascend to the peak of meaning, become the worst interruption nightmare, or both, depending on how brands use it.

It could be argued that Google is the first major media channel in the marketing with meaning future, given that the company rose to

> The "Google Life" future might well either ascend to the peak of meaning, become the worst interruption nightmare, or both.

prominence by delivering an incredibly useful search tool funded by advertisers' paid search ads. When people are searching for information, they sometimes find these small search advertisements helpful and click on them. The result is a win for the consumer (who gets the information he is looking for), the marketer (who generates traffic and sales), and Google (which charges a fee for each click). Clearly, these search ads are marketing that people choose to engage with, and that can provide value without requiring a purchase.

Google has become a $100 billion company thanks almost entirely to profits driven by its search business. However, the company sees a peak in search revenue in the future, and it is working to diversify and grow through new markets. Seeing the number of businesses that are searching for a new marketing model, the company has chosen to pursue new ways of generating advertising revenue.

Google's brilliant in-house software developers continue to create new services like Gmail, Google Maps, and Android—a software platform for mobile devices—all of which do or can feature text and display advertising. And the company is actively spending its hoard of billions in cash on such acquisitions as YouTube ($1.65 billion in 2006) and the online ad server DoubleClick ($3.1 billion in 2007). Google has also bought small players for niche needs in areas such as online gaming, Internet telephony, microblogging, and mobile social networking.

And its deeper moves into the advertising industry are not limited to digital. After purchasing a system for buying radio ads, Google experimented with reselling ad space in magazines, and recently added a feature that allows brands to upload and place television ads through its AdWords interface (a partnership with EchoStar). Meanwhile, Google is building up a large in-house media sales team that is starting to rival those of the biggest players in the industry.

The overall consensus in the industry is that Google is working to become an integrated advertising platform that can enable marketers of any size to target consumers on an individual basis. Today, it is putting all the pieces together and allowing businesses to place and measure ads easily. But tomorrow, it could link all of its services together into something much more powerful. For example, the company could use your online activity and searches as the trigger for myriad marketing alternatives. Let's say you and your spouse start thinking about vacation options for the summer. You open up Google's Web browser and search for family-friendly trip options. Along the way, Google is building a profile and triggering advertising campaigns on its other media services. Suddenly, when you turn on your radio or television, you hear ads for brands like Carnival Cruise Lines and Expedia.com, which have bid for the chance to present their messages to people who are specifically in trip-planning mode.

This is a very intriguing concept, and it's probably something that Google can achieve in the next three to five years. The idea is basically a deeper form of what is referred to as "addressable advertising," which essentially means any system of serving ads to specific individuals within the household. In 2008, media agency Starcom MediaVest ran a test marketing with addressable ads (with companies like GM, P&G, and Discover participating) in Huntsville, Alabama, and found that homes there skipped or changed channels on ads 38 percent less than average. In the spring of 2009, Cablevision rolled out a similar program in 500,000 homes in New York and New Jersey. Google could go even further by not just targeting the right demographic, but using other data to observe—and maybe even predict—what are currently the most important needs in a person's life.

Google might even become a force that drives improvement in advertising creativity itself. In its new TV commercial platform, ad placement will be based not only on which brand pays the most, but on the quality of the ad. This system mirrors the way Google prioritizes search ads—after all, if the ad is so bad that no one clicks on it, Google doesn't make any money. To begin with, the company will measure quality by the percentage of the program audience that changes the channel or skips the ads. Combined, these moves might lead to a resurgence in the traditional advertising model.

Vincent Dureau, head of TV technology at Google, says, "We are confident we are going to revive the television advertising industry by bringing new advertising to it. You can actually make more money, because you can increase the relevance of your ads. At the end of the day, you're changing the attitude of the consumer. They've reached a point where they expect the ad to be relevant and they're more likely to watch it." Hey! Keep those 30-second boards coming!

But not so fast. To date, the theory that personally targeted ads will break through is far from proven. Take advertising on Facebook, for example. The company got marketers excited with the promise of reaching people who are sharing their lives with their friends. Facebook created a Google-like ad-serving interface that allows marketers to go in and target people based on everything from their age and zip code to what pets they have and what type of beer they love. The hope was that marketers would grab these consumers' attention by presenting extremely relevant ads when they logged on to Facebook each day. But that's just not happening. So far, the company has been unable to generate the huge revenue growth it hoped for because people do not pay attention to the advertising it serves—no matter how personally relevant it is. Based on a handful of experiments at our agency, click rates for Facebook ads are typically around 0.02 percent, and there is no significant improvement from microtargeting audiences. Marketers are quickly discovering that people are far more interested in their friends' photos and status updates than they are in margin ads that they can easily tune out.

Ilya Vedrashko, emerging media strategist at ad agency Hill Holliday, has a great analogy for this. Vedrashko, whose company has been running the future-focused Ad Lab blog since 2004, suggests that TV commercials are really no different from a buddy grabbing your remote control and changing the channel in the middle of your favorite show. "You can't create a consistently smarter interruption," he says. "It's not the problem of what is interrupting, it's the interruption itself that's the problem." He goes on to remark that "meaningful marketing is about building trust without waterboarding consumers with promises."

And even when these advertisements are perfectly relevant and targeted, there are concerns about consumer privacy. What happens when Dad does a Google search for erectile dysfunction or daughter looks up birth control? That could lead to a lot of discomfort when ads for Viagra and Trojan end up on the family's nightly news program. These are extreme scenarios, to be sure, but they demonstrate that people do not like to have their personal information "broadcasted" in any way. As a result, government legislation may kill the targeting dream scenario before it even gets off the ground.

> Meaningful marketing is about building trust without waterboarding consumers with promises.
> —ILYA VEDRASHKO

The problem that Google Life will face is that it is still aiming to polish an interruptive advertising model that no longer rules people's lives. It may indeed become the best form of traditional advertising— and some amount of interruptive marketing will probably always exist—but it is a small whiff of oxygen for a dying model, rather than the major transfusion we need.

• • •

Try as I might to serve up predictions for the advancing paradigm of marketing with meaning, the future remains something that we can see only when it is upon us. But not everyone experiences what's next at the same time, and marketers can get ahead of the game by personally engaging and testing the waters. To quote science fiction author William Gibson, "The future is already here, it is just unevenly divided."

Whether as a classic brand marketer or a digital agency strategist, I have always found myself attracted to "the new" in hopes of getting an edge on my competitors and reaping improved returns on advertising investment. I believe that a natural curiosity and a desire to learn quickly are skills that will benefit the aspiring meaningful marketer. I found some of the best guidance for this next generation of brand marketers from Dave Knox, a digital brand strategist at Procter & Gamble and a thought-leading blogger (www.hardknoxlife.com). Knox suggests that his fellow brand managers must "combine the skills of a marketer, technologist, and social anthropologist to study how digital advances are changing culture and media." He goes on to suggest that his peers should "be as comfortable talking about new technology as they are reviewing creative with their agency." I believe Knox is on to something powerful.

If you thrive on change and love to figure out how the world works, this is the greatest time to be in business, and specifically in marketing. The legacy rules have expired, and those who have historically been leaders are losing their protection; it has never been easier to launch a new product or service into the global marketplace. The fall of the traditional interruptive model of success may leave us exposed and looking for an answer, but I believe that marketing with meaning can be the model that helps you successfully shift to a new path to growth, both in sales and in stature.

In a speech to aspiring dot-com millionaires in the Stanford Technology Ventures Program, serial start-up success and marketing guru Guy Kawasaki advised his audience that the real essence of entrepreneurship is about making meaning. That's right—not "setting up for IPO success" nor "maximizing return on invested capital," but rather setting out to make the world a better place. As Kawasaki advises, "If you make meaning you will probably make money. But if you set out to make money, you probably won't make meaning and you won't make money."

May you make a bunch of money for your brand and a successful career for yourself by making marketing with meaning.

EPILOGUE

ADDING MEANING
TO YOUR LIFE

From the more than two years of preparation for this book, one example of marketing with meaning sticks out most in my mind. Luxottica's OneSight charity is less a program that is about external sales than it is a tool for inspiring a united company culture. There is a good chance that you have never heard of this program, because it is not something that the company has chosen to thump its chest about. But it presents a final lesson on how marketing with meaning can add something deeper to your company and your life.

Luxottica is one of the world's leading designers, manufacturers, and distributors of prescription frames and sunglasses in the premium and luxury eyewear market. Its strong brand portfolio includes North American retail brands such as Pearle Vision, LensCrafters, and Sunglass Hut as well as other licensed and house brands including Oakley, Ray-Ban, and Versace to name just a few. I first learned about One-Sight during a keynote presentation by Greg Hare, executive director of the program, in 2007. OneSight is a family of charitable vision-care programs dedicated to improving vision through outreach, research, and education. The program is designed to help the more than 250 million adults and children around the world who suffer from poor vision because they lack access to basic vision care. Through OneSight, teams of employees travel to developing nations, where they conduct free eye health screenings and provide gently used eyeglasses to people who are in desperate need. Over the past 20 years, OneSight has helped more than 7 million underprivileged people in developing nations and in North America see more clearly. Consumers can help by donating their gently used glasses at any one of Luxottica's retail vision-care centers—including Pearle Vision and LensCrafters.

Hare described how the OneSight "employee engagement model" enrolls everyone in the company in this important cause. In vision-care offices, employees get together over pizza a few nights a year while fixing up donated glasses for shipment. And at Luxottica's corporate headquarters in Cincinnati, Ohio, all employees are invited to help out in the OneSight recycle center by processing donated frames and preparing them to ship out to events around the world. Luxottica asks its vendors and agency partners to get involved as well. The people who prepare the glasses often include a card with their name and store number, in hopes that one of the clinic team members will snap a photo of a person wearing the glasses they sent on.

For a chosen few, the program becomes an even more special experience. All employees around the world have an opportunity to apply to join one of the 20 or so global trips per year where the eye-glasses are passed out. They travel to places in Central and South America, Africa, and Asia, living and working in rural conditions and experiencing the incredible process of helping people to see clearly again—or maybe for the first time in their lives. Many of the chosen few come back with life-changing experiences and amazing stories, like that of the 95-year-old Mexican man whose new glasses allowed him to really see his grandchildren for the first time. When employees return to their offices and stores after such experiences, they feel that their everyday job is more life-affirming than they had thought before. They realize that instead of just "selling frames," they are actually "providing the gift of better vision." This new attitude improves service quality and positively influences those around them as well.

Instead of promoting its special program with a multi-million-dollar television campaign, Luxottica has run this program quietly for 20 years, with the main company benefit being to build up the organization's morale. Greg Hare described how this charity and the deep personal involvement shown by every employee adds something special to a dispersed network of 64,000 workers in 130 countries who speak 55 languages. He told the story of two prized recruits in Japan who had turned down jobs at a more prestigious company for a chance to join Luxottica—specifically because of its OneSight program. The program has also been a way for employees in newly acquired companies (like Sunglass Hut, Pearle Vision, and Oakley) to feel better about their new parent company, proving that Luxottica, although large, is "one company with one passion: basic eye care for everyone."

> **Marketing with meaning... will build your company's morale and personal satisfaction at the same time it builds your business.**

The story of OneSight begins my final pitch for your adoption of marketing with meaning: it will build your company's morale and personal satisfaction at the same time it builds your business.

Clearly, those of us who are in marketing and advertising could use such a boost. Many of us feel ashamed every year when Gallup publishes its survey of the most- and least-trusted professions; without fail, advertisers ranks at the bottom of the list, along with car salesmen and politicians. In another study, conducted by J. Walter Thompson/*Adweek* in 2007, only 14 percent of people said that they respect those in advertising, ranking them just above car salesmen (5 percent) and national politicians (10 percent), but far behind military personnel (79 percent), physicians (75 percent), and teachers (71 percent). Only 12 percent said that we have improved in recent years, and only 31 percent said that we provide a "necessary good."

If this annual ranking doesn't make your heart ache, maybe the endless stream of antiadvertising rhetoric will. Philosophers and comedians alike cannot resist making fun of advertising, a profession that many people love to hate. Just punch "advertising" into an online quotation search service and you can find a who's who of famous people deriding the very cause to which we commit our days.

Few of us like to talk about society's judgment. In a rare example of an open discussion of the merits of our work, Maureen Hall, an agency owner, recently wrote in the *Advertising Age Small Agency Diary*[1] that her friends ask, "How could you spend your life perpetuating unhealthy consumerism?" Like Hall, I and many other people I know have been put on the spot to defend what we do. At best, we claim that advertising "stimulates the economy," "underwrites free content," and "sometimes helps you solve a problem." Maureen Hall adds, "While not all advertising is good, none of it is intrinsically evil." Hmm, not intrinsically evil—that's a start, I guess.

Authors John A. Quelch and Katherine E. Jocz take a different tack in their book *Greater Good: How Good Marketing Makes for Better Democracy*. They claim that "marketing itself is marketed poorly and that the social value created by the 17 million Americans who are employed in marketing deserves more credit." Their view follows the line that, like democracy, marketing is not perfect, but it is a very efficient system that contributes to a productive society. Perhaps, to paraphrase Churchill, marketing today is the worst form of communication, except for all the others.

Since all the signs are pointing to the belief that the marketing model we follow today is not good enough, I say that if we are going to revolutionize the marketing model, we might as well salvage our reputations at the same time. But we had better move quickly, or we will lose the competition for the talent that is needed to build the new model of brand marketing and agency success.

We already have our work cut out for us. In *Fortune*'s "Most Admired Companies" list, SC Johnson is the only marketing-focused company that's in the top twenty-five. Among advertising agencies, only Integer Group, at number eight in the medium-sized-company list, and my own Bridge Worldwide, at number six in the small-company list, make the cut. In *BusinessWeek*'s annual "Best Places to Launch a Career" list, the highest-ranking traditional marketing-focused company on the list is General Mills at number twenty. There are no advertising agencies on this list. Kevin Roberts, CEO of ad agency Saatchi & Saatchi, laments that we are losing big thinkers to today's more sexy professions like strategic consulting.[2] Ad agencies have lost their role as trusted guide to CEOs—a clear outcome of our mounting focus on producing television commercials instead of business results.

But at least one company shows a glimmer of hope. Google stands at number eight on the most admired list, and is number five on the list of best places to launch a career. Google should actually be considered an advertising and marketing-focused company, since it makes nearly all of its money from search term advertising. But Google is not a traditional marketing company in any sense of the word. Because it is revolutionizing the advertising and marketing business by providing a service that people find valuable, Google is considered the most valuable brand in the world today,[3] even though it spends almost nothing on advertising.

Google and Luxottica are not the only companies to see a culture boost from meaningful marketing—in fact, the people behind nearly every case study in this book have experienced both greater return on investment and higher personal satisfaction because of their work. In his survey of purpose-driven brands at both P&G and outside companies, Jim Stengel claimed that he could see a remarkable positive difference in these employees from the time he walked in the door. Commenting on our marketing with meaning blog, Carrie Schiff, a producer of the television show *Designing Spaces*, claims, "The best stories come from brand managers, presidents, and CMOs that really believe they can make a difference in people's lives."

Schiff goes on to suggest, "Don't we all just want to help people in some way to lead better lives, and be able to make good money doing it?" This is a concept close to what Bill Gates recently referred to as "creative capitalism." In his book *Tribes*, Seth Godin nails the general feeling that is catching hold in our boardrooms and cubicles:

> Many people are starting to realize that they work a lot and that working on stuff they believe in (and making things happen) is much more satisfying than just getting a paycheck and waiting to get fired (or die). "How was your day?" is a question that matters a lot more than it seems. It turns out that the people who like their jobs the most are also the ones who are doing the best work, making the greatest impact, and changing the most. Changing the way they see the world, sure, but also changing the world.

As our basic desires for material possessions are met, we feel a natural urge to improve the world around us.

Increasingly in our society, we feel less motivated by a paycheck and a pat on the back, but instead wish to devote ourselves to work that we find meaningful in our own lives. To return to Maslow's hierarchy of needs, as our basic desires for material possessions are met, we feel a natural urge to improve the world around us. And while we can contribute money or time outside of the office, people would prefer to spend their days doing work that is itself more rewarding.

Maslow believed that the path to human happiness was best achieved through worthwhile work. Management theorist Douglas McGregor has found that people want their companies to stand for something, and that they will give their best effort when they are working toward a cause they believe in. In his bestselling book *The Dream Manager*, Matthew Kelly suggests, "When employees believe that what they are doing is helping them to accomplish their personal dreams they can tolerate quite a bit. Highly engaged employees tend to have a vision that they are working toward."

For me, our company, and the other managers who have adopted a meaningful marketing model, the shared vision is to create work that makes the world a better place. By creating marketing that people choose to engage with, and that itself improves people's lives, we are reaching the highest level of personal success.

I began this book by describing my personal desire to follow Steve Jobs's mantra to "make a dent in the world." I think it is only fitting to end with another Jobs quote that I hope can provide the tipping point in your personal choice to pursue marketing with meaning; whether you have been a marketer for four months or forty years, now is as good a time as any to put your talents toward this most meaningful of directions:

We don't get a chance to do that many things, and every one should be really excellent. Because this is our life. Life is brief, and then you die. We've all chosen to do this with our lives. So it'd better be damn good.

I wish you much happiness and success in your business and marketing careers, and I hope that this book, and marketing with meaning, will have the positive influence on you that it should. And if you ever need some extra help or motivation, you can always track me down at www.marketingwithmeaning.com.

ENDNOTES

Introduction

1. http://en.wikipedia.org/wiki/Michelin_guide.

Chapter 1

1. Bob Garfield, "Bob Garfield's 'Chaos Scenario,'" *Advertising Age*, April 13, 2005.
2. www.mangiamedia.com/pizza_box.html.
3. www.bbidisplays.com/gallery2/main.php?g2_itemId=202.
4. Eric Pfanner, "At 30,000 Feet, Finding a Captive Audience for Advertising," *New York Times*, August 26, 2007.
5. Eric Pfanner, "The View from Your Airplane Window, Brought to You By . . . ," *New York Times*, September 25, 2007.
6. http://media.guardian.co.uk/advertising/0,,2197672,00.html.
7. Wendy A. Lee, "As the Fall Season Arrives, TV Screens Get More Cluttered," *New York Times*, September 24, 2007.
8. http://youtube.com/watch?v=UFYhupmhhBw.
9. www.tvweek.com/news/2007/11/world_series_2007_ratings_aver.php.
10. Frederik Balfour, "Catching the Eye of China's Elite," *BusinessWeek*, January 31, 2008.
11. Moshe Bar, "To Get Inside Their Minds, Learn How Their Minds Work," *Advertising Age*, November 26, 2007.
12. http://gawker.com/news/the-future/schizophrenia-is-the-new-ad-gimmick-329133.php.
13. "Cookie-Scented Ads Cause Stink in S.F.," CBSNews.com, December 6, 2006.
14. http://money.cnn.com/2007/02/09/news/companies/gm_robotad/.
15. Rebecca Dana and Stephanie King, "Answer to Vexing Question: Who's Not Watching Ads," *Wall Street Journal*, October 17, 2007.
16. Rob McGann, "Study: Consumers Delete Cookies at Surprising Rate," ClickZ, March 14, 2005.
17. Noam Cohen, "Whiting Out the Ads, but at What Cost?" *New York Times*, September 3, 2007.

18. www.computerworld.com/action/article.do?command=viewArticleBasic&
articleId=9060002&intsrc=hm_list.
19. Pamela Parker, "Interactive Ads Play Big Role in 'Minority Report,'"
ClickZ, June 21, 2002.
20. Bob Sullivan, "Do Not Call Entries Won't Expire, After All," Red Tape
Chronicles, October 23, 2007.
21. http://en.wikipedia.org/wiki/Adbusters.
22. www.commercialalert.org/theater_ads.html.
23. www.vss.com/news/index.asp?d_News_ID=166.
24. Bob Garfield, "Bob Garfield's Chaos Scenario 2.0," *Advertising Age*, March
26, 2007.
25. "How Many Friends Can You Have?" Ad Age Digital Conference session,
April 8, 2009.
26. www.emarketer.com/Article.aspx?id=1006799.

Chapter 2

1. http://en.wikipedia.org/wiki/Burger_king.
2. Daniel Gross, "Unhappy Meal," *Slate*, June 24, 2004.
3. Andrew Martin, "Gulp! Burger King Is on the Rebound," *New York Times*,
February 10, 2008.
4. Emily Bryson York, "No Offense, But This Guy's Got Your Number," *Advertising Age*, March 2, 2009.
5. "Burger King, Helped by 'Freakout' Ad, Posts Sales Gains," Dow Jones
Newswires, January 31, 2008.

Chapter 3

1. Brian F. Martin (founder-CEO of Brand Connections, a specialty media
and marketing company), "Give It a Try: Put Brands in Consumers' Hands
(Literally)," *Advertising Age*, October 22, 2007.
2. Emily Bryson York and Natalie Zmuda, "Sampling: The New Mass
Medium," *Advertising Age*, May 12, 2008.
3. www.brooklynvegan.com/archives/2008/10/radiohead_in_ra.html.
4. Source of some insights: Ellen Reid Smith, author of *e-Loyalty*.
5. *Advertising Age*, August 28, 2007.
6. SAS Institute.
7. Louise Story, "Online Pitches Made Just for You," *New York Times*, March 6,
2008.
8. www.renegade.com.
9. Company press release.
10. www.prweekus.com/Promotional-Event-of-the-Year-2008/article/104095/.
11. David Ogilvy, *Ogilvy on Advertising* (Vintage, 1985), p. 74.
12. Pew Internet and American Life Project.
13. "Discovering the Pivotal Point Consumer," The CMO Council and Pointer
Media Network, 2008.
14. www.bazaarvoice.com/pressrelease.php?id=18.
15. *Marketing Experiments Journal*, July 2007.
16. All statistics from Baazarvoice.
17. http://marketingroi.wordpress.com/2007/06/07/a-little-knowledge-is
-great-marketing/.

Chapter 4

1. http://en.wikipedia.org/wiki/BMW_films#History; http://www.imediaconnection.com/content/546.asp; http://wiki.media-culture.org.au/index.php/Viral_Marketing_-_Case_Study_-_BMW_Films.
2. Laura Lorber, "Marketing Videos Became a Hit in Their Own Right." *Wall Street Journal*, July 2, 2007.
3. http://www.gamedaily.com/articles/features/study-women-gamers-outnumber-men-in-25-34-age-group/68821/?biz1.
4. http://www.imediaconnection.com/content/1060.asp.
5. http://dchpl.blogspot.com/2007/07/great-results-for-get-glass.html.
6. http://arstechnica.com/news.ars/post/20071121-your-song-in-guitar-hero-equals-a-big-jump-in-digital-sales.html.
7. Steve Lohr, "Apple, a Success at Stores, Bets Big on Fifth Avenue," *New York Times*, May 19, 2006.
8. Pete Blackshaw, "How Apple Is Blurring the Line between Marketing and Service," *Advertising Age*, June 23, 2008.
9. "Apple's New U.S. Store Hints at Global Plans," *Boston Globe*, May 15, 2008.
10. Aaron O. Patrick, "Heineken Set to Keep Shop," *Wall Street Journal*, July 4, 2008.
11. Tim Parry, "Following Up with the Meow Mix Café," *Chief Marketer*, October 11, 2005.
12. Mickey Alam Khan, "Embed Marketing in Products: Crispin Porter + Bogusky CEO," *DMNews*, October 25, 2006.
13. http://creativity-online.com/?action=news:article&news=Id119089&sectionId=the_creativity_awards.
14. Jay Greene, "This Social Network Is Up and Running," *BusinessWeek*, November 17, 2008.
15. Bob Garfield, *Advertising Age*, July 9, 2007.
16. Ken Robinson, *Out of Our Minds: Learning to Be Creative* (Capstone Publishing Limited, 2001).
17. 2008 Reggie Awards—Special Advertising Section to *Brandweek*.
18. John Gerzema and Edward Lebar, *The Brand Bubble* (Jossey-Bass, 2008).
19. Charlene Li and Josh Bernoff, "Groundswell," Forrester Research, 2008.
20. Jean Halliday, "Saturn Brand Expands Orbit with Its Own Social Network," *Advertising Age*, April 28, 2008.
21. Edmund Lee, "Amazon Relied on Customers to Pimp the Kindle," Portfolio.com, August 26, 2008.
22. Andrew McMains, "Mercedes Readies Second Exclusive Online Community," *Brandweek*, November 17, 2008.
23. http://searchenginewatch.com/3631269.
24. http://worldofusability.wordpress.com/2008/10/08/why-zappos-works/.

Chapter 5

1. Jack Aaronson, "Education as a CRM Tool," ClickZ, January 2, 2003.
2. Stuart Elliott, "1,200 Marketers Can't Be Wrong: The Future Is in Consumer Behavior," *New York Times*, October 15, 2007.
3. www.homedepot.com.
4. Powered.com Case Studies.

5. "Chronic, A Report on the State of Teen Driving," Allstate Foundation, 2005.
6. Ron Nixon, "Bottom Line for (Red)," *New York Times*, February 6, 2008.
7. Jerry C. Welsh, "Good Cause, Good Business," *Harvard Business Review*, September–October 1999.
8. Jonah Bloom, "Agencies Will Have to Steer Marketers toward the Big Ideal," *Advertising Age*, October 8, 2007.
9. David Holthaus, "P&G: Doing Good Is Good for Business," *Cincinnati Enquirer*, April 24, 2009.
10. Michael Bush, "Consumers Continue to Stand by Their Causes during Downturn," *Advertising Age*, November 17, 2008.
11. "TBWA's Pedigree Effort Ahead of Pack at Kelly Awards," *Advertising Age*, June 4, 2008.
12. Elaine Wong, "Tide's Charitable Makeover," *Brandweek*, April 10, 2009.
13. Michael Bush, "Häagen-Dazs Saves the Honey Bees," *Advertising Age*, May 7, 2009.
14. Tiffany Meyers, "Häagen-Dazs: A Marketing 50 Case Study," *Advertising Age*, November 17, 2008.
15. Diana Barrett, "The Rise of Cause-Related Marketing," *Harvard Business Review*, April 4, 2002.
16. Chip Conley and Eric Friedenwald-Fishman, *Marketing That Matters* (Berrett-Koehler Publishers, 2006).
17. Ibid.
18. "BP Touts Greenness, Then Asks to Dump Ammonia," adage.com, August 20, 2007.

Chapter 6

1. Emily Steel, "Marketers Reach Out to Loyal Customers," *Wall Street Journal*, November 26, 2008.
2. www.PGA.com.
3. Netflix 2008 Investor Day slides.
4. Millward Brown's annual equity survey.
5. www.web-strategist.com/blog/2008/10/25/community-marketing-fishing-where-the-fish-are/ and www.adweek.com/aw/content_display/news/client/e3ie2cfa53a4f085a60558894f6f99295cc.

Chapter 7

1. "Consumer Revolution," keynote address by Mark Addicks, senior vice president and CMO, General Mills, HBS Marketing Conference, November 23, 2008.
2. Gerald Zaltman, *How Customers Think: Essential Insights into the Mind of the Market* (Harvard Business School Press, 2003).
3. Ibid.
4. Ibid.
5. Brian Morrissey, "Sears Aids Prom-Dress Sharing on Facebook," *Brandweek*, March 21, 2008.
6. Copyright 2009 Effie Worldwide Inc. All rights reserved.
7. IRI Scanner Data, January/February 2007 vs. 2006.

Chapter 8

1. www.advertisingourselvestodeath.com/2007/06/full_contact_br.html.
2. Todd Wasserman, "Westin Not Ambivalent about Ambient Ads," *Brandweek*, December 15, 2008.
3. Jack Neff, "J&J's BabyCenter to Close Online Store," *Advertising Age*, January 6, 2009.
4. The JCPenney deal lapsed in 2008, and Federated Media was itself shopping for a new sponsor for this content.
5. Stephanie Kang, "BMW Ran Risk with Silent Role in Mockumentary," *Wall Street Journal*, June 20, 2008.
6. Joan Voight, "Appetite for Disruption," *OMMA* magazine, March 2009.
7. www.digitalpodcast.com/podcastnews/2008/04/22/social-marketing-case-study-levis-project-501/.

Chapter 9

1. Brian Haven, "Marketing's New Key Metric: Engagement," Forrester Research, August 8, 2007.
2. Christopher Vollmer, "Digital Darwinism," *Strategy+Business*, Spring 2009.
3. Nina Lentini, "Plugged into the Electorate." *OMMA* magazine, April 2009.
4. John Gaudiosi, "Mountain Dew Makes MMO More Than Just a Game," *Advertising Age*, January 28, 2008.

Chapter 10

1. John Gerzema and Ed Lebar, *The Brand Bubble* (Jossey-Bass, 2008).
2. Abbey Klaassen, "Sephora Simplifies Selection Process with Mobile Reviews," *Advertising Age*, January 19, 2009.

Epilogue

1. http://adage.com/smallagency/post?article_id=120054.
2. www.saatchikevin.com/C-_to_A/.
3. "2007 BrandZ Top 100 Most Powerful Brands," Millward Brown Optimor.

INDEX

ABOUT THE AUTHOR

Bob Gilbreath is chief marketing strategist at Bridge Worldwide, one of the largest digital and relationship-marketing agencies in North America and a wholly owned subsidary of WPP. He has been quoted in publications including the *Wall Street Journal* and the *New York Times* and has spoken at Harvard Business School and Ad:Tech. Bob began his marketing career at Procter & Gamble, where he was named an *Advertising Age* Top 50 Marketer. He is a graduate of Duke University and New York University and lives in Cincinnati, Ohio, with his wife, Stephanie, and his daughters, Grace and Ella.

**Ready to create
marketing that adds
value to people's lives?**

So are we.

Let's create meaningful
marketing together.

Our place or yours?

BRIDGE WORLDWIDE

OUR PLACE:

info@bridgeworldwide.com
302 W. Third Street Suite 900
Cincinnati, OH 45202
513.381.1380
www.bridgeworldwide.com
www.twitter.com/BridgeWorldwide